7/10

FIFTH EDITION

POST OFFICE JOBS

EXPLORE AND FIND
JOBS, PREPARE
FOR THE 473
POSTAL EXAM,
AND LOCATE
ALL JOB
OPPORTUNITIES

DENNIS V. DAMP

POST OFFICE JOBS

Explore and Find Jobs, Prepare for the 473 Postal Exam,
and Locate ALL Job Opportunities
By Dennis V. Damp

BOOKHAVEN PRESS LLC

249 Field Club Circle

Mckees Rocks, PA 15136

http://bookhavenpress.com and http://postalwork.net

First edition 1996. Fifth edition/eleventh printing 2009, completely revised
Printed and bound in the United States of America

Disclaimer of All Warranties and Liabilities

This book provides information on post office employment, preparing for the 473 postal exam, and preparing for interviews. It is sold with the understanding that the publisher and author are not engaged in rendering legal, general counseling, or other professional services. If expert assistance is required, the services of a competent professional should be sought. The author and publisher make no warranties, either expressed or implied, with respect to the information contained herein. The information in this book was obtained from multiple sources including the U.S. Postal Service and government reports, and conveyed to the publisher either in writing, by telephone interview, or through Web searches. The author and publisher shall not be liable for any incidental or consequential damages in connection with, or arising out of, the use of material in this book. This book and its companion Web site at www.postalwork.net are not affiliated with or endorsed by the U.S. Postal Service.

Publisher's Cataloging-in-Publication Data
(Provided by Quality Books, Inc.)

Damp, Dennis V.
   Post Office jobs : explore and find jobs, prepare for the 473 postal exam, and locate all job opportunities /
Dennis V. Damp.-- 5th ed.
      p. cm.
      Includes bibliographical references and index.
      ISBN-13: 978-0-943641-27-0
      ISBN-10: 0-943641-27-6
   1. Postal service--Vocational guidance--United States.
   2. Postal service--United States-- Employees.
   3. Postal service--United States--Examinations, questions, etc. I. Title.
HE6499.D18 2009   383'.4973'023   QBI09-233

For information on distribution or quantity discount rates, Telephone 412/494-6926 or write to: Sales Department, Bookhaven Press LLC, 249 Field Club Circle, McKees Rocks, PA 15136. Distributed to the trade by Midpoint Trade Books, 27 West 20th Street, Suite 1102, New York, NY 10011, Tel: 212-727-0190.

Table of Contents

Chapter Three

Chapter Four

Chapter Five

Chapter Six

Chapter Seven

Chapter Eight

The [...] entered the 21st century when it recently expanded its eC[...] to new hires. It shed its arcane mass testing program for en[...] [in]stituted an automated online hiring process that offers job h[...] [en]trance tests are still required; however, you now apply for s[...] complete much of the initial assessment, including exam[...] ply. Applicants take proctored exams at designated testi[ng...] s instead of lengthy written tests that were previously used[...] cover this new system, and older books that included th[...] now outdated.

This new[...] opportunities to job seekers. Previously, you had to sign up t[...] ea that was offered only every two to three years. If you mi[...] ment you couldn't apply for jobs until the register that wa[...] revious exam was exhausted. Many were locked out by t[...] pply for job vacancies as they occur, and exams are adm[...] ed by contractors.

The Pos[...] 75 billion in sales and employed 765,000 workers nation[...] ver 203 billion pieces of mail in 2008. The average annual pay and benefits for career bargaining unit employees increased $10,000 since the previous edition was published in 2005, to $66,929, and the jobs remain highly competitive.

Unfortunately, even with its new and improved recruiting program the Postal Service provides little career guidance for applicants. This book fills the gap, taking readers step-by-step through the Postal Service's new eCareer recruiting system and providing the information needed to explore and find jobs, prepare for the 473 Postal Exam, and locate all job opportunities. Dennis Damp, the author, writes from first-hand experience; he spent 35½ years working for Uncle Sam. He provides an insider's perspective on what it takes to go from job hunter to hired,

Pass it On
Tips for Preserving Your Treasures

1. HANDLE WITH A CLEAN, GENTLE TOUCH
2. STORE SAFELY IN STABLE CONDITIONS
3. FORESEE AND AVOID POSSIBLE RISKS
4. MAKE A DUPLICATE
5. ASK A PROFESSIONAL
6. VISIT YOUR LIBRARY
7. PASS IT ON!

Celebrate Preservation Week
www.ala.org/preservationweek
American Library Association | www.alastore.ala.org
Design by Distillery Design Studio

and everything in between, to improve your chances of landing a high-paying government job.

The all-new Fifth Edition provides an overview of what is available, including many jobs that don't require written tests and how to apply for them. Over half of all workers are mail carriers and clerks; however, postal workers are employed in hundreds of diverse occupations, from janitors and truck drivers to accountants, personnel specialists, electronics technicians, and engineers.

The Postal Service eliminated the 460 Battery exam for rural carriers in 2008. Rural carriers must now take the 473 Major Entry-Level Exam, the same exam that all mail carriers, clerks, mail handlers, and sales, service, and distribution associates take.

Post Office Jobs is the only Post Office career guide that includes a comprehensive 473 Battery Test study guide and job descriptions for the top 28 Post Office occupations. It also lists major Postal Service job classifications, offers guidance on how to explore alternative Civil Service occupations, and includes a chapter on how to apply for Postal Inspector positions.

Postal employees are interviewed prior to appointment by the selecting official, and Chapter Six provides detailed guidance on how to successfully handle this often nerve-racking face-to-face encounter. The interview chapter provides sample questions to help you prepare and reduce your stress level.

Professional and administrative occupations do not require written examinations. Your background, work experience and education will be used to determine your eligibility for the job. You'll learn how to locate vacancies and apply for these positions nationwide. An updated list of Customer Service Districts is included in Appendix C that you can contact concerning test results and to learn when jobs will be advertised in your area.

Visit www.postalwork.net, the companion Web site for the new 5th edition for up-to-date guidance on Postal Service job options including direct links to key Postal Service recruiting sites. Also visit www.federaljobs.net to explore other Civil Service opportunities. This site includes extensive assistance for job seekers and covers many topics for people interested in exploring all federal careers.

If you are seeking a job with the Postal Service you should also be aware of the many scams that offer or guarantee postal employment for a fee. The Postal Service does not charge application fees, and no one can guarantee you a federal or postal job. All jobs are filled competitively.

If you're looking for good pay with excellent benefits, explore the Postal Service job market. Use this book's resources, including the Job Hunter's Checklist in Appendix A, to begin your personal job search.

Chapter One
The U.S. Postal Service

Hundreds of thousands apply each year for postal jobs, and those who understand the hiring process and study for entrance exams – when required – will dramatically improve their chances. The Postal Service never charges fees to take an exam or to apply for jobs. Don't be misled by ads that offer postal employment and charge a fee for their services. You will find all you need in this book, its companion Web site at www.postalwork.net and on the official USPS Web site at www.usps.com/employment.

The Postal Service is huge by any standard, employing over 765,000 workers with an annual budget of $75 billion. It pays over $2 billion in salaries and benefits every two weeks to workers in 300 occupations for positions at 37,000 post offices, branches, and stations throughout the United States. Approximately 40,000 postal workers are hired yearly to backfill for retirements, transfers, deaths and to replace employees who choose to leave for other reasons.

Starting pay in 2009 was $20.94 per hour, $43,555 per year, for part-time flexible mail carriers. Mail handlers start at $15.65 per hour, $32,553 per year, and clerks start at $19.19 per hour, $39,915 per year.[1] Workers are initially hired under the part-time flexible pay scale and typically work 40 or more hours per week.

Adding benefits, overtime, and premiums, the average bargaining unit annual compensation rate was $66,929 in 2008.

www.postalwork.net
www.usps.com/employment

---

[1] Beginning salary figures obtained from the Pittsburgh USPS human resource office.

The average pay and benefits for career bargaining unit employees was $66,929 per year, excluding corporate-wide expenses, in 2008.[2] The largest pay system in the Postal Service is predominantly for bargaining unit employees. There are also executive and administrative annual Pay-For-Performance schedules for non-bargaining unit members that pay from $21,293 up to an authorized maximum of $110,329.

Significant changes were implemented in 2008 that simplified, centralized, and streamlined the recruiting process. Now applicants apply for specific job vacancies online instead of testing to get on a local hiring register. Under the new process, exams are often two parts, an online assessment tool and a proctored section that you take at a designated location in your area. The 473 Major Entry Level Jobs Exam is now equally divided into a 90-minute unproctored online assessment and a 90-minute standard proctored test. The proctored exams are contracted out to local testing facilities, providing greater access for applicants.

BENEFITS

Postal employees receive the same general benefits provided to federal employees for the most part. However, USPS employees pay considerably less health care bi-weekly premiums than the competitive Civil Service does.

Vacation and Sick Leave

All employees receive: 10 paid holidays, 13 days of vacation for the first three years, twenty days of vacation with three to fifteen years service, and after fifteen years, twenty-six days. Additionally, 13 sick days are accrued each year regardless of length of service. Military time counts toward benefits. If you have three years of military service, you begin with four weeks paid vacation and three years toward retirement.

Health Benefits and Life Insurance

Medical health plans and the Federal Employees' Group Life Insurance (FEGLI) programs are available to all employees. The medical plan is an employee-employer contribution system and includes HMO and Blue Cross and Blue Shield programs. There are hundreds of plans to choose from. The FEGLI program offers low-cost term life insurance for the employee and basic coverage for the family. FEGLI offers up to five times the employee's salary in death benefits.

---

[2] Comprehensive Statement on Postal Operations, 2008 — USPS

One of the primary benefits of Postal Service employment is the satisfaction you experience from working in a challenging and rewarding position. Positions are available with the level of responsibility and authority that you desire.

Retirement

The Postal Service retirement system was significantly changed for individuals hired after January 1, 1984. There are three components to the Federal Employees Retirement System (FERS). Retirees receive a fixed annuity based on the number of years served, typically 1% of an employee's high three years average earnings for each year of service, Social Security, and there is an employee contribution system that is fashioned after a 401k defined contribution plan. You can elect to contribute into a *THRIFT savings 401k plan*. The government will match your contribution up to 5 percent. Your contributions are tax deferred and reduce your taxable income by the amount contributed. The retirement benefit is determined by the amount that has accumulated during the employee's career. This includes the interest earned and capital gains realized from the retirement fund. Go to www.federalretirement.net to learn more about the FERS retirement system

There are many withdrawal options, including lump sum and various fixed-term annuities. The contribution plan payout is in addition to the Social Security and fixed annuity benefits that you will be eligible for at retirement. Postal workers pay considerably less for their health benefits than competitive federal Civil Service employees due to their negotiated union contracts.

EMPLOYEE CLASSIFICATIONS

Initial appointments are either casual or transitional (temporary) or Part-Time Flexible (Career). Hourly rates for Part-Time Flexible employees vary depending upon the position's rate schedule. Some positions are filled full-time, such as the Maintenance (Custodial) classification.

- Full-Time and Part-Time Flexible (career) employees compose the *Regular Work Force*. This category includes security guards. Part-Time Flexible employees are scheduled to work fewer than 40 hours per week and they must be available for flexible work hours as assigned. Part-Time Flexible employees are paid by the hour. Hourly rates vary from $16.72 for PS Grade 3 Step BB to $31.62 for PS Grade 11 step P. See page 15 for a complete pay scale listing.

- A *Supplemental Work Force* is needed by the Postal Service for peak mail periods and offers casual (temporary) employees two 89-day employment terms in a calendar year. During Christmas an additional 21 days of employment can be offered to Supplemental Work Force employees. Transitional (temporary) employees can work up to 360 days in carrier positions.

Entrance exams are not required for supplemental work force jobs, and these positions can not be converted to full-time positions. However, you will be able to apply for future job vacancies and take the 473 Postal Exam in your area when they are advertised. Many, if not the majority of, postal workers today start out in casual or transitional positions and eventually apply, pass the exam, and get hired.

College students may be considered for casual (temporary) employment with the Postal Service during the summer months. The rate of pay is from $6.55 to $22.50 per hour. Tests are not required and appointments cannot lead to a career position. Apply early for summer work. Contact post offices in your area no later than February for summer employment applications. Casual temporary positions are also advertised on the Postal Service's employment and job listing Web site at www.usps.com/employment.

QUALIFICATION REQUIREMENTS

Various standards from age restrictions to physical requirements must be met before you can take one of the Postal Service exams.

Age Limit

You must be at least eighteen to apply. Certain conditions allow applicants as young as sixteen to apply. Carrier positions, requiring driving, are limited to age 18 or older. High school graduates or individuals who terminated high school education for sufficient reason are permitted to apply at age 16.

Entrance Exams

Clerks, carriers, rural carriers and other mail-handling job applicants must pass an entrance exam. Specialties such as mechanic, electronic technician, machinist, and trades must also pass a written test. The overall rating is based on the test results and your qualifying work experience and education. Professionals and certain administrative positions don't require an entrance exam or written test. They are rated and hired strictly on their prior work experience and education. The clerk and carrier exam was updated in December of 2004 to the new 473 and 473 C and 473 E Battery Exams. The only difference among the three is the occupational title and the methods of taking the exams.

The **473 Major Entry Level Jobs Exam** covers the following positions:

- ✔ **City Carrier**
- ✔ **Rural Carrier**
- ✔ **Mail Processing Clerk**
- ✔ **Sales, Service, and Distribution Associate**
- ✔ **Mail Handler**

This exam, also referred to as the *473 Battery Examination,* covers the vast majority of entry-level hiring. Custodial positions are reserved for veteran preference eligibles by federal law. The USPS also requires *motor vehicle* and *tractor trailer operators,* and highly skilled maintenance positions such as *Building Equipment Mechanic, Engineman, Electronics Technician, and General Mechanic* to successfully pass an entrance exam. All of the skilled maintenance positions require examination 931. A separate announcement, examination 932, is required for Electronics Technician positions. A list of exams is included on page 23, and Chapter Four provides sample tests for major occupations.

Eight sample exams are presented in Chapter Four and a sample *473 Battery Examination* is included in Chapter Five to help you prepare for this test. The 473 examination and completion of forms will require approximately three hours and fifteen minutes, with half of the exam taken online when you first apply and a second proctored exam at a local testing facility in your area. Jobs with the U.S. Postal Service are highly competitive due to the excellent salary and benefits offered. It's essential that you pass the test with the highest score possible to improve your chances. Applicants scoring between 90% and 100% will get called sooner than lower graded applicants and they have a better chance of being hired.

Citizenship

Applicants do not have to be U.S. citizens. If you have permanent alien resident status in the United States of America or owe allegiance to the United States of America you can apply for Postal Service jobs.

Physical Requirements

Physical requirements are determined by the job. Carriers must be able to lift a 70-pound mail sack and all applicants must be able to efficiently perform assigned duties. Eyesight and hearing tests are required. Applicants must have at least 20/40 vision in the good eye and no worse than 20/100 in the other eye. Eyeglasses are permitted.

State Driver's License

Applicants must have a valid state driver's license for positions that require motor vehicle operation. A safe driving record is required and a Postal Service road test is administered for the type of vehicle that you will operate.

DRUG TESTING (SUBSTANCE ABUSE)

The Postal Service maintains a comprehensive program to ensure a drug-free workplace. A qualification for postal employment is to be drug free, and this qualification is determined through the use of a urinalysis drug screen. When you are determined to be in the area of consideration for employment, you will be scheduled for a drug screening test.

APPLICATION PROCEDURES

Positions Requiring Written Examinations

The Postal Service significantly changed the application process in 2008, and you now apply for specific job vacancies. Previously, you had to sign up for a test that was administered every two to three years in your area. Applicants who passed the exam were placed on a hiring register in rank order by exam score. When vacancies occurred in an area, the Postal Service would contact the highest ranked candidates and call them in for an interview. You could be on the list for two years or more and never get called, and when the list was closed you had to reapply by retaking the same test.

Exam registers became outdated quickly as applicants found other employment, and they were difficult to maintain. The hiring process was decentralized, and many were excluded from the list because they missed the exam testing notification in their area. Now, when a vacancy exists the Postal Service advertises the job on its centralized Web site and you apply for a specific job that will be filled between four and six weeks of the job announcement's closing date.

To apply for postal positions, first visit www.postalwork.net/jobs.htm, this book's companion Web site, and review the step-by-step instructions with helpful hints on how to apply for post office jobs on the official Web site. This site shows screen shots of the official application pages with instructions to help you successfully navigate the new *eCareer* application system. Don't be sidetracked by major private-sector jobs board ads. The Postal Service seldom advertises on any of the large online jobs boards, and if it does you are linked directly to the official site at **http://usps.com/employment** to apply at no cost.

There are many postal job scams online and in newspaper classifieds that list toll-free numbers and charge fees ranging from $70 to over $200 for exam study guides. The application process is free to all who apply and this book provides a comprehensive 473 exam study guide in Chapter Five.

You can also call **1/478-757-3199** or TTY 1-800-800-8776 to apply, take an assessment, or to apply for temporary and casual employment. You must have the job announcement number to use the phone system, and it can be confusing. If you don't have an announcement number, which is readily available for current openings on the Internet, contact your local post office, Management Sectional Center (MSC), General Mail Facilities, or call your local Customer Service District Office that is listed in Chapter Four.

Apply online at www.usps.com/employment. Most libraries offer online access. Job opportunities are also advertised at local post offices, in national and local newspapers, journals and periodicals. Read the caution notice above prior to calling any toll-free number.

A passing score of 70 percent or better is required for your name to be added to the register. The highest-rated applicants will be called to complete additional paperwork, take a drug screening test, and an interview. Your score determines your placement on the list.

Apply for each job separately. However, after you initially register online, pass the test, and obtain an **Exam History Code,** you can enter this code at the beginning of the application process to avoid having to retest. To improve your chances, apply for all positions that you qualify for. Your exam results are valid through the exam date shown on your Notice of Rating.

Positions That Don't Require a Written Exam

Vacancies in these positions — generally professional and administrative — are announced (advertised) first within the Postal Service. Postal employees who have the knowledge, education, credentials, and skills may apply for these openings. If there aren't any qualified internal applicants (called bidders in the federal sector), then the postal service will advertise the vacancies to the general public and accept résumés and applications for rating. All applicants must pass an entrance examination and/or an evaluation process to be considered for a job. Corporate positions that don't require entrance exams are covered in Appendix B.

It is generally recommended that job applicants seeking entry-level professional and administrative positions take the 473 Battery Exam to get their foot in the door. Once hired, as vacancies open in their specialty such as accounting, budget, and engineering, they will have first crack at the jobs through internal Postal Service job announcements. You can view the diverse lists of job advertisements online at www.usps.com/employment. There are lists of jobs reserved for current postal employees only. Once you get your foot in the door you can bid on these restricted announcements, and the experience that you will gain from the entry-level position will help you better understand the postal system.

Realistically, many professional jobs won't be filled internally. Few postal clerks and non-professional employees will have law degrees, engineering credentials or doctorates, for example. Visit the employment Web site to explore all the available jobs, and review the job classifications list in Chapter Ten.

These job openings will be advertised on the USPS Web site. You should also contact local Customer Service and Sales District (CSSD) personnel offices listed in Appendix C to identify upcoming job vacancies for your specialty. You can also call your local CSSD office to check on the status of your application or to follow up on interviews.

You will be rated on a point system (maximum of 100 points) plus veterans preference points if applicable, even without a written test. Therefore, your résumé and *Application for Employment* (PS Form 2591) or online submission must be thoroughly completed and include all key information such as degrees, training, credentials, and detailed work experience. Only the top three candidates will generally be referred to the selecting official for consideration.

I suggest compiling your résumé and application offline first and spend quality time drafting your work experiences, collecting the required employment and education history, and spell and grammar check your application. Then, and only after thorough review, copy and paste it to the online résumé builder. Use the PS Form 2591 that is available at www.postalwork.net to make sure you capture all required information. If you omit key information your application may be rejected, and at the very least you stand to lose points. Corporate applicants need to spend quality time compiling their federal style resume and application. You will find *The Book of U.S. Government Jobs*, Chapter Six, very helpful. This book takes applicants step-by-step through the process from evaluating the job announcement to compiling work histories and Knowledge, Skills & Abilities (KSAs) statements. This book's companion Web site at www.federaljobs.net will also prove helpful.

VETERANS PREFERENCE

Veterans receive five or ten point preference. Those with a 10% or greater compensable service-connected disability are placed at the top of the register in the order of their scores. All other eligibles are listed below the disabled veterans group in rank order. The Veterans Preference Act applies to all Postal Service positions. Refer to Chapter Eight for detailed information on veterans preference.

Custodial exams for the position of cleaner, custodian, and custodial laborer are exclusively for veterans and present employees. These jobs are open only to veterans preference candidates.

PAY SCALES

The Postal Service (PS) pay scale for bargaining unit employees and the Executive and Administrative Schedule (EAS) pay scale for non-bargaining unit employees are presented in this chapter.

Special pay scales are also used for rural letter carriers, city carriers, mail handlers and others. Full-time mail carriers earn between $41,167 and $53,853 annually and transitional temporary carriers earn between $20.58 and $21.49 per hour. Rural carriers are paid on an equivalent annual rate dependent on hours worked each week. If they work a 12-hour work week they earn $11,808 to $15,194 a year. Working a 48-hour work week increases earning to between $51,170 and $65,831 a year.

The Postal Service also pays extra compensation, overtime, and night shift differential to workers. A Cost of Living Adjustment (COLA) is added to the base salary of employees at the rate of one cent per hour for each .4 point increase in the Consumer Price Index. Postal pay scales are posted on www.postalwork.net and are updated as changes occur. You will find General Schedule federal pay schedules posted on www.federaljobs.net.

| Steps | Grades | | | | | | | | |
	3	4	5	6	7	8	9	10	11
BB	33,443	34,621							
AA	34,448	35,616							
A	35,453	36,611	38,377	40,122	41,964	42,802			
B	36,458	37,606	39,314	41,008	42,800	43,644			
C	37,463	38,601	40,251	41,894	43,636	44,526			
D	38,468	39,596	41,188	42,780	44,472	45,388	49,120	52,298	53,473
E	39,473	40,591	42,125	43,666	45,308	46,250	49,765	53,065	54,287
F	40,478	41,586	43,062	44,552	46,144	47,112	50,410	53,832	55,101
G	41,483	42,581	43,999	45,438	46,980	47,974	51,055	54,599	55,915
H	42,488	43,576	44,936	46,324	47,816	48,836	51,700	55,366	56,729
I	43,493	44,571	45,873	47,210	48,652	49,698	52,345	56,133	57,543
J	44,498	45,566	46,810	48,096	49,488	50,560	52,990	56,900	58,357
K	45,503	46,561	47,747	48,982	50,324	51,422	53,635	57,667	59,171
L	46,508	47,556	48,684	49,868	51,160	52,284	54,280	58,434	59,985
M	47,513	48,551	49,621	50,754	51,996	53,146	54,925	59,201	60,799
N	48,518	49,546	50,558	51,640	52,832	54,008	55,570	59,968	61,613
O	49,518	50,541	51,495	52,526	53,668	54,870	56,215	60,735	62,247
P							56,860	61,502	63,241

POSTAL SERVICE (PS) Full Time Annual Rates (8/30/2008)

Step Increases BB-P are awarded on time in service and range from 24 weeks to 96 weeks between increases.

EXECUTIVE & ADMINISTRATIVE STEP SCHEDULE (EAS) 2008			
EAS Grade	Min / Max	EAS GRADE	Min / Max
1	$21,293 / $28,137	15	$37,862 / $59,123
2	$21,999 / $29,060	16	$39,206 / $66,122
3	$22,714 / $30,016	17	$40,945 / $69,053
4	$23,630 / $31,226	18	$42,743 / $72,085
5	$24,418 / $32,267	19	$44,769 / $75,502
6	$25,298 / $33,413	20	$47,197 / $79,598
7	$26,334 / $34,800	21	$49,490 / $83,465
8	$27,390 / $36,195	22	$52,433 / $90,459
9	$28,460 / $37,608	23	$55,291 / $95,388
10	$39,510 / $38,997	24	$58,027 / $100,109
11	$31.102 / $48,566	25	$60,913 / $105,088
12	$32,594 / $50,898	26	$63,952 / $110,329
13	$34,115 / $53,272		
14	$35,896 / $56,054		

POSTAL OCCUPATIONS
With Over 400 Employees

Occupation	Number Employed	Average Salary
Accounting Specialist / Tech	478	$57,120
Address Management Specialist	528	$57,787
Auto Technician	2,267	$47,454
Auto Technician (Lead)	1,202	$56,932
Bldg. Equipment Mechanic	2,370	$55,962
Bulk Mail Technician	3,017	$53,521
Carrier City	181,909	$51,063
Carrier (Temporary Relief)	4,715	$26,101
Carrier Technician	27,217	$51,529
Casual Temporary	11,368	$25,160
Clerk Special Delivery Services	466	$52,528
Criminal Investigators	429	$75,464
Customer Service Analyst	605	$64,426
Data Collection Technician	1,352	$53,401
Data Conversion Operator	4,953	$30,956
Distributions Windows & Markup Clerk	2,033	$52,448
Electronics Technician	7,783	$60,479
Flat Sorting Mach. Operator	2,958	$52,139
Human Resource Specialists	648	$61,873
Laborer Custodial, Custodian	16,279	$47,831
Mail Handler/Tech/Operator	52,918	$47,330
Mail Processing Clerk	81,511	$51,907
Mail Processing Machine Operators	1,422	$50,250
Maintenance Support Clerk/Tech	1,435	$51,623
Maintenance Mechanic & MPE	9,230	$55,485
Motor Vehicle Operator	2,759	$50,533
Parcel Post Dist-Machine	8,737	$51,765
PM/Relief/Replacement	12,951	$24,355
Postal Inspector	1,494	$78,950
Postal Police	581	$51,114
Postmaster	22,876	$65,000
Review Clerk	621	$53,655
Rural Carrier Associates	53,064	$37,493
Rural Delivery Carriers	68,812	$52,843
Sales Services Associates	50,993	$50,269
Secretary	836	$50,980
T&A Payroll Clerks	413	$53,661
Tractor Trailer Operator	5,530	$52,599
Training Technicians	450	$53,598
Transitional Employee	13,232	$41,166

Source: Employee Master File/RDL/OCCLIST/ Occupation Code Listing

Chapter Two
The Hiring Process

The Postal Service implemented major changes to its recruiting program in 2008 to improve operational efficiency and automate the hiring process. It expanded its internal **eCareer** application system to include new hires. Instead of applying to take a standardized exam for a specific occupation, you now apply for an actual job vacancy. This is far more efficient, and you will know within two to six weeks of the job announcement's closing date whether or not you are being considered for the position. Up to a million or more apply for post office jobs each year. Their new system collects background information, education, and work history when you first apply. This information is saved in your personal online profile and can be reused to apply for all jobs that you choose to apply for.

Previously, the Postal Service scheduled regional examinations for major occupational groups. Applicants who passed the exams with a score of 70 or higher were added in rank order to a hiring list for each area. These lists became outdated quickly as applicants found other employment, and it often took up to two years or longer before you were called for an interview, depending on when the Postal Service needed to hire and where you were on the list.

The majority of positions, approximately 80 percent of all postal jobs, require passing a postal exam. Most tested positions are for city and rural carriers, mail processing specialists, mail handlers, sales, service, and distribution associates. There are also examinations for vehicle operators, mechanics, electronics technicians and others. A list of tested occupations is on page 23, and sample examinations are presented in Chapter Four. Chapter Five includes a comprehensive study guide for the 473 Postal Exam that is required for most mail handling positions.

The majority of positions, approximately 80 percent of all postal jobs, require passing a postal exam.

The remaining 20 percent of jobs, mostly corporate positions, do not require a written entrance exam. Your work experience, education and accomplishments are evaluated to rate you for positions. These jobs require that applicants prepare a detailed professional *postal style résumé*. A postal style résumé is considerably different from a standard one-page private sector résumé. More information on this application process is included in Appendix B.

The U.S. Postal Service is an Equal Opportunity Employer. Hiring and advancement in the Postal Service is based on qualifications and performance regardless of race, color, creed, religion, sex, age, national origin, or disability. Applicants do not have to be U.S. citizens. If you have permanent alien resident status in the United States or owe allegiance to the United States you can apply for Postal Service jobs.

Postal installation managers are generally appointing officials and are delegated the authority to fill vacancies by transfer, reassignment, reinstatement of a former federal or postal employee, promotion, or from a current job announcement. Regardless of the recruitment source, applicants must meet the position's qualifications, including passing the appropriate examination if required. Examinations can be either written or a *rated application process* such as that used for professional positions.

EMPLOYEE CLASSIFICATIONS

There are two employee classifications for the largest tested occupational group, the Regular and Supplemental Work Force. The regular work force includes full-time, part-time flexible, and part-time regular pay schedules. Most new hires except technicians, professionals and other corporate employees start as part-time flexibles. Part-time flexibles are not guaranteed 40 hours per week but generally work five to six days per week and will be required to work up to 50 hours per week during peak periods.

The Postal Service's hiring process is composed of the following components, the suitability and selection components of which are separated into sub groups as specified below:[1]

- Recruitment / Job announcement
- Examinations (if required)
- Suitability review
  - The applicant's work history
  - Criminal conviction history[2]
  - Personal interviews (see Chapter Seven)
  - Medical assessment
- Selection

---

[1] Reference the U.S. Postal Service's Self-Instruction Module.

[2] Suitability screening, evaluation activities continue after you are hired.

RECRUITMENT OPTIONS

Noncompetitive *(Internal Hiring)*

Noncompetitive hiring for current employees and select groups may include reassignment, a change to lower level, or a promotion from a lower level, the reinstatement of eligible former postal or federal employees, or the transfer of career or career-conditional employees from other federal agencies.

Additionally, the options exist for the noncompetitive appointment of veterans with 30 percent or more disabilities, or noncompetitive appointment of Veterans' Readjustment Appointment (VRA) eligibles. Regardless of the choice of action, the appointee must meet the qualification standards of the position, including the examination requirement, if any. Noncompetitive hiring options also include the Postal Service's program for employment of persons with severe disabilities.[3]

Competitive *(External Hiring)*

Job vacancies are announced to the public and entrance examinations administered when necessary to meet the staffing needs of the Postal Service. During the period the job announcement is open, persons who meet the qualifications stated in the job announcement may apply. For age and citizenship eligibility, applicants do not have to meet these requirements at the time of application if they will become eligible during the time their ratings are on the register. When the job announcement is closed, applications are no longer accepted unless the applications are covered by one of the exceptions due to military service and other situations. Selections are made from a register of eligibles composed of scores on the basis of a written examination or a rated application examination. If veterans' preference is claimed, the basic scores are increased by 5 or 10 points.

Scores are converted to ratings on a scale of 100. Scores lower than passing are given ratings of ineligible. Claimed veterans' preference points are added only to eligible ratings.

A rated application examination is an evaluation of an application and résumé that will be rated on a scale of 100 based on your work experience, education, certifications and special skills. About 20 percent of postal jobs, mostly non-bargaining unit and corporate jobs, don't require a written exam. However, your application will be evaluated against the job announcement's required duties and specialized experience. Applicants must tailor their application and postal style résumé to the job announcement to achieve the highest score possible and improve their chances of being called for an interview. Additional information on how to tailor your application to the job announcement is including in Appendix B.

---

[3] Excerpts from Handbook EL-312, Updated With Postal Bulletin Revisions Through April 24, 2008

Advertising Job Vacancies

The Postal Service uses many avenues to advertise job vacancies, depending on the labor pool in each area. They typically post vacancy announcements in postal facility lobbies, on the Web site, and in federal, state, and municipal buildings open to the public. They may also:

- Send press releases to newspapers and other periodicals, including those directed toward women, minorities, veterans, and people with disabilities.

- Supply information to public and nonprofit employment services and to other social service agencies, veterans' organizations, state employment agencies, and organizations that represent special emphasis groups.

- Use public service advertisements or spots on radio or television to reach the members of the community.

- Advertise on the Internet.

- Partner with appropriate State Employment and Job Service Offices to promote maximum publicity of recruitment efforts and to increase the pool of qualified applicants through the employment service network.

- Conduct and participate in job fairs, open houses, or other recruitment activities to reach the community.

Positions Restricted to Applicants Eligible for Veterans' Preference

Certain positions are restricted to applicants eligible for veterans' preference under the Veterans' Preference Act of 1944. This rule applies only to appointments from external recruitment sources (whether competitive or noncompetitive). The following are restricted positions in the Postal Service:[4]

- Building maintenance custodian
- Custodian laborer
- Custodian
- Elevator operator
- Laborer custodial
- Window cleaner

Applicants who are not entitled to veterans' preference may be considered for positions restricted to preference eligibles only when preference eligibles are not available for appointment.

EXAMINATIONS

The majority of applicants must pass an entrance test, with mail carriers, clerks, and mail handlers – the largest group – taking the 473 examination. The examinations help identify applicants that meet pre-established qualification

---

[4] Postal Handbook EL-312, Section 232.52

requirements for filling vacant positions. Examinations measure or evaluate knowledge, skills, and abilities to predict probable future work performance. Passing examination scores are between 70 and 100. Applicants will be advised when applying for jobs whether or not a written examination is required. Most complete at least part of the exam online. A monitored exam will be scheduled at a local testing facility within 14 days from the date you apply. You are given 14 days to complete your application and assessments, and most do this online.

A list of exams follows, and you will find sample exams in Chapter 4 for the 710 (Clerical Abilities), 714 (Data Conversion), 931 (Maintenance Specialists / Technician), 932 (Electronics Technician), 933 (Maintenance Mechanic), 943 (Auto Mechanic), and 741 (Accounting Technician) exams. A comprehensive 473 exam study guide is offered in Chapter 5. The Postal Service also sends an Assessment Information Package to applicants when they apply via an e-mail attachment.

The application process was consolidated online under the eCareer program. Applicants develop a Candidate Profile and establish a user name and password when they first apply that is used when applying for all other jobs.

Examination List: (Partial List)

	Exam #	Exam Title	Occupational Groups
•	98X	Examinations 98X	Basic Mechanical Electrical
•	230	Motor Vehicle Operator	Motor Vehicle Operators
•	238	Motor Vehicle / Tractor Trailer Operator	Tractor Trailer Operators
•	240	Tractor Trailer Operator	Tractor Trailer Operators
•	473	473-473C Postal Exam	Carriers, Mail Handlers, Clerks
•	630	Postal Police Officer	Police Officer
•	710	Clerical Abilities	Secretary, Clerks, Admin.
•	711	Stenography	Transcription, Stenography
•	712/713	CBT Ver 2.0	Typing Test
•	714	Computer Based Test	Data Entry
•	715	715 Ver 2.0	Data Entry
•	720	Examination 720	General
•	725	Examination 725	General
•	741	Accounting Tech Junior	Accounting Technicians
•	744	Accounting Tech Senior	Accounting Technicians
•	804	Orientation Guide	Drivers Orientation
•	916	Custodial Maintenance	Custodian and Laborer
•	931	General Maintenance	Most Maintenance Positions
•	932	Electronics Group	Electronics Technicians
•	933	Mail Processing Equipment	Maintenance Mechanics
•	943	Automotive Mechanic	Automotive Mechanics
•	944	Automotive Technician	Automotive Technicians
•	950	Mechanical Test M/N 950	Mechanical and Trades

REGISTERS

Registers are lists containing applicant names and other information, including an examination rating and/or results of an evaluation process. The names of applicants who pass an entrance examination and/or evaluation process are placed on the register in numerical score order. That is why it is important for applicants to score as high as possible on their entrance exams. Passing grades are between 70 and 100; however, the higher your score the better chance you have of being called for an interview.

Eligible applicants are ranked on a register according to final ratings (including veterans preference points – see Chapter 7) and divided into two groups. The first group is made up of veterans who have a compensable service-connected disability. The second group is made up of everyone else.

An alternative recruitment source, called the general application file, can be used to fill temporary positions when it isn't feasible to announce an examination. A general application file is comparable to a one-time use or temporary register. Because no examination is given and to comply with the provisions of veteran preference, applicants must be considered for employment by priority groups. Persons entitled to 10-point veteran preference who have a compensable service-connected disability are placed ahead of all other persons entitled to veteran preference and then placed ahead of all other applicants on the list.

> Under the previous recruitment system, large registers were maintained for each major metropolitan area and used to hire for a period of from one to three years. Now, registers are compiled for each job vacancy as they occur.

SUITABILITY

Applicants are screened and evaluated to determine their overall suitability for postal employment prior to selection. This evaluation includes a review of:

- ✔ The applicant's work history
- ✔ Criminal conviction history
- ✔ Personal interviews (See Chapter Seven)
- ✔ Medical assessment

Medical assessment occurs after the job offer. The Rehabilitation Act of 1973 prohibits the Postal Service from inquiring into an applicant's medical suitability until a bona fide job offer is made. Medical assessment is done after selecting an applicant who has met all other suitability requirements.

After an applicant is hired, a career employee's job performance is evaluated during the probationary period. Fingerprints are submitted for a special agency check to ensure that there is no derogatory information about the individual that has not been discovered in the screening process. Thorough screening is done to ensure that individuals who do not meet Postal Service requirements are eliminated from the hiring process.

SELECTION

Selection is the process of identifying the best-qualified applicant for employment. Employing officials make selection decisions based on an evaluation of all information obtained during suitability screening. It is important to understand that a decision to select does not guarantee that the applicant will be appointed to the Postal Service. The applicant's medical assessment, which is completed after selection, or the identification of derogatory information about the applicant, may disqualify the individual before the appointment is effected.

APPOINTMENT

Appointment is the process of placing a selected applicant on the Postal Service rolls. The appointment is made after suitability is confirmed. Before a selection has been made or the medical assessment scheduled, an interview is scheduled for the applicant. Wherever feasible, the applicant must be given the opportunity to visit the actual job site and to observe working conditions. The selecting official or certified interviewer discusses the following with the eligible:[5]

- Duties of the position.
- Working hours including reporting times, overtime, holidays, and weekends.
- An explanation of the Equal Employment Opportunity and Affirmative Action policy.
- Required dress code.

---

[5] Postal Handbook EL-312, Section 621.1

GETTING IN THE FRONT DOOR

Getting in is half the battle. If you are qualified as a computer systems analyst and there are currently no openings, apply for positions that require the 473 exam for entry level positions such as Postal Clerks and Mail Carriers to get in the door. You can also apply for related occupations that you meet the qualifications for. The Postal Service generally advertises jobs in-house first to offer qualified workers opportunities for advancement. If the position can't be filled in-house it advertises the jobs to the public. You will have the opportunity to bid on other jobs if you have the qualifications and a good track record.

Another option is to apply for supplemental work as a casual or transitional part time employee. The Postal Service hires many casual workers to assist with mail-delivery during peak periods, and hires transitional employees to backfill for career carrier positions. You don't have to pass an exam to be hired, and if you do well in the position you will be able to take the 473 exam when jobs do open up. Many current employees started out as supplemental workers. Casuals can work two 89-day employment terms and 21 days during the Christmas holiday each year and transitional employees can work up to one year to backfill for letter carriers. Also consider applying for rural carrier positions in your area.

Supplemental workers earn a fair wage, and you will get exposure to what the Postal Service has to offer. These jobs are demanding and have flexible schedules and often require long hours on short notice.

*There are two things to aim at in life: first, to
get what you want; and after that to enjoy it.
Only the wisest of people achieve the second.*
— **Logan Smith**

INTERVIEWS

The Postal Service conducts interviews as part of the suitability recruitment process. You need to be prepared for these interviews. There are generally a good number of high scoring applicants, and the selecting official will use the interview process to determine the best candidates for the jobs. Refer to Chapter Seven for guidance on how to prepare for interviews.

Chapter Three
What Jobs Are Available

This chapter describes the nature of work, working environment, training, other qualifications, employment, jobs outlook, and average earnings potential. You will also find occupational descriptions for the most common Postal Service jobs. A list of occupations with more than 1,000 employees and their average salary is listed on page 18. Chapter Eight provides comprehensive job descriptions for 28 diverse occupations, Chapter Nine lists each job occupational group, the number employed, and average salaries, and Chapter Ten features Postal Inspector jobs. You should also explore related occupations with the competitive federal Civil Service in Chapter Eleven. Use the *Job Hunters Checklist* in Appendix A to assist you with your job search.

The Postal Service launched its *eCareer* hiring system recently to simplify, consolidate, and improve recruitment functions. Job vacancy announcements are now posted on-line **at http://usps.com/employment** where you apply for specific jobs. Additional guidance, updated information, and related Web links are available on this book's companion Web site at **www.postalwork.net**.

Applicants can also apply by calling **1-478-757-3199** or TTY 1-800-800-8776 to access the *Interactive Voice Response System* to locate job vacancies and to apply for exams by phone. Callers will need the job announcement number, which can be obtained from the published job announcement, on the Web site, or by calling your local Post Office. You can also call your local Customer Service District Sales office; they are listed in Appendix C.

Postal recruitment notices may also be advertised in national and local newspapers, publications, journals and periodicals. Visit www.postalwork.net for direct links to the Postal Service's Web site and guides to the postal application process. Explore other related federal jobs by visiting http://federaljobs.net/. This

Our business in life is not to get ahead of others, but to get ahead of ourselves — to break our own records, to outstrip our yesterdays by our today.

Susan B. Johnson

site provides links to 141 federal recruiting Web sites. If there are no vacancies listed on the sites mentioned above, contact individual mail facilities in your area to find out when they intend to recruit. Otherwise you will have to visit these sites weekly to check for new job announcements.

IMPROVING YOUR CHANCES

The more contacts you make, the greater your chances. **Don't get lost in the process.** Too many job seekers pin all their hopes on one effort. They apply for one job, then forget about the process until they receive a reply. Post office jobs are highly competitive. The more positions you apply for and examinations you take, the better your chances. There are also jobs that don't require entrance exams. Visit the USPS Web site to explore all occupations that you may qualify for. A list of exams is located on page 23. Also explore related occupations in the competitive federal Civil Service in Chapter Eleven.

The interviewing techniques presented in Chapter Six will help you prepare for the suitability screening process discussed in Chapter Two. Prepare for the interview. The Postal Service requires that each individual be interviewed prior to making an offer of appointment. It will verify your education, job history, and specialized skills, and clarify reasons for leaving previous jobs.

Take time to thoroughly complete your job application online and use the sample PS Form 2591 available on www.postalwork.net as a guide for completing your online application. Collect all the data requested on this form and compile your work histories and education on your desktop prior to starting your online application. You can copy and paste your work histories into the online résumé builder after registering. This will save time when you actually apply. Online applications time out after 30 minutes without any activity, and if you are searching for this information and making calls the system may time out.

You aren't locked into the first job or, for that matter, the first location that you are originally selected for. Once hired, you'll have opportunities to bid for jobs in-house. Post Offices, General Mail Facilities, and District Offices are located throughout the country and you can bid to many locations for future promotions or to enter a related or new career field. There are over 37,000 postal facilities nationwide.

POSTAL SERVICE WORKERS

Nature of the Work

Each week, the U.S. Postal Service delivers billions of pieces of mail, including letters, bills, advertisements, and packages, through heat, snow, or rain. To do this in an efficient and timely manner, the Postal Service employs about 615,000 individuals who process, sort, and deliver mail and packages as well as provide customer services and supplies in post offices. Most Postal Service workers are clerks, mail carriers, or mail sorters, processors, and processing machine operators. Postal clerks wait on customers at post offices, whereas mail sorters, processors, and processing machine operators sort incoming and outgoing mail at post offices and mail processing centers. Mail carriers deliver mail to urban and rural residences and businesses throughout the United States.[1]

Postal Service clerks, also known as window clerks, sell stamps, money orders, postal stationery, and mailing envelopes and boxes in post offices throughout the country. They also weigh packages to determine postage and check that packages are in satisfactory condition for mailing. These clerks register, certify, and insure mail and answer questions about postage rates, post office boxes, mailing restrictions, and other postal matters. Window clerks also help customers file claims for damaged packages.

Postal Service mail sorters, processors, and processing machine operators prepare incoming and outgoing mail for distribution at post offices and at mail processing centers. These workers are commonly referred to as mail handlers, distribution clerks, mail processors, or mail processing clerks. They load and unload postal trucks and move mail around a mail processing center with forklifts, small electric tractors, or hand-pushed carts. They also load and operate mail processing, sorting, and canceling machinery.

Postal Service mail carriers deliver mail, once it has been processed and sorted, to residences and businesses in cities, towns, and rural areas. Although carriers are classified by their type of route—either city or rural—the duties of city and rural carriers are similar. Most travel established routes, delivering and collecting mail. Mail carriers start work at the post office early in the morning, when they arrange the mail in delivery sequence. Automated equipment has reduced the time that carriers need to sort the mail, causing them to spend more of their time delivering it.

Mail carriers cover their routes on foot, by vehicle, or a combination of both. On foot, they carry a heavy load of mail in a satchel or push it on a cart. In most urban and rural areas, they use a car or small truck. Although the Postal Service provides vehicles to city carriers, most rural carriers must use their own automobiles, for whose use they are reimbursed. Deliveries are made house-to-house, to roadside mailboxes, and to large buildings such as offices or apartments, which generally have all of their tenants' mailboxes in one location.

Besides delivering and collecting mail, carriers collect money for postage-due and COD (cash-on-delivery) fees and obtain signed receipts for registered, certified, and insured mail. If a customer is not home, the carrier leaves a notice that tells where special mail is being held. After completing their routes, carriers return to the post office with mail gathered from homes, businesses, and sometimes street collection boxes, and turn in the mail, receipts, and money collected during the day.

---

[1] Bureau of Labor Statistics, U.S. Department of Labor, Occupational Outlook Handbook, 2008-09 Edition

Some city carriers may have specialized duties such as delivering only parcels or picking up mail from mail collection boxes. In contrast to city carriers, rural carriers provide a wider range of postal services, in addition to delivering and picking up mail. For example, rural carriers may sell stamps and money orders and register, certify, and insure parcels and letters. All carriers, however, must be able to answer customers' questions about postal regulations and services and provide change-of-address cards and other postal forms when requested.

Work Environment.

Window clerks usually work in the public portion of post offices. They have a variety of duties and frequent contact with the public, but they rarely work at night. However, they may have to deal with upset customers, stand for long periods, and be held accountable for an assigned stock of stamps and funds. Depending on the size of the post office, they also may be required to sort mail.

Despite the use of automated equipment, the work of mail sorters, processors, and processing machine operators can be physically demanding. Workers may have to move heavy sacks of mail around a mail processing center. These workers usually are on their feet, reaching for sacks and trays of mail or placing packages and bundles into sacks and trays. Processing mail can be tiring and tedious. Many sorters, processors, and machine operators work at night or on weekends, because most large post offices process mail around the clock, and the largest volume of mail is sorted during the evening and night shifts. Workers can experience stress as they process mail under tight production deadlines and quotas.

Most carriers begin work early in the morning—those with routes in a business district can start as early as 4 a.m. Overtime hours are frequently required for urban carriers. Carriers spend most of their time outdoors, delivering mail in all kinds of weather. Though carriers face many natural hazards, such as extreme temperatures, wet and icy roads and sidewalks, and even dog bites, serious injuries are often due to the nature of the work, which requires repetitive movements, as well as constant lifting and bending. These types of repetitive injuries occur as various kinds of injuries to joints and muscles, as well as carpal tunnel syndrome.

Training, Other Qualifications, and Advancement

All applicants for Postal Service jobs are required to take a Postal Service examination. After passing the exam, it may take one to two years or longer before being hired, as the number of applicants is generally much greater than the number of jobs that open up.

Education and training. There are no specific education requirements to become a Postal Service worker; however, all applicants must have a good command of the English language. Upon being hired, new Postal Service workers are trained on the job by experienced workers. Many post offices offer classroom instruction on safety and defensive driving. Workers receive additional instruction when new equipment or procedures are introduced. In these cases, workers usually are trained by another postal employee or a training specialist.

Other qualifications. Postal Service workers must be at least 18 years old. They must be U.S. citizens or have been granted permanent resident-alien status in the United States, and males must have registered with the Selective Service upon reaching age 18.

All applicants must pass a written examination that measures speed and accuracy at checking names and numbers and the ability to memorize mail distribution procedures. Job seekers should contact the post office or mail processing center where they wish to work to determine when job vacancies are anticipated. Applicants who pass the exam are listed in order of their examination scores. Five points are added to the score of an honorably discharged veteran, and 10 points are added to the score of a veteran who was wounded in combat or is disabled. The appointing officer chooses one of the top three applicants on the job vacancy list. Applicants must reapply for other job vacancies as they occur.

When accepted, applicants must pass a physical examination and drug test, and may be asked to show that they can lift and handle mail sacks weighing 70 pounds. Applicants for mail carrier positions must have a driver's license and a good driving record, and must receive a passing grade on a road test.

Postal clerks and mail carriers should be courteous and tactful when dealing with the public, especially when answering questions or receiving complaints. A good memory and the ability to read rapidly and accurately are important. Good interpersonal skills are important, particularly for mail clerks and mail carriers who deal closely with the public.

Advancement. Postal Service workers often begin on a part-time, flexible basis and become regular or full time in order of seniority, as vacancies occur. Full-time workers may bid for preferred assignments, such as the day shift or a high-level nonsupervisory position. Carriers can look forward to obtaining preferred routes as their seniority increases. Postal Service workers can advance to supervisory positions on a competitive basis.

Employment

The U.S. Postal Service employed 80,000 clerks, 338,000 mail carriers, and 198,000 mail sorters, processors, and processing machine operators in 2006. Most of them worked full time. Most postal clerks provide window service at post office branches. Many mail sorters, processors, and processing machine operators sort mail at major metropolitan post offices; others work at mail processing centers. The majority of mail carriers work in cities and suburbs; others work in rural areas.

Postal Service workers are classified as casual, part-time flexible, part-time regular, or full time. Casuals are hired for 90 days at a time to help process and deliver mail during peak mailing or vacation periods. Part-time flexible workers do not have a regular work schedule or weekly guarantee of hours but are called as the need arises. Part-time regulars have a set work schedule of fewer than 40 hours per week, often replacing regular full-time workers on their scheduled days off. Full-time postal employees work a 40-hour week over a 5-day period.

Job Outlook

Employment of Postal Service workers is expected to experience little or no change through 2016. Still, many jobs will become available for mail clerks and carriers, because these positions are expected to add workers, and because of the need to replace those who retire or leave the occupation.

Employment change. The stable employment overall of Postal Service mail carriers and Postal Service clerks will be offset by declines in Postal Service mail sorters, processors, and processing machine operators, which will likely cause overall employment of Postal Service workers to decline 2 percent over the 2006-2016 period. An increasing population, the greater use of third class, or bulk, mail by businesses, and more electronic shopping will generate more business for the Postal Service. However, demand will be moderated by the fact that people are sending out fewer pieces of first class mail because of the growing use of electronic communication.

These changes will affect Postal Service occupations in different ways. Efforts by the Postal Service to provide better service and meet the needs of a growing population will increase the demand for Postal Service clerks. However, the declining use of first class mail as the use of electronic communication grows will hold growth in this occupation to a minimum.

Employment of mail sorters, processors, and processing machine operators is expected to decline moderately because of the increasing use of automated materials handling equipment and optical character readers, barcode sorters, and other automated sorting equipment. In addition, companies that mail in bulk have an economic incentive to presort the mail before it arrives at the Post Office to qualify for a reduction in the price.

Employment of mail carriers is expected to grow, but only by about 1 percent through 2016. As the population continues to rise, the need for mail carriers will grow. In addition, businesses are using the mail more to deliver advertising, which is making up for the reduced use of first class mail. Also, the Postal Service is moving toward more centralized mail delivery, such as the use of cluster mailboxes, to cut down on the number of door-to-door deliveries. The best employment opportunities for mail carriers are expected to be in less urbanized areas as the number of addresses to which mail must be delivered continues to grow, especially in fast-growing rural areas. However, increased use of the "delivery point sequencing" system, which allows machines to sort mail directly by the order of delivery, should reduce the amount of time that carriers spend sorting their mail, allowing them to spend more time on the streets delivering mail. This will mitigate the demand for more mail carriers.

Job prospects. Those seeking jobs as Postal Service workers can expect to encounter keen competition. The number of applicants usually exceeds the number of job openings because of the occupation's low entry requirements and attractive wages and benefits.

The role of the Postal Service as a government-approved monopoly continues to be a topic of debate. However, in 2003 the Presidential Commission on Postal Services, and in 2006 Congress, both rejected the idea of privatizing the United States Postal Service. Employment and schedules in the Postal Service fluctuate with the demand for its services. When mail volume is high, full-time employees work overtime, part-time workers get additional hours, and casual workers may be hired. When mail volume is low, overtime is curtailed, part-timers work fewer hours, and casual workers are discharged.

Earnings

Starting pay in 2009 was $20.94 per hour, $43,555 per year, for part time flexible mail carriers. Mail handlers start at $15.65 per hour, $32,553 per year, and clerks start at $19.19 per hour, $39,915 per year.[2] Mail handlers are initially hired under the part time flexible pay scale and work 40 or more hours per week. The average pay and benefits for career bargaining unit employees was $66,929 per year, excluding corporate-wide expenses, in 2008.[3] The largest pay system is predominantly for bargaining unit employees. There are also executive and administrative annual Pay-for-Performance schedules for non-bargaining unit members that range from $21,293 up to an authorized maximum of $110,329.

---

[2] Beginning salary figures obtained from the Pittsburgh USPS human resource office.

[3] Comprehensive Statement on Postal Operations, 2008 — USPS

Sources of Additional Information

Review Chapter Four and Five for specific exam information and visit http://usps.com/employment for complete information on all occupations including jobs that don't require entrance examination. Also visit www.postalwork.net, the companion Web site for this book, for additional information and updates. Explore http://federaljobs.net including links to 141 federal agency personnel recruiting offices and for guidance on how to locate related jobs in the competitive federal Civil Service. If you are looking for secretarial, general or entry-level healthcare work visit http://healthcarejobs.org for other viable hiring options.

NOTE: The above occupational description was excerpted from the Bureau of Labor Statistics, U.S. Department of Labor, Occupational Outlook Handbook, 2008-09 Edition, Postal Service Workers. The content was amended with updated information that was compiled in early 2009.

MAJOR OCCUPATIONS

The following occupational descriptions are provided for a variety of postal jobs. You will find job descriptions for 28 of the more common occupations in Chapter Eight that you can review along with the following to evaluate which occupations would be best suited for you. The occupations reviewed in this chapter include:

- Custodian and Custodial Laborer
- Data Conversion Operator
- Maintenance Positions
- Vehicle Operator / Tractor-Trailer Operator
- Processing, Distribution & Delivery
- City Carrier & Clerk
- Distribution Clerk, Machine & Flat Sorting Machine Operators
- Mail Handler
- Mail Processor
- Automated Mark Up Clerk

Custodian and Custodial Laborer

Note: These positions are restricted to veteran preference eligibles.

The Job:

Custodian duties include manual cleaning, housekeeping, and buildings and grounds maintenance. Custodial laborers perform manual labor in connection with the maintenance and cleaning of the buildings and grounds. All positions may include irregular hours.

General Qualifications:

All applicants will be required to take a written examination. The examination and completion of forms will require approximately one hour and 30 minutes.

Custodial positions require prolonged standing, walking, climbing, bending, reaching and stooping. Employees must lift and carry heavy objects on level surfaces, on ladders and/or stairways. Custodial positions may require the use of hand tools and power cleaning equipment.

A qualification for postal employment is to be drug-free. This is determined through the use of a urinalysis drug screen. Applicants who qualify on the examination and are in the area of consideration for employment will be scheduled for the drug test.

Applicants must have vision of 20/40 (Snellen) in one eye and the ability to read without strain printed material the size of typewritten characters; glasses permitted.

How to Apply:

Visit http://usps.com/employment or call 1-478-757-3199 for job vacancy announcements and application procedures. If you call you must first have the announcement number to apply by phone. You can now apply online for many entrance exams.

Applicants will be notified of the date, time, and place of the examination and will be sent material to prepare for the examination.

Selection Process:

A minimum score of 70 points (exclusive of Veteran Preference) on the examination places the applicant's name on a list of eligibles for two years. Names are placed on the hiring list according to the score on the examination.

Data Conversion Operator

The Job

Data Conversion Operators extract information from source documents, transfer that information to computer input forms, and enter data using a keyboard.

General Qualifications

All applicants will be required to take a written examination. The examination and completion of forms will require approximately two hours.

Applicants must have six months or equivalent of clerical or office machine operating experience, preferably on a data conversion machine. Typing is required.

A qualification for postal employment is to be drug-free. This is determined through the use of a urinalysis drug screen. Applicants who qualify on the examination and are in the area of consideration for employment will be scheduled for the drug-test.

Applicants must have vision of 20/40 (Snellen) in one eye and the ability to read without strain, printed material the size of typewritten characters, corrective lenses permitted. The ability to distinguish basic colors and shades is desirable.

Applicants must be able to hear the conversational voice; hearing aids permitted.

How to Apply

Visit http://usps.com/employment or call 1-478-757-3199 for job vacancy announcements and application procedures. If you call you must first have the announcement number to apply by phone. You can now apply online for many entrance exams.

Applicants will be notified of the date, time, and place of the examination and will be sent material to prepare for the examination.

Selection Process

Applicants must first attain a minimum score of 70 points (exclusive of Veteran Preference) on the written examination. The applicants' names are then placed, by score, on a hiring list of eligibles for a period of two years. Applicants who qualify on the examination and are in the area of consideration for employment will be scheduled for a job-simulated typing performance test.

Maintenance Positions

The Job

Maintenance positions require highly skilled and experienced individuals. All applicants must meet the Knowledge, Skills, and Abilities listed on the job description.

General Qualifications

All applicants will be required to pass a three-hour written examination, complete a Candidate Supplemental Application booklet and successfully complete an interview.

A qualification for postal employment is to be drug-free. This is determined through the use of a urinalysis drug screen. Applicants who qualify on the examination and are in the area of consideration for employment will be scheduled for the drug test.

Maintenance positions require prolonged standing, walking, climbing, bending, reaching and stooping. Employees must lift and carry heavy objects on level surfaces, on ladders and/or stairways.

For positions requiring driving, applicants must have a valid state driver's license and a safe driving record. They must be able to obtain a Government Motor Vehicle Operator's Identification Card. Applicants may be required to qualify on industrial powered lifting equipment.

Applicants must have vision of 20/40 (Snellen) in one eye and the ability to read without strain, printed material the size of typewritten characters; glasses permitted. The ability to distinguish basic colors and shades is required.

How to Apply

Visit http://usps.com/employment or call 1-478-757-3199 for job vacancy announcements and application procedures. If you call you must first have the announcement number to apply by phone. You can now apply online for many entrance exams.

Applicants will be notified of the date, time, and place of the examination and will be sent material to prepare for the examination.

Selection Process

Applicants must first attain a minimum score of 70 points (exclusive of Veteran Preference) on the written examination. They must then complete a Candidate Supplemental Application booklet and successfully complete an interview. The applicants' names are then placed, by score, on a hiring list of eligibles for a period of two years.

Vehicle Operator/ Tractor-trailer Operator

The Job:

Motor Vehicle Operators operate mail trucks to pick up and transport mail in bulk. Tractor-Trailer Operators operate heavy duty tractor-trailers either in over-the-road service, city shuttle service or trailer operations. May include irregular hours.

General Qualifications:

Applicants for Motor Vehicle Operator and Tractor-Trailer Operator positions must have at least two years of driving experience, with at least one year of full-time experience (or equivalent) driving at least a seven-ton capacity truck or 24-passenger bus.

For Tractor-Trailer Operators, at least six months of the truck driving experience must be with tractor-trailers. Only driving experience in the United States, its possessions, territories, or in any United States military installation worldwide will be considered.

At the time of appointment, applicants must have a valid commercial driver's license, with air brakes certification, for the type(s) of vehicle(s) used on the job from the state in which they live. After being hired, applicants must be able to obtain the appropriate certification to operate specific postal vehicles.

Applicants will be required to pass a two-hour and 30-minute written examination and must also complete forms detailing their employment history, driving record, and other qualifying factors, to demonstrate possession of the following abilities: 1) Ability to drive trucks safely. 2) Ability to drive under local conditions. 3) Ability to follow instructions and prepare trip and other reports.

A qualification for postal employment is to be drug-free. This is determined through the use of a urinalysis drug-screen. Applicants who qualify on the examination, and are in the area of consideration for employment, will be scheduled for the drug test.

Applicants must have a vision of at least 30/30 (Snellen) in one eye and 20/50 (Snellen) in the other eye and the ability to read, without strain, printed material the size of typewritten characters; corrective lenses permitted. Operators must also be able to hear the conversational voice, hearing aids permitted.

How to Apply:

Visit http://usps.com/employment or call 1-478-757-3199 for job vacancy announcements and application procedures. If you call you must first have the announcement number to apply by phone. You can now apply online for many entrance exams.

Applicants will be notified of the date, time, and place of the examination and will be sent material to prepare for the examination.

Selection:

Applicants receive scores based on their examination results and a rating of their qualifications process listed on the U.S. Postal Service Application for Employment Form, Driving Record, and Supplemental Experience Statement. The application must contain pertinent information detailed enough to establish that the applicant meets all the requirements listed in this announcement. Applicants must provide full details about the types and weight of vehicles they have driven and the companies for which they worked as well as the length of their experience. A score of 70% (exclusive of Veteran Preference) places the applicant's name on a list of eligibles for two years. Names are placed on the hiring list in the order of their scores.

Processing, Distribution and Delivery Positions

All eligibilities previously established will be canceled upon receipt of the new examination results. Therefore, all applicants must reapply and compete in the new examination to reestablish eligibility.

General Qualifications:

A qualification for postal employment is to be drug-free. This is determined through the use of a urinalysis drug screen. Applicants who qualify on the examination and are in the area of consideration for employment will be scheduled for the drug test. All applicants will be required to take a written examination. The examination and completion of forms will require approximately two hours and fifteen minutes.

At the time of the examination, the applicant may select any or all of the seven different jobs listed below.

Job Choices:

CITY CARRIER	**MAIL HANDLER**
CLERK	**MAIL PROCESSOR**
DIST. CLERK, MACHINE	**MARK UP CLERK**
FLAT SORTING MACH. OPER.	

How to Apply:

Visit http://usps.com/employment or call 1-478-757-3199 for job vacancy announcements and application procedures. If you call you must first have the announcement number to apply by phone. You can now apply online for many entrance exams.

Applicants will be notified of the date, time, and place of the examination and will be sent material to prepare for the examination.

City Carrier and Clerk

The Jobs:

Clerks work indoors sorting and distributing mail. They may be required to work with the public selling stamps and weighing parcels, and are responsible for all money and stamps. May include irregular hours.

City Carriers collect and deliver mail in all kinds of weather, and walk and/or drive on their route.

Carrier and clerk positions require prolonged standing, walking, reaching and the ability to lift 70 pounds. Carriers are also required to carry a mail bag weighing as much as 35 pounds.

For positions requiring driving, applicants must have a valid state driver's license and a safe driving record. They must be able to obtain a Government Motor Vehicle Operator's Identification Card.

Applicants must have a vision of 20/40 (Snellen) in one eye and the ability to read without strain, printed material the size of typewritten characters; glasses permitted. Clerks working with the public must be able to hear the conversational voice.

Distribution Clerk, Machine and Flat Sorting Machine Operators

The Jobs:

Distribution Clerk, Machine and Flat Sorter Machine Operators are required to operate machinery which sorts and distributes letters or flats (magazines, over-sized envelopes etc.). Individuals must read address ZIP Codes and enter codes, using special purpose keyboards. Operators must also load and unload the machines, and the job may include irregular hours.

Distribution Clerk, Machine applicants must pass a vision test and possess the manual dexterity required to operate a two-handed keyboard. Vision requirements are: 20/40 (Snellen) in one eye and at least 20/100 (Snellen) in the other, and the ability to read without strain printed material the size of typewritten characters; corrective lenses permitted.

Flat Sorting Machine Operator applicants must pass a vision test and possess the manual dexterity required to operate a one-handed keyboard. Vision requirements are: 20/30 (Snellen) in one eye and 20/50 (Snellen) in the other; corrective lenses permitted. The ability to distinguish basic colors and shades is desirable.

Mail Handler

The Job:

Mail Handlers work in an industrial environment. Duties include the loading, unloading and moving of sacks of mail and packages weighing up to 70 pounds. May include irregular hours.

Prior to appointment, applicants will be required to pass a test of physical abilities. Applicants must demonstrate they can lift and carry up to 70 pounds.

Applicants must have a vision of 20/40 (Snellen) in one eye and the ability to read without strain, printed material the size of typewritten characters; corrective lenses permitted. The ability to distinguish basic colors and shades is desirable.

Mail Processor

The Job:

Mail Processors are required to stand for prolonged periods of time loading and unloading mail from a variety of automated mail processing equipment. May include irregular hours.

Applicants must have a vision of 20/40 (Snellen) in one eye and the ability to read without strain, printed material the size of typewritten characters; corrective lenses permitted. The ability to distinguish basic colors and shades is desirable.

Automated Mark up Clerk

The Job:

Automated Mark Up Clerks enter change of address data into a computer data base, process mail and perform other clerical functions. May include irregular hours.

Applicants must have six (6) months or equivalent of clerical or office machine operating experience. Typing is required.

Applicants must have a vision of 20/40 (Snellen) in one eye and the ability to read without strain, printed material the size of typewritten characters; corrective lenses permitted. The ability to distinguish basic colors and shades is desirable.

Selection Process:

A minimum score of 70 points (exclusive of Veteran Preference) on the examination places the applicant's name on a list of eligibles for two years. Names are placed on the hiring list according to the score on the examination. An applicant who qualifies on the examination and is in the area of consideration for employment for a certain job will be scheduled for job simulated performance exercises or an additional test. Distribution Clerk, Machine and Flat Sorter Machine Operators will be scheduled for Dexterity Exercises, Mail Handlers for a Strength and Stamina Test, and Automated Mark Up Clerks for a Typing Test.

Veteran Preference:

Veteran preference is granted for employment in the Postal Service. Those with a 10-percent or greater compensable service-connected disability are placed at the top of the hiring list in the order of their scores. Other eligibles are listed below this group in rank order.

Age Requirement:

The general minimum age requirement for positions in the Postal Service is 18 at the time of appointment or a high school graduate.

Citizenship:

All applicants must be citizens of or owe allegiance to the United States of America, or have been granted permanent resident alien status in the United States. Verification is required.

Selective Service:

To be eligible for appointment to a position in the Postal Service, males born after December 31, 1959 must (subject to certain exceptions) be registered with the Selective Service System in accordance with Section 3 of the Military Selective Service Act. Males between 18 and 26 years of age (have not reached their 26th birthday) can register with the Selective Service System at any U.S. Post Office, or consular officer if outside the United States. Your registration status can be verified with the Selective Service System by calling (708) 688-6888 for information.

OCCUPATIONS LIST
(Partial List)

Craft and Wage per-hour positions:

Administrative Clerk

Auto Mechanic

Blacksmith-Welder

Building Equipment Mechanic

Carpenter

Carrier

Cleaner, Custodian

Clerk Stenographer

Data Conversion Operator

Distribution Clerk

Electronic Technician

Elevator Mechanic

Engineman

Fireman

Garageman-Driver

General Mechanic

Letter Box Mechanic

Letter Carrier

LSM Operator

Machinist

Mail Handler

Maintenance Mechanic

Mark Up Clerk

Mason

Mechanic Helper

Motor Vehicle Operator

Painter

Plumber

Scale Mechanic

Security Guard

Professional

Accounting Technician

Architect/Engineer

Budget Assistant

Computer Programmer

Computer System Analyst

Electronic Engineer

Transportation Specialist

Industrial Engineer

Technical Writer

Stationary Engineer

Management

Administrative Manager

Foreman of Mail

General Foreman

Labor Relations Representative

Manager-Bulk Mail

Manager-Distribution

Manager-Station/Branch

Postmaster-Branch

Safety Officer

Schemes Routing Officer

Supervisor-Accounting

Supervisor-Customer Service

System Liaison Specialist

Tour Superintendent

Chapter Four
Postal Exams

Clerks, carriers, mail handlers, and other job applicants such as mechanics, electronic technicians, motor vehicle operators, machinists, clerical, and trades must pass a written test when applying for jobs. The rating is based on the test results and your qualifying work experience and education. Certain occupations, including many professionals, don't require a written exam. These groups are evaluated under the Postal Service's *Rated-Application Examinations* process. They are rated and hired through an extensive evaluation of their prior work experience, education, and how well they do on the interview.

Helpful Web Sites:
www.usps.com/employment
www.postalwork.net

Locate job vacancies for your area online, or if you know the announcement number you can call the Postal Service's job hotline at **1/478-757-3199.** Go to **www.usps.com/employment** and select the "search jobs" link located on this page. This will take you to the employment section of the Web site. You can also go to **www.postalwork.net,** the companion Web site for this book, to review the Postal Service's online application system with helpful hints to get you started.

Review Chapters Two and Three to understand the hiring process and what to expect. The Postal Service changed the application process significantly, and you now apply for specific jobs rather than applying to take a standardized test for occupations in each major metropolitan area.

All tests, including the 473 and 473-C/E exams, are scheduled when you apply online. When you apply you will be asked to register, complete an application, and take an initial online unproctored exam. Many occupations also require you to take a proctored exam at a testing facility in your area. The Postal Service will schedule you for the exam, and you have 14 days to complete your application, assessment, and exams from the date you apply.

*R*ural carriers mus[t] take the 473 exam instead of the 460 exam. **The old 460 exam is no longer used.**

473 MAJOR-ENTRY LEVEL EXAM

The **New 473 and 473-C/E Exam** covers the following positions:

> ✔ **City Carrier**
> ✔ **Rural Carrier**
> ✔ **Mail Processing Clerk**
> ✔ **Mail Handler**
> ✔ **Sales, Services, and Distribution Associate**

The **473 Major Entry Level Jobs Exam** may also be referred to as the 473 Battery Exam. The main difference between the 473 and 473-C/E exam is the target audience. The 473-C exam is used when the Postal Service is recruiting large numbers of City Letter Carriers, and the 473 and 473 E exam is used to cover all the job categories listed above. All of these exams are essentially the same.

Examinations cover the majority of entry level hiring although some offices also maintain custodial registers which, by law, are reserved for veteran preference eligibles. The postal service no longer uses the *460 Battery Examination* for rural mail carrier positions, rural carriers now must take the 473 exam. The USPS also administers exams for *motor vehicle* and *tractor trailer operators* and some highly skilled maintenance positions such as *building equipment mechanic, engineman, electronics technician, and general mechanic.* All skilled maintenance positions require examination 931. A separate announcement, examination number 932, is required for electronics technician positions.

Sample exams and test questions are provided in this chapter for most job categories except for the *473 Battery Test.* The *473 Battery Test* and completion of forms is covered in Chapter Five with additional practice exams and study tips.

SKILLS TESTS

Ability and skills tests (*performance tests*) are designed to predict future success, both in job training and job performance. The Postal Service uses these tests to obtain an indication of your potential to learn and perform particular job responsibilities. Skills tests measure specifically what you know about and can perform in a particular job—they test your mastery of tasks. The Postal Service administers skills tests when it is interested in filling a position with an applicant who knows the basics of the job and can perform job tasks as soon as he or she starts. Some performance tests are: the road test for operators of postal vehicles, the typing test, and the test of strength and stamina for mail handlers.

ROAD TEST EXAMINATION

The initial road test is a systematic way to measure an individual's ability and skill to drive safely and properly under normal operating conditions. This test is an important part of the overall selection process for positions that require motor vehicle operation, and it is also a practical test to determine whether or not an individual is a skilled and safe driver. The test includes items that have been reported as actual causes of accidents and gives special emphasis to the driving deficiencies identified as major causes of postal motor vehicle accidents.

There is a comprehensive table of disqualifications that apply to the Road Test Examination such as:

1. Applicant doesn't have at least two years of documented driving experience.
2. Applicant has had driving permit suspended once (or more) in the last three years, OR twice (or more) in the last five years.
3. Applicant has had driving permit revoked once (or more) in the last five years.

Specific offenses such as reckless driving, hit-and-run offense, or use of drugs also are disqualifying factors. For the purpose of determining disqualifying violations, consider only offenses followed by a conviction.

STUDY HABITS

It's often helpful to study with a partner, someone to read the question and check your responses. It can be a fellow worker, a spouse, or just a good friend.

Try various study routines until you hit a combination that works. Try studying in 20 to 30-minute sessions, with 5-minute breaks in between, or stretch it out to hour intervals. A good study routine will improve your test scores.

TEST-TAKING STRATEGIES

The following strategies will help you improve your grades. Use these strategies on the practice tests in this book and when you take your actual Postal Service exam. If you practice these techniques now, when you take the postal exam they will become second nature.

- Eliminate the answers in multiple-choice questions that make no sense at all. You can often eliminate half of the answers through this method. If you have to guess an answer, you improve your chances through the process of elimination.
- Be skeptical when an answer includes words like "always, never, all, none, generally," or "only." These words can be a trap. Only

select an answer with these words in it if you are absolutely sure it is the right answer.

✎   If two answers have opposite meanings, take your time and look closer. Many times one of the two is correct.

✎   Place a mark next to answers that you are unsure about. After completing the remainder of the exam, go back and review these questions and make a final selection. Often, other questions that you've answered will jog your memory.

✎   One word can dramatically change the meaning of a sentence. Read each question word-for-word before answering.

✎   Don't let the test get the best of you. Build your confidence by answering the questions you know first. If the first question you read stumps you, skip it and go on to the next one. When you've completed most of the exam you can go back – if time permits – to the questions that you couldn't answer.

✎   Get plenty of rest the night before the exam.

SAMPLE EXAMS

Sample practice exams are provided to applicants when you apply for jobs. An expanded list of exams is available in Chapter Two on page 23. Postal Service sample exams are presented in this chapter for the following occupational groups:

Exam 91 - Motor Vehicle Operator Exam
(Garageman, Motor Vehicle and Tractor Trailer Operators)

Exam 710 - Clerical Abilities Exam
(Data Conversion Operator, Clerk-Typist, Clerk Stenographer)

Exam 714 - Data Conversion Operator

Exam 931 - Maintenance Specialists/Technicians, Engineman, Blacksmith-welder, Custodian, Building Equipment Mechanics, Carpenter, Elevator Mechanic, Fireman, General Mechanic, Machinist, Electrician, Mason, Painter, Oiler, Plumber, Stationary Engineer.

Exam 932 - Electronic Technician Positions

Exam 933 - Measures 16 Knowledge, Skills, and Abilities (KSAs) used by a variety of maintenance positions including Maintenance Mechanic and Overhaul Specialist.

Exam 943 - Automotive Mechanic

Exam 741 - Accounting Technician Junior Exam

SAMPLE EXAM 91

Motor Vehicle Operator Exam
(Garageman, Motor Vehicle & Tractor Trailer Operators)

The sample exam that follows illustrates the types of questions that will be used in Test M/M 91. The samples will also show how the questions in the test are to be answered. Job descriptions for these occupations are included in Chapter Nine.

T0352 000000   SQ 91

SAMPLE QUESTIONS FOR TEST 91

The sample questions in this booklet show the kinds of questions that you will find in the written test. By reading and doing these questions, you will find out how to answer the questions in the test and about how hard the questions will be.

Read the questions carefully. Be sure you know what the questions are about and then answer the questions in the way you are told to do. If you are told the answer to a question, be sure you understand why the answer is right.

Here are the sample questions for you to answer.

Question 1 is about picture 1, below. Look at the picture.

PICTURE 1

1.   How many vehicles are shown in the picture,

(Write your answer for question 1 here.)

GO ON TO THE NEXT PAGE.

Questions 2 and 3 are about picture 2, below. Look at the picture.

PICTURE 2

2.   Who is sitting on the motorcycle ?

(Write your answer for question 2 here.)

3.   What is the policeman probably doing ?

(Write your answer for question 3 here.)

Questions 4 and 5 are about picture 3, below. Look at the picture.

PICTURE 3

4.   What is happening in this picture ?

(Write your answer for question 4 here.)

5.   Show the positions of the truck and the passenger car by drawing boxes like those shown below. (Your boxes will not be the same position as these.)

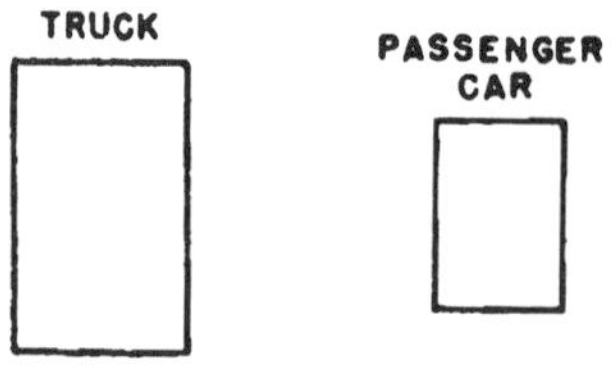

TRUCK   PASSENGER
              CAR

Draw your boxes in the space below.

GO ON TO THE NEXT PAGE.

Questions 6 and 7 are about pictures of oilcans. Each picture has a letter. You are to tell what each picture shows by writing a short description of the picture on the answer line that goes with the question.

Now look at picture X.
6. What does picture X show ?

(Write your answer for question 6 here.)

Picture X shows two oilcans. So, you should have written something like "two oilcans" on the line under question 6.

Now look at picture Y.
7. What does picture Y show?

(Write your answer for question 7 here.)

Question 8 is filling in a chart. You are given the following information to put in the chart. Truck, license number 48-7128, had its oil changed last at speedometer reading 96,005.

Truck, license number 858-232, was greased last at speedometer reading 89,564.

Look at the chart below. The information for the first truck has already been filled in. For question 8, fill in the information for the other truck. You are to show, in the proper columns, the license number of the truck, the kind of service, and the speedometer reading when serviced.

Truck License Number	Kind of Service	Speedometer Reading When Serviced
48-7128	Oil Change	96,005

(For question 8, write the information for the second truck in the proper columns above.)

GO ON TO THE NEXT PAGE.

Questions 9 and 10 are about words that might appear on traffic signs.

In questions like 9, there is one numbered line and then, just below that line, four other lines which are lettered A, B, C, and D. Read the first line. Then read the other four linea. Decide which line—A, B, C, or D—means most nearly the same as the first line in the question. Write the letter of the line that means the same as the numbered line in the answer space.

Here is another example.
9.   Speed Limit—20 Miles
A)   Do Not Exceed 20 Miles per Hour
B)   Railroad Crossing
C)   No Turns
D)   Dangerous Intersection
_____
(Write your answer for question 9 here.)

The first line says "Speed Limit—20 Miles." Line A says "Do Not Exceed 20 Miles per Hour." B says "Railroad Crossing." C says "No Turns." D says "Dangerous Intersection." The line that says almost the same thing as the first line is line A. That is, the one that means most nearly "Speed Limit—20 Miles" is "Do Not Exceed 20 Miles per Hour." The answer to question 9 is A. You should have marked A on the answer line for question 9.

Here is another example.
10. Dead End
A)   Merging Traffic
B)   No U-Turns
D)   Turn on Red
D)   No Through Traffic
_____
(Write your answer for question 10 here.)

After you answer questions like the ones you have just finished, you will be asked other questions to see how well you understand what you have written. To answer the next questions, you will use the information that you wrote for the first 10 questions. Mark your answers to the next questions on the Sample Answer Sheet on page 6.

The Sample Answer Sheet has spaces that look like these:

If you wanted to mark D for your answer to question 1, you would mark it like this:

If you wanted to mark C for your answer to question 2, you would mark it like this:

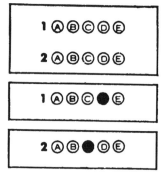

GO ON TO THE NEXT PAGE.

Each of the questions in the next part is about something you should have written on your answer lines.

In answering the next questions in this booklet, you may look back to what you have already written as often as you wish. You may look back while you are marking the Sample Answer Sheet. In the actual test, the pictures and their questions will be taken away from you before you mark the answer sheet, but you will keep what you wrote about the pictures while marking your answer sheet. So, for this practice, try not to look at the pictures but look at what you wrote about them.

Answer each of the following questions by darkening completely space A, B, C, D, or E beside the number that you are told in the question. Mark all your answers on the Sample Answer Sheet.

Question 11 is about question 1. Use what you wrote under question 1 to answer question 11. Mark your answer on the Sample Answer Sheet at the foot of the next page.

11. For number 11 on the Sample Answer Sheet,
    mark space A if only one vehicle is shown in the picture
    mark space B if only two vehicles are shown in the picture
    mark space c if only three vehicles are shown in the picture
    mark space D if only four vehicles are shown in the picture
    mark space E if only five vehicles are shown in the picture

If you look at the answer you gave for question 1, you will see that you wrote that three vehicles were shown in the picture. The question above tells you to mark space C on the Sample Answer Sheet if only three vehicles are shown. So you should have marked space C for number 11 on the Sample Answer Sheet.

Question 12 below is about question 2, and question 13 below is about question 3.
12. For number 12 on the Sample Answer Sheet, mark space
    A if a policeman is sitting on the motorcycle
    B if a man in overall is sitting on the motorcycle
    C if a boy in a sport shirt is sitting on the motorcycle
    D if a nurse is sitting on the motorcycle
    E if a man with a white beard is setting on the motorcycle

Be sure to mark your answer on the Sample Answer Sheet.
13. For number 13 on the Sample Answer Sheet, mark space
    A if the policeman is probably fixing a tire
    B if the policeman is probably using a telephone
    C if the policeman is probably taking off his cap
    D if the policeman is probably blowing a whistle
    E if the policeman is probably writing a "ticket"

Question 14 below is about question 4, and question 15 below is about question 5.
14. For number 14 on the Sample Answer Sheet, mark space
    A if a bus is passing a fire truck
    B if a motorcycle is hitting a fence
    C if a truck is backing up to a platform
    D if a passenger car is getting gas
    E if a passenger car is hitting a truck

15. Look at the boxes you drew for question 5. For number 15 on the Sample Answer Sheet, mark space

A if a truck is on a ramp and a passenger car is on the street
B if a truck is to the rear of a passenger car
C if the front bumpers of a passenger car and a truck are in line
D if a passenger car is to the rear of a truck
E if a motorcycle is between a truck and a passenger car

Question 16 below is about question 6 under picture X, and question 17 below is about question 7 under picture Y.

16. For number 16 on the Sample Answer Sheet, mark space

A if there is only one oilcan in picture X
B if there are only two oilcans in picture X
C if there are only three oilcans in picture X
D if there are only four oilcans in picture X
E if there are only five oilcans in picture X

17. For number 17 on the Sample Answer Sheet, mark space

A if there is only one oilcan in picture Y
B if there are only two oilcans in picture Y
C if there are only three oilcans in picture Y
D if there are only four oilcans in picture Y
E if there are only five oilcans in picture Y

Question 18 below is about the chart you filled in. For this question, mark on the Sample Answer Sheet the letter of the suggested answer—A, B, C, or D—that best answers the question.

18. What is the license number of the truck that was greased? (Look at what you wrote on the chart. Don't answer from memory.)

A) 89,564   C) 858-232
B) 48 - 7128   D) 96,005

For number 19 on the Sample Answer Sheet, mark the space that has the same letter as the letter you wrote on the answer line for question 9.

For number 20 on the Sample Answer Sheet, mark the space that has the same letter as the letter you wrote on the answer line for question 10.

Now see if the answers you have marked on the Sample Answer Sheet are the same as the answers marked in Correct Answers to Sample Questions. If the answers you have picked are the same as the answers in Correct Answers to Sample Questions, you are showing that you can pick right answers. If the answers you have picked are not the same as the answers in Correct Answers to Sample Questions, go back to the questions to see why your answers are wrong.

EXAM 710 - Clerical Abilities Exam
(Data Conversion Operator, Clerk-Typist, Clerk Stenographer)

The sample exam that follows illustrates the types of questions that will be used in Examination 710. The samples will also show how the questions in the test are to be answered. Job descriptions for these occupations are included in Chapter Nine.

SAMPLE QUESTIONS FOR EXAMINATION 710
CLERICAL ABILITIES

The following questions are samples of the types of questions that will be used on Examination 710. Study these questions carefully. Each question has several suggested answers. You are to decide which one is the best answer. Next, on the Sample Answer Sheet below, find the answer space that is numbered the same number as the question, then darken the space that is lettered the same as the answer you have selected. After you have answered all the questions, compare your answers with the ones given in the Correct Answers to Sample Questions below the Sample Answer Sheets

Sample Questions 1 through 14 - Clerical Aptitude

In Sample Questions 1 through 3 below, there is a name or code in a box at the left, and four other names or codes in alphabetical or numerical order at the right. Find the correct space for the boxed name or number so that it will be in alphabetical and/or numerical order with the others and mark the letter of that space as your answer on your Sample Answer Sheet below.

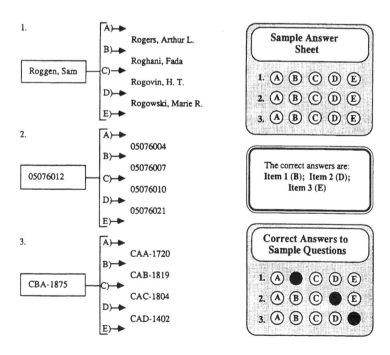

Sample Questions 4 through 8 require you to compare names, addresses, or codes. Ln each line across the page, there are three names, addresses or codes that are much alike. Compare the three and decide which ones are exactly alike. On the Sample Answer Sheet at the bottom, mark the answers:

A   if **ALL THREE** names, addresses, or codes are exactly **ALIKE**
B   if only the **FIRST** and **SECOND** names, addresses, or codes are exactly **ALIKE**
C   if only the **FIRST** and **THIRD** names, addresses, or codes are exactly **ALIKE**
D   if only the **SECOND** and **THIRD** names, addresses, or codes are exactly **ALIKE**
E   if **ALL THREE** names, addresses, or codes are **DIFFERENT**

4. Helene Bedell	Helene Beddell	Helene Beddell
5. F. T. Wedemeyer	F. T. Wedemeyer	F. T. Wedmeyer
6. 3214 W. Beaumont St.3214	Beaumount St.	3214 Beaumont St.
7. BC 3105T-5	BC 3015T-5	BC 3105T-5
8. 4460327	4460327	4460327

For the next two questions, find the correct spelling of the word and darken the appropriate answer space on your Sample Answer Sheet. If none of the alternatives are correct, darken Space D.

9.   A) accomodate
      B) acommodate
      C) accommadate
      D) none of the above

10.   A) manageble
      B) manageable
      C) manageable
      D) none of the above

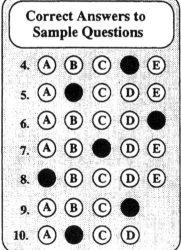

Sample Answer Sheet

4. Ⓐ Ⓑ Ⓒ Ⓓ Ⓔ
5. Ⓐ Ⓑ Ⓒ Ⓓ Ⓔ
6. Ⓐ Ⓑ Ⓒ Ⓓ Ⓔ
7. Ⓐ Ⓑ Ⓒ Ⓓ Ⓔ
8. Ⓐ Ⓑ Ⓒ Ⓓ Ⓔ
9. Ⓐ Ⓑ Ⓒ Ⓓ
10. Ⓐ Ⓑ Ⓒ Ⓓ

The correct answers are:
Item 4 (D);
Item 5 (B);
Item 6 (E);
Item 7 (C);
Item 8 (A);
Item 9 (D);
Item 10 (B)

Correct Answers to Sample Questions

4. Ⓐ Ⓑ Ⓒ ● Ⓔ
5. Ⓐ ● Ⓒ Ⓓ Ⓔ
6. Ⓐ Ⓑ Ⓒ Ⓓ ●
7. Ⓐ Ⓑ ● Ⓓ Ⓔ
8. ● Ⓑ Ⓒ Ⓓ Ⓔ
9. Ⓐ Ⓑ Ⓒ ●
10. Ⓐ ● Ⓒ Ⓓ

For Questions 11 through 14, perform the computation as indicated in the question and find the answer among the list of alternative responses. Mark your Sample Answer Sheet A, B, C, or D for the correct answer; or, if your answer is not among these, mark E for that question.

11. $32+26 =$

A) 69
B) 59
C) 58
D) 54
E) none of the above

12. $57-15 =$

A) 72
B) 62
C) 54
D) 44
E) none of the above

13. $23 \times 7 =$

A) 164
B) 161
C) 154
D) 141
E) none of the above

14. $160/5 =$

A) 32
B) 30
C) 25
D) 21
E) none of the above

Sample Answer Sheet

11. Ⓐ Ⓑ Ⓒ Ⓓ Ⓔ
12. Ⓐ Ⓑ Ⓒ Ⓓ Ⓔ
13. Ⓐ Ⓑ Ⓒ Ⓓ Ⓔ
14. Ⓐ Ⓑ Ⓒ Ⓓ Ⓔ

The correct answers are:
**Item 11 (C); Item 12 (E);
Item 13 (B); Item 14 (A)**

Correct Answers to Sample Questions

11. Ⓐ Ⓑ ● Ⓓ Ⓔ
12. Ⓐ Ⓑ Ⓒ Ⓓ ●
13. Ⓐ ● Ⓒ Ⓓ Ⓔ
14. ● Ⓑ Ⓒ Ⓓ Ⓔ

Sample Questions 15 through 22 - Verbal Abilities

Sample items 15 through 17 below test the ability to follow instructions. They direct you to mark a specific number and letter combination on your Sample Answer Sheet. The answers that you are instructed to mark are, for the most part, NOT in numerical sequence (i.e., you would not use Number 1 on your answer sheet to answer Question 1; Number 2 for Question 2, etc.). Instead, you must mark the number and space specifically designated in each test question.

Sample Answer Sheet

15. Ⓐ Ⓑ Ⓒ Ⓓ Ⓔ

16. Ⓐ Ⓑ Ⓒ Ⓓ Ⓔ

17. Ⓐ Ⓑ Ⓒ Ⓓ Ⓔ

15.   Look at the letters below. Draw a circle around the middle letter. Now, on your Sample Answer Sheet, find Number 16 and darken the space for the letter you just circled.

R   C   H

16.   Draw a line under the number shown below that is more than 10 but less than 20. Find that number on your Sample Answer Sheet, and darken Space A.

5   9   17   22

The correct answers are:
**Item 15 (B); Item 16 (C);
Item 17 (A)**

17.   Add the numbers 11 and 4 and write your answer on the blank line below. Now find this number on your Sample Answer Sheet and darken the space for the second letter in the alphabet.

**Correct Answers to
Sample Questions**

15. Ⓐ ● Ⓒ Ⓓ Ⓔ

16. Ⓐ Ⓑ ● Ⓓ Ⓔ

17. ● Ⓑ Ⓒ Ⓓ Ⓔ

Answer the remaining Sample Test Questions on the Sample Answer Sheet in numerical sequence (i.e., Number 18 on the Sample Answer Sheet for Question 18; Number 19 for Question 19, etc.).

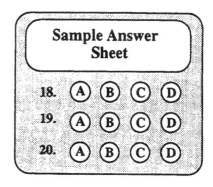

Select the sentence below which is most appropriate with respect to grammar, usage, and punctuation suitable for a formal letter or report.

18. A) He should of responded to the letter by now.
     B) A response to the letter by the end of the week.
     C) The letter required his immediate response.
     D) A response by him to the letter is necessary.

In questions 19 and 20 below, you will be asked to decide what the highlighted word means.

19. The payment was **authorized** yesterday. **Authorized** most nearly means

     A) expected
     B) approved
     C) refunded
     D) received

> The correct answers are:
> **Item 18 (C); Item 19 (B);**
> **Item 20 (D)**

20. Please **delete** the second paragraph. **Delete** most nearly means

     A) type
     B) read
     C) edit
     D) omit

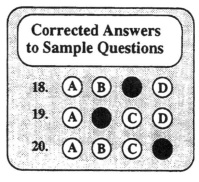

In questions 21 and 22 below, you are asked to read a paragraph, then answer the question that follows it.

21.   "Window Clerks working for the Postal Service have direct financial responsibility for the selling of postage. In addition, they are expected to have a thorough knowledge concerning the acceptability of all material offered by customers for mailing. Any information provided to the public by these employees must be completely accurate."

The paragraph best supports the statement that Window Clerks

A) must account for the stamps issued to them for sale
B) have had long training in other Postal Service jobs
C) must help sort mail to be delivered by carriers
D)   inspect the contents of all packages offered for mailing

22.   "The most efficient method for performing a task is not always easily determined. That which is economical in terms of time must be carefully distinguished from that which is economical in terms of expended energy. In short, the quickest method may require a degree of physical effort that may be neither essential nor desirable."

The paragraph best supports the statement that

A) it is more efficient to perform a task slowly than rapidly
B) skill in performing a task should not be acquired at the expense of time
C) the most efficient execution of a task is not always the one done in the shortest time
D) energy and time cannot both be considered in the performance of a single task

---

Sample Answer Sheet

21. Ⓐ Ⓑ Ⓒ Ⓓ
22. Ⓐ Ⓑ Ⓒ Ⓓ

The correct answers are:
Item 21 (A); Item 22 (C);

Corrected Answers to Sample Questions

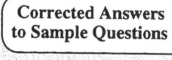

21. ● Ⓑ Ⓒ Ⓓ
22. Ⓐ Ⓑ ● Ⓓ

SAMPLE ITEMS FOR COMPUTER BASED TEST 714

The CB 714 is a computer administered and scored exam. Applicants are assisted with the start-up of the exam and with the exam instructions. You do MI need prior experience on a computer terminal to take this test.

The exam contains a list of alphanumeric postal data entry items just as you see in the sample items below. Applicants must demonstrate that they can type these items on the computer terminal at the following rate(s) based on the requirements of the position. The lower level passing rate is 5 correct lines per minute. The higher level passing rate is 7 correct lines per minute. Credit is given only for correctly typed lines. Practice for the exam by typing the sample provided below.

Type each line as shown in the exercise, beginning with the first column. You may use lower-case or capital letters when typing the sample exercise. When you reach the end of a line, single space and begin typing the next line. If you reach the end of the sample items in the first column, continue with the items in the second column. If you finish both columns, simply begin again with the first column and continue to type until the five minutes have elapsed.

See whether you can copy the entire Sample Test once in a five minute timing. Now count the number of lines you typed correctly and divide this number by five to determine your per minute score. Correctly typing only the items in column 1 is approximately equal to typing 5 correct lines per minute. Correctly typing all of the items in both columns is approximately equal to typing 7 correct lines per minute.

In the exam you will have five minutes in which to type the test material. Keep in mind that in order to pass the test you must type both rapidly and accurately.

SAMPLE TEST COPY

4.90 STEERING DAMPER	18.25 DOWN SPRING
16.55 REAR DOOR LATCH	3.10 VC GASKET
23.80 TIMING CHAIN	35.45 ROCKER ARM
8721 8906	4973 5261
2013 2547	6057 7352
5972 6841	2783 4195
HANOVER RD. 600 - 699	GREENBRIAR DR. 1100 - 1399
ARKANSAS AVE. 4000 - 4199	MADISON ST. 3700 - 3799
SO. MAIN ST. 1200 - 1299	BRUNSWICK AVE. 8100 - 8199
CAPITOL DR. 500 - 599	INDUSTRIAL RD. 2300 - 2499
L ON MAPLEWOOD PL.	
RETRACE TO 421	
R ON MOHICAN TO TOWER	
4478267 LSM/LSM	
4478271 MPLSM	
4478289 EGR SECONDARY	
KNIGHT, J.R. 04/17/67	
CHARLES, S.M. 11/19/68	
JEFFERSON, W.A. 08/20/69	
SPRINGFIELD 07215	
GREENSBORO 07098	
LEXINGTON 07540	
FOURTH CLASS 363	
INTN. SECTION 27	
200 BOX 10	

EXAM 931 - Maintenance Specialists/Technicians, Engineman, Blacksmith-welder, Custodian, Building Equipment Mechanics, Carpenter, Elevator Mechanic, Fireman, General Mechanic, Machinist, Electrician, Mason, Painter, Oiler, Plumber, Stationary Engineer

Test M/N 931 covers the following Knowledge, Skills, and Abilities:

✔ *Knowledge of basic mechanics* refers to the theory of operation, terminology, usage, and characteristics of basic mechanical principles as they apply to such things as gears, pulleys, cams, pawls, power transmissions, linkages, fasteners, chains, sprockets, and belts; and including hoisting, rigging, roping, pneumatics, and hydraulic devices.

✔ *Knowledge of basic electricity* refers to the theory, terminology, usage, and characteristics of basic electrical principles such as ohm's Law, Kirchoff's Law, and magnetism, as they apply to such things as AC-DC circuitry and hardware, relays, switches, and circuit breakers.

✔ *Knowledge of basic electronics* refers to the theory, terminology, usage, and characteristics of basic electronic principles concerning such things as solid state devices, vacuum tubes, coils, capacitors, resistors, and basic logic circuitry.

✔ *Knowledge of safety procedures and equipment* refers to the knowledge of industrial hazards (e.g., mechanical, chemical, electrical, electronic) and procedures and techniques established to avoid injuries to self and others such as lock-out devices, protective clothing, and waste disposal techniques.

✔ *Knowledge of refrigeration* refers to the theory, terminology, usage, and characteristics of refrigeration principles as they apply to such things as the refrigeration cycle, compressors, condensers, receivers, evaporators, metering devices, and refrigerant oils.

✔ *Knowledge of heating, ventilation, and air conditioning (HVAC) equipment operation* refers to the knowledge of equipment operation such as safety considerations, start-up, shut-down, and mechanical and electrical operating characteristics of HVAC equipment (e.g., chillers, direct expansion units, window units, heating equipment). This does not include the knowledge of refrigeration.

✔ *Ability to perform basic mathematical computations* refers to the ability to perform basic calculations such as addition, subtraction, multiplication and division with whole numbers, fractions and decimals.

✔ *Ability to perform more complex mathematics* refers to the ability to perform calculations such as basic geometry, scientific notation, and number conversions, as applied to mechanical, electrical and electronic applications.

✔ *Ability to apply theoretical knowledge to practical applications* refers to mechanical, electrical and electronic maintenance applications such as inspection, troubleshooting equipment repair and modification, preventive maintenance, and installation of electrical equipment.

✔ *Ability to detect patterns* refers to the ability to observe and analyze qualitative factors such as number progressions, spatial relationships, and auditory and visual patterns. This includes combining information and determining how a given set of numbers, objects, or sounds are related to each other.

✔ *Ability to use written reference materials* refers to the ability to locate, read, and comprehend text material such as handbooks, manuals, bulletins, directives, checklists and route sheets.

✔ *Ability to follow instructions* refers to the ability to comprehend and execute written and oral instructions such as work orders, checklists, route sheets, and verbal directions and instructions.

✔ *Ability to use hand tools* refers to knowledge of, and proficiency with, various hand tools. This ability involves the safe and efficient use and maintenance of such tools as screwdrivers, wrenches, hammers, pliers, chisels, punches, taps, dies, rules, gauges, and alignment tools.

✔ *Ability to use technical drawings* refers to the ability to react and comprehend technical materials such as diagrams, schematics, flow charts, and blueprints.

✔ *Ability to use test equipment* refers to the knowledge of, and proficiency with, various mechanical, electrical and electronic test equipment such as VOMS, oscilloscopes, circuit tracers, amprobes, and tachometers.

✔ *Ability to solder* refers to the knowledge of, and the ability to safely and effectively apply, the appropriate soldering techniques.

The sample exam that follows illustrates the types of questions that will be used in Test M/M 931. The samples will also show how the questions in the test are to be answered. Job descriptions for these occupations are included in Chapter Nine.

UNITED STATES POSTAL SERVICE

SAMPLE QUESTIONS - TEST M/N 931

The purpose of this booklet is to illustrate the types of questions that will be used in Test M/M 931. The samples will also show how the questions in the test are to be answered.

Test M/N 931 measures 16 Knowledge, Skills, and Abilities (KSAs) used by a variety of maintenance positions. Exhibit A lists the actual KSAs that are measured, and Exhibit B lists the positions that use this examination. However, not all KSAs that are measured in this test are scored for every position listed. The qualification standard for each position lists the KSAs required for the position. Only those questions that measure KSAs required for the positions) for which you are applying will be scored for the position(s).

The suggested answers to each question are lettered A, B, C, etc. Select the BEST answer and make a heavy pencil mark in the corresponding space on the Sample Answer Sheet. Each mark must be dense black. Each mark must cover more than half the space and must not extend into neighboring spaces. If the answer to Sample 1 is B, you would mark the Sample Answer Sheet like this:

After recording your answers, compare them with those in the Correct Answers to Sample Questions. If they do not agree, carefully re-read the questions that were missed to get a clear understanding of what each question is asking.

During the test, directions for answering questions in Part I will be given orally, either by a cassette tape or by the examiner. You are to listen closely to the directions and follow them. To practice for this part of the test you might have a friend read the direction to you while you mark your answers on the Sample Answer Sheet. Directions for answering questions in Part II will be completely described in the test booklet.

STUDY CAREFULLY BEFORE YOU GO TO THE EXAMINATION ROOM

PART I

In Part I of the test, you will be told to follow directions by writing in a test booklet and then on an answer sheet. The test booklet will have lines of material like the following five samples:

SAMPLE   1.   5 _____

SAMPLE   2.   1 6 4 3 7

SAMPLE   3.   D B A E C

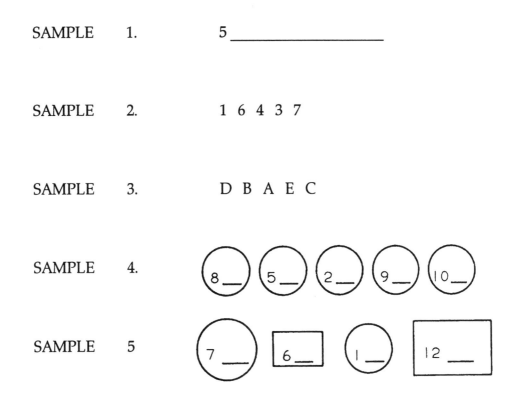

SAMPLE   4.

SAMPLE   5

To practice this test, have someone read the instructions on the **next page** to you and you follow the instructions. When they tell you to darken the space on the Sample Answer Sheet, use the one on this page.

SAMPLE ANSWER SHEET

1	Ⓐ Ⓑ Ⓒ Ⓓ Ⓔ	5	Ⓐ Ⓑ Ⓒ Ⓓ Ⓔ	9	Ⓐ Ⓑ Ⓒ Ⓓ Ⓔ
2	Ⓐ Ⓑ Ⓒ Ⓓ Ⓔ	6	Ⓐ Ⓑ Ⓒ Ⓓ Ⓔ	10	Ⓐ Ⓑ Ⓒ Ⓓ Ⓔ
3	Ⓐ Ⓑ Ⓒ Ⓓ Ⓔ	7	Ⓐ Ⓑ Ⓒ Ⓓ Ⓔ	11	Ⓐ Ⓑ Ⓒ Ⓓ Ⓔ
4	Ⓐ Ⓑ Ⓒ Ⓓ Ⓔ	8	Ⓐ Ⓑ Ⓒ Ⓓ Ⓔ	12	Ⓐ Ⓑ Ⓒ Ⓓ Ⓔ

Instructions to be read (the words in parentheses should not be read aloud).

You are to follow the instructions that I shall read to you. I cannot repeat them.

Look at the samples. Sample 1 has a number and a line beside it. On the line write an A. (Pause 2 seconds.) Now on the Sample Answer Sheet, find number 5 (pause 2 seconds) and darken the space for the letter you just wrote on the line. (Pause 2 seconds.)

Look at Sample 2. (Pause slightly.) Draw a line under the third number. (Pause 2 seconds.) Now look on the Sample Answer Sheet, find the number under which you just drew a line and darken space B as in baker for that number. (Pause 5 seconds.)

Look at Sample 3. (Pause slightly.) Draw a line under the third letter in the line. (Pause 2 seconds.) Now on your Sample Answer Sheet, find number 9 (pause 2 seconds) and darken the space for the letter under which you drew a line. (Pause 5 seconds.)

Look at the five circles in Sample 4. (Pause slightly.) Each circle has a number and a line in it. write D as in dog on the blank in the last circle. (Pause 2 seconds.) Now on the Sample Answer Sheet, darken the space for the number-letter combination that is in the circle you just wrote in. (Pause 5 seconds.)

Look at Sample 5. (Pause slightly.) There are two circles and two boxes of different sizes with numbers in them. (Pause slightly.) If 4 is more than 2 and if 5 is less than 3, write A in the smaller circle. (Pause slightly.) Otherwise write C in the larger box. (Pause 2 seconds.) Now on the Sample Answer Sheet, darken the space for the number-letter combination in the circle or box in which you just wrote. (Pause 5 seconds.)

Now look at the Sample Answer Sheet. (Pause slightly.) You should have darkened spaces 4B, 5A, 9A, 10D, and 12C on the Sample Answer Sheet. (If the person preparing to take the examination made any mistakes, try to help him or her understand why the mistakes are wrong.)

SAMPLE ANSWER QUESTIONS

1 Ⓐ Ⓑ Ⓒ Ⓓ Ⓔ

2 Ⓐ Ⓑ Ⓒ Ⓓ Ⓔ

3 Ⓐ Ⓑ Ⓒ Ⓓ Ⓔ

4 Ⓐ Ⓑ Ⓒ Ⓓ Ⓔ

5 Ⓐ Ⓑ Ⓒ Ⓓ Ⓔ

6 Ⓐ Ⓑ Ⓒ Ⓓ Ⓔ

7 Ⓐ Ⓑ Ⓒ Ⓓ Ⓔ

8 Ⓐ Ⓑ Ⓒ Ⓓ Ⓔ

9 Ⓐ Ⓑ Ⓒ Ⓓ Ⓔ

10 Ⓐ Ⓑ Ⓒ Ⓓ Ⓔ

11 Ⓐ Ⓑ Ⓒ Ⓓ Ⓔ

12 Ⓐ Ⓑ Ⓒ Ⓓ Ⓔ

13 Ⓐ Ⓑ Ⓒ Ⓓ Ⓔ

14 Ⓐ Ⓑ Ⓒ Ⓓ Ⓔ

15 Ⓐ Ⓑ Ⓒ Ⓓ Ⓔ

16 Ⓐ Ⓑ Ⓒ Ⓓ Ⓔ

17 Ⓐ Ⓑ Ⓒ Ⓓ Ⓔ

18 Ⓐ Ⓑ Ⓒ Ⓓ Ⓔ

19 Ⓐ Ⓑ Ⓒ Ⓓ Ⓔ

20 Ⓐ Ⓑ Ⓒ Ⓓ Ⓔ

21 Ⓐ Ⓑ Ⓒ Ⓓ Ⓔ

22 Ⓐ Ⓑ Ⓒ Ⓓ Ⓔ

23 Ⓐ Ⓑ Ⓒ Ⓓ Ⓔ

24 Ⓐ Ⓑ Ⓒ Ⓓ Ⓔ

25 Ⓐ Ⓑ Ⓒ Ⓓ Ⓔ

26 Ⓐ Ⓑ Ⓒ Ⓓ Ⓔ

27 Ⓐ Ⓑ Ⓒ Ⓓ Ⓔ

28 Ⓐ Ⓑ Ⓒ Ⓓ Ⓔ

29 Ⓐ Ⓑ Ⓒ Ⓓ Ⓔ

30 Ⓐ Ⓑ Ⓒ Ⓓ Ⓔ

31 Ⓐ Ⓑ Ⓒ Ⓓ Ⓔ

32 Ⓐ Ⓑ Ⓒ Ⓓ Ⓔ

33 Ⓐ Ⓑ Ⓒ Ⓓ Ⓔ

34 Ⓐ Ⓑ Ⓒ Ⓓ Ⓔ

PART II

1. Which device is used to transfer power and rotary mechanical motion from one shaft to another?

A) Bearing
B) Lever
C) Idler roller
D) Gear
E) Bushing

2. Lead anchors are usually mounted in

A) steel paneling.
B) drywall construction.
C) masonry construction.
D) wood construction.
E) gypsum board.

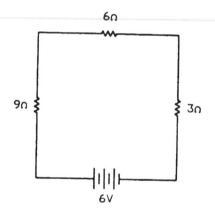

Figure III-A-22

3. Which of the following circuits is shown in Figure III-A-22?

A) Series circuit
B) Parallel circuit
C) Series, parallel circuit
D) Solid state circuit
E) None of the above

4. Which component would BEST simulate the actions of the photocell in Figure 24-3-1?

A) Variable resistor
B) Variable capacitor
C) Variable inductor
D) Auto transformer
E) Battery

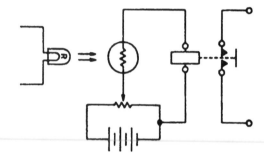

Figure 24-3-1

5. The semi-conductor materials contained in a transistor are designated by the letter(s)

A) Q
B) N, P
C) CR
D) M, P, M
E) None of the above

6. Which of the following circuits or devices always has inductance?

A) Rectifier
B) Coil
C) Current limiter
D) Condenser
E) Filter

7. Crowbars, light bulbs and vacuumbags are to be stored in the cabinet shown in Figure 75-25-1. Considering the balance of weight, what would be the safest arrangement?

A) Top Drawer - Crowbars
   Middle Drawer - Light Bulbs
   Bottom Drawer - Vacuum bags
B) Top Drawer - Crowbars
   Middle Drawer - Vacuum bags
   Bottom Drawer - Light Bulbs
C) Top Drawer - Vacuum Bags
   Middle Drawer - Crowbars
   Bottom Drawer - Light Bulbs
D) Top Drawer - Vacuum Bags
   Middle Drawer - Light Bulbs
   Bottom Drawer - Crowbars
E) Top Drawer - Light Bulbs
   Middle Drawer - Vacuum Bags
   Bottom Drawer - Crowbars

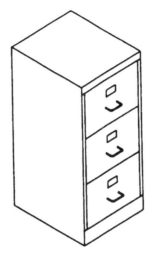

Figure 75-25-1

8. Which is most appropriate for pulling a heavy load?

A) Electric lift
B) Fork lift
C) Tow Conveyor
D) Dolly
E) Pallet truck

9. What measuring device is illustrated in Figure 75-26-1?

A) Screw pitch gage
B) Vernier calipers
C) Inside calipers
D) Outside calipers
E) Outside micrometer

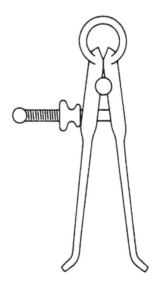

Figure 75-26-1

10. A screw pitch gauge can be used for

   A) determining the pitch and number of internal threads.
   B) measuring the number of gages available for use.
   C) measuring the depth of a screw hole.
   D) checking the thread angle.
   E) cleaning the external threads.

11. What measuring device is illustrated in Figure 75-20-17?

   A) Screw pitch gage
   B) Vernier caliper
   C) Inside calipers
   D) Outside calipers
   E) Outside micrometer

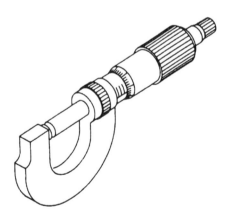

Figure 75-20-17

12. One characteristic of the breast drill is that it

   A) is gearless.
   B) is hand operated.
   C) has a 3 and 1/4 hp motor.
   D) has 4 speeds.
   E) is steam powered.

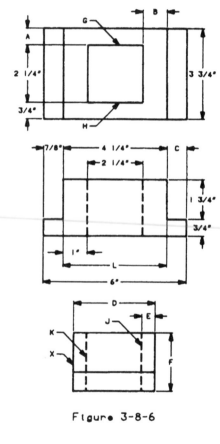

Figure 3-8-6

13. In Figure 3-8-6, what is the measurement of dimension F?

   A) 1 3/4 inches
   B) 2 1/4 inches
   C) 2 ½ inches
   D) 3 3/4 inches
   E) None of the above

14. The device pictured in Figure 36 is in a rest position. Which position, if any, is the normal closed?

A) A
B) B
C) C
D) Devices of this sort have no normal closed position
E) The normal closed is not shown in this diagram

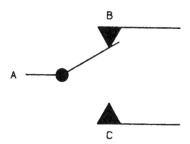

Figure 36

15. Which of the following test equipment would most likely be used in determining amplifier band width?

A) Clamp-on ammeter
B) Tube tester
C) Watt meter
D) Frequency analyzer
E) Sweep frequency generator

16. Which instrument is used to test insulation breakdown of a conductor?

A) Ohmmeter
B) Ammeter
C) Megger
D) Wheatstone bridge
E) Woltmeter

17. The primary purpose of soldering is to

A) melt solder to a molten state.
B) heat metal parts to the right temperature to be joined.
C) join metal parts by melting the parts.
D) harden metal.
E) join metal parts.

18. Which of the following statements is correct of a soldering gun?

A) Tip is not replaceable
B) Cannot be used in cramped places
C) Heats only when trigger is pressed
D) Not rated by the number of watts they use
E) Has no light

19. Contaminants have caused bearings to fail prematurely. Which pair of the items listed below should be kept away from bearings?

A) Dirt and oil
B) Grease and water
C) Oil and grease
D) Dirt and moisture
E) Water and oil

20. The electrical circuit term "open circuit" refers to a closed loop being opened. When an ohmmeter is connected into this type of circuit, one can expect the meter to

A) read infinity.
B) read infinity and slowly return to ZERO.
C) read ZERO.
D) read ZERO and slowly return to infinity.
E) none of the above

21. A change from refrigerant vapor to liquid while the temperature stays constant results in a

A) latent pressure loss.
B) sensible heat loss.
C) sensible pressure loss.
D) latent heat loss.
E) super heat loss.

22. The mediums normally used in condensing refrigerants are

A) air and water.
B) air and vapor.
C) water and gas.
D) liquid and vapor.
E) vapor and gas.

23. Most condenser problems are caused by

A) high head pressure.
B) high suction pressure.
C) low head pressure.
D) low suction pressure.
E) line leaks.

24. Most air conditioners with motors of 1 horsepower, or less, operate on which type of source?

A) 110-volt, single-phase
B) 110-volt, three-phase
C) 220-volt, single-phase
D) 220-volt, three-phase
E) 220-440-volt, three-phase

25. 2.6 - .5 =

A) 2.0
B) 2.1
C) 3.1
D) 3.3
E) None of the above

26. ½ of 1/4 is

A) 1/12
B) 1/8
C) 1/4
D) ½
E) 8

27. A drawing of a certain large building is 10 inches by 15 inches. On this drawing, 1 inch represents 5 feet. If the same drawing had been made 20 inches by 30 inches, 1 inch on the drawing would represent

A) 2 ½ feet.
B) 3 1/3 feet.
C) 5 feet.
D) 7 ½ feet.
E) 10 feet.

28. In a shipment of bearings, 51 were defective. This is 30 percent of the total number of bearings ordered. What was the total number of bearings ordered?

A) 125
B) 130
C) 153
D) 171
E) None of the above

In sample question 29 below, select the statement which is most nearly correct according to the paragraph.

"Without accurate position descriptions, it is difficult to have proper understanding of who is to do what and when. As the organization obtains newer and different equipment and as more and more data are accumulated to help establish proper preventive maintenance routines, the organization will change. When changes occur, it is important that the organization chart and the position descriptions are updated to reflect them."

29. <u>According to the above paragraph</u>, which of the following statements is most nearly correct?

   A) Job descriptions should be general in nature to encourage job flexibility.

   B) The organizational structure is not dependent upon changes in preventive maintenance routines.

   C) As long as supervisory personnel are aware of organizational changes, there is no need to constantly update the organization chart

   D) Organizational changes can result from procurement of new, advanced equipment.

   E) Formal job descriptions are not needed for an office to function on a day-to-day basis. The supervisor knows who is to do what and when.

30. A small crane was used to <u>raise</u> the heavy part. Raise MOST nearly means

   A) lift
   B) drag
   C) drop
   D) deliver
   E) guide

31. <u>Short</u> MOST nearly means

   A) tall
   B) wide
   C) brief
   D) heavy
   E) dark

In each of the sample questions below, look at the symbols in the first two boxes. Something about the three symbols in the first box makes them alike; something about the two symbols in the other box with the question mark makes them alike. Look for some characteristic that is common to all symbols in the same box, yet makes them different from the symbols in the other box. Among the five answer choices, find the symbol that can best be substituted for the question mark, because it is <u>like</u> the symbols in the second box, and, <u>for the same reason</u>, different from those in the first box.

32.

In the sample question above, all the symbols in the first box are vertical lines. The second box has two lines, one broken and one solid. Their <u>likeness</u> to each other consists in their being horizontal; and their being horizontal makes them <u>different</u> from the vertical lines in the other box. The answer must be the only one of the five lettered choices that is a horizontal line, either broken or solid. NOTE: There is not supposed to be a series or progression in these symbol questions. If you look for a progression in the first box and the second box, you will be wasting time. Remember, look for a <u>likeness</u> within each box and a <u>difference</u> between the two boxes. Now do sample question 33.

33.

In sample question 34 below, there is at the left a drawing of a flat piece of paper and at the right, four figures labeled A, B, C, and D. When the paper is rolled, it will form one of the figures at its right. Decide which figure can be formed from the flat piece. Then on the Answer Sheet darken the space which has the same letter as your answer.

34.

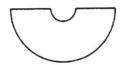

A   B   C   D

CORRECT ANSWERS TO
SAMPLE QUESTIONS

1.	D		18.	C
2.	C		19.	D
3.	A		20.	A
4.	A		21.	D
5.	B		22.	A
6.	B		23.	A
7.	E		24.	A
8.	E		25.	B
9.	C		26.	B
10.	A		27.	A
11.	E		28.	E
12.	B		29.	D
13.	C		30.	A
14.	B		31.	C
15.	D		32.	A
16.	C		33.	A
17.	E		34.	B

EXHIBIT B

The following positions use Test M/N 931:

Position Title	Register Number
Area Maintenance Specialist	M11
Area Maintenance Technician	M12
Assistant Engineman	M01
Blacksmith-Welder	M36
Building Maintenance Custodian	M13
Building Equipment Mechanic	M02
Carpenter	M14
Elevator Mechanic	M37
Engineman	M03
Fireman	M04
Fireman-Laborer	M05
General Mechanic	M38
Industrial Equipment Mechanic	M39
Letter Box Mechanic (Shop)	M40
Machinist	M41
Maintenance Electrician	M15
Mason	M21
Mechanic Helper	M42
Oiler, MPE	M43
Painter	M22
Painter/Finisher	M23
Plumber	M24
Postal Machines Mechanic	M44
Postal Maintenance Trainee A&B	M45
Scale Mechanic	M46
Stationary Engineer	M06

EXAM 932 - Electronic Technician Positions

Test M/N 932 covers the following Knowledge, Skills, and Abilities:

✔ *Knowledge of basic mechanics* refers to the theory of operation, terminology, usage, and characteristics of basic mechanical principles as they apply to such things as gears, pulleys, cams, pawls, power transmissions, linkages, fasteners, chains, sprockets, and belts; and including hoisting, rigging, roping, pneumatics, and hydraulic devices.

✔ *Knowledge of basic electricity* refers to the theory, terminology, usage, and characteristics of basic electrical principles such as ohm's Law, Kirchoff's Law, and magnetism, as they apply to such things as AC-DC circuitry and hardware, relays, switches, and circuit breakers.

✔ *Knowledge of basic electronics* refers to the theory, terminology, usage, and characteristics of basic electronic principles concerning such things as solid state devices, vacuum tubes, coils, capacitors, resistors, and basic logic circuitry.

✔ *Knowledge of digital electronics* refers to the terminology, characteristics, symbology, and operation of digital components as used in such things as logic gates, registers, adders, counters, memories, encoders and decoders.

✔ *Knowledge of safety procedures and equipment* refers to the knowledge of industrial hazards (e.g., mechanical, chemical, electrical, electronic) and procedures and techniques established to avoid injuries to self and others such as lock-out devices, protective clothing, and waste disposal techniques.

✔ Knowledge of basic computer concepts refers to the terminology, usage, and characteristics of digital memory storage/processing devices such as internal memory, input-output peripherals, and familiarity with programming concepts.

✔ *Ability to perform basic mathematical computations* refers to the ability to perform basic calculations such as addition, subtraction, multiplication and division with whole numbers, fractions and decimals.

✔ *Ability to perform more complex mathematics* refers to the ability to perform calculations such as basic geometry, scientific notation, and number conversions, as applied to mechanical, electrical and electronic applications.

✔   *Ability to apply theoretical knowledge to practical applications* refers to mechanical, electrical and electronic maintenance applications such as inspection, troubleshooting equipment repair and modification, preventive maintenance, and installation of electrical equipment.

✔   *Ability to detect patterns* refers to the ability to observe and analyze qualitative factors such as number progressions, spatial relationships, and auditory and visual patterns. This includes combining information and determining how a given set of numbers, objects, or sounds are related to each other.

✔   *Ability to use written reference materials* refers to the ability to locate, read, and comprehend text material such as handbooks, manuals, bulletins, directives, checklists and route sheets.

✔   *Ability to follow instructions* refers to the ability to comprehend and execute written and oral instructions such as work orders, checklists, route sheets, and verbal directions and instructions.

✔   *Ability to use hand tools* refers to knowledge of, and proficiency with, various hand tools. This ability involves the safe and efficient use and maintenance of such tools as screwdrivers, wrenches, hammers, pliers, chisels, punches, taps, dies, rules, gauges, and alignment tools.

✔   *Ability to use technical drawings* refers to the ability to react and comprehend technical materials such as diagrams, schematics, flow charts, and blueprints.

✔   *Ability to use test equipment* refers to the knowledge of, and proficiency with, various mechanical, electrical and electronic test equipment such as VOMS, oscilloscopes, circuit tracers, amprobes, and tachometers.

✔   *Ability to solder* refers to the knowledge of, and the ability to safely and effectively apply, the appropriate soldering techniques.

The sample exam that follows illustrates the types of questions that will be used in Test M/M 932. The samples will also show how the questions in the test are to be answered. Job descriptions for these occupations are included in Chapter Nine.

UNITED STATES POSTAL SERVICE

SAMPLE QUESTIONS - TEST M/N 932

The purpose of this booklet is to illustrate the types of questions that will be used in Test M/M 932. The samples will also show how the questions in the test are to be answered.

Test M/N 931 measures 16 Knowledge, Skills, and Abilities (KSAs) used by a variety of maintenance positions. Exhibit A lists the actual KSAs that are measured, and Exhibit B lists the positions that use this examination. However, not all KSAs that are measured in this test are scored for every position listed. The qualification standard for each position lists the KSAs required for the position. Only those questions that measure KSAs required for the position(s) for which you are applying will be scored for the position(s).

The suggested answers to each question are lettered A, B, C, etc. Select the BEST answer and make a heavy pencil mark in the corresponding space on the Sample Answer Sheet. Each mark must be dense black. Each mark must cover more than half the space and must not extend into neighboring spaces. If the answer to Sample 1 is B, you would mark the Sample Answer Sheet like this:

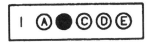

After recording your answers, compare them with those in the Correct Answers to Sample Questions. If they do not agree, carefully re-read the questions that were missed to get a clear understanding of what each question is asking.

During the test, directions for answering questions in Part I will be given orally, either by a cassette tape or by the examiner. You are to listen closely to the directions and follow them. To practice for this part of the test you might have a friend read the direction to you while you mark your answers on the Sample Answer Sheet. Directions for answering questions in Part II will be completely described in the test booklet.

STUDY CAREFULLY BEFORE YOU GO TO THE EXAMINATION ROOM

PART I

In Part I of the test, you will be told to follow directions by writing in a test booklet and then on an answer sheet. The test booklet will have lines of material like the following five samples:

SAMPLE   1.   5 _____

SAMPLE   2.   1 6 4 3 7

SAMPLE   3.   D B A E C

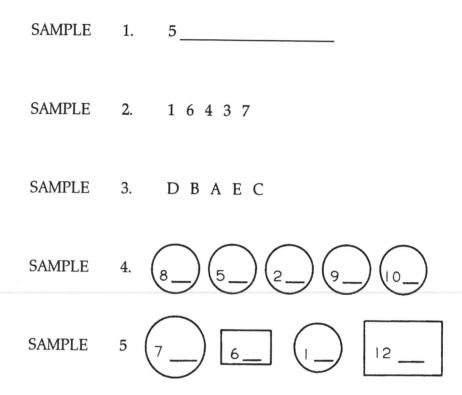

SAMPLE   4.

SAMPLE   5

To practice this test, have someone read the instructions on the **next page** to you and you follow the instructions. When they tell you to darken the space on the Sample Answer Sheet, use the one on this page.

```
                    SAMPLE ANSWER SHEET

  1 Ⓐ Ⓑ Ⓒ Ⓓ Ⓔ      5 Ⓐ Ⓑ Ⓒ Ⓓ Ⓔ       9 Ⓐ Ⓑ Ⓒ Ⓓ Ⓔ
  2 Ⓐ Ⓑ Ⓒ Ⓓ Ⓔ      6 Ⓐ Ⓑ Ⓒ Ⓓ Ⓔ      10 Ⓐ Ⓑ Ⓒ Ⓓ Ⓔ
  3 Ⓐ Ⓑ Ⓒ Ⓓ Ⓔ      7 Ⓐ Ⓑ Ⓒ Ⓓ Ⓔ      11 Ⓐ Ⓑ Ⓒ Ⓓ Ⓔ
  4 Ⓐ Ⓑ Ⓒ Ⓓ Ⓔ      8 Ⓐ Ⓑ Ⓒ Ⓓ Ⓔ      12 Ⓐ Ⓑ Ⓒ Ⓓ Ⓔ
```

Instructions to be read (the words in parentheses should not be read aloud).

You are to follow the instructions that I shall read to you. I cannot repeat them.

Look at the samples. Sample 1 has a number and a line beside it. On the line write an A. (Pause 2 seconds.) Now on the Sample Answer Sheet, find number 5 (pause 2 seconds) and darken the space for the letter you just wrote on the line. (Pause 2 seconds.)

Look at Sample 2. (Pause slightly.) Draw a line under the third number. (Pause 2 seconds.) Now look on the Sample Answer Sheet, find the number under which you just drew a line and darken space B as in baker for that number. (Pause 5 seconds.)

Look at Sample 3. (Pause slightly.) Draw a line under the third letter in the line. (Pause 2 seconds.) Now on your Sample Answer Sheet, find number 9 (pause 2 seconds) and darken the space for the letter under which you drew a line. (Pause 5 seconds.)

Look at the five circles in Sample 4. (Pause slightly.) Each circle has a number and a line in it. write D as in dog on the blank in the last circle. (Pause 2 seconds.) Now on the Sample Answer Sheet, darken the space for the number-letter combination that is in the circle you just wrote in. (Pause 5 seconds.)

Look at Sample 5. (Pause slightly.) There are two circles and two boxes of different sizes with numbers in them. (Pause slightly.) If 4 is more than 2 and if 5 is less than 3, write A in the smaller circle. (Pause slightly.) Otherwise write C in the larger box. (Pause 2 seconds.) Now on the Sample Answer Sheet, darken the space for the number-letter combination in the circle or box in which you just wrote. (Pause 5 seconds.)

Now look at the Sample Answer Sheet. (Pause slightly.) You should have darkened spaces 4B, 5A, 9A, 10D, and 12C on the Sample Answer Sheet. (If the person preparing to take the examination made any mistakes, try to help him or her understand why the mistakes are wrong.)

SAMPLE ANSWER QUESTIONS

1 Ⓐ Ⓑ Ⓒ Ⓓ Ⓔ		18 Ⓐ Ⓑ Ⓒ Ⓓ Ⓔ
2 Ⓐ Ⓑ Ⓒ Ⓓ Ⓔ		19 Ⓐ Ⓑ Ⓒ Ⓓ Ⓔ
3 Ⓐ Ⓑ Ⓒ Ⓓ Ⓔ		20 Ⓐ Ⓑ Ⓒ Ⓓ Ⓔ
4 Ⓐ Ⓑ Ⓒ Ⓓ Ⓔ		21 Ⓐ Ⓑ Ⓒ Ⓓ Ⓔ
5 Ⓐ Ⓑ Ⓒ Ⓓ Ⓔ		22 Ⓐ Ⓑ Ⓒ Ⓓ Ⓔ
6 Ⓐ Ⓑ Ⓒ Ⓓ Ⓔ		23 Ⓐ Ⓑ Ⓒ Ⓓ Ⓔ
7 Ⓐ Ⓑ Ⓒ Ⓓ Ⓔ		24 Ⓐ Ⓑ Ⓒ Ⓓ Ⓔ
8 Ⓐ Ⓑ Ⓒ Ⓓ Ⓔ		25 Ⓐ Ⓑ Ⓒ Ⓓ Ⓔ
9 Ⓐ Ⓑ Ⓒ Ⓓ Ⓔ		26 Ⓐ Ⓑ Ⓒ Ⓓ Ⓔ
10 Ⓐ Ⓑ Ⓒ Ⓓ Ⓔ		27 Ⓐ Ⓑ Ⓒ Ⓓ Ⓔ
11 Ⓐ Ⓑ Ⓒ Ⓓ Ⓔ		28 Ⓐ Ⓑ Ⓒ Ⓓ Ⓔ
12 Ⓐ Ⓑ Ⓒ Ⓓ Ⓔ		29 Ⓐ Ⓑ Ⓒ Ⓓ Ⓔ
13 Ⓐ Ⓑ Ⓒ Ⓓ Ⓔ		30 Ⓐ Ⓑ Ⓒ Ⓓ Ⓔ
14 Ⓐ Ⓑ Ⓒ Ⓓ Ⓔ		31 Ⓐ Ⓑ Ⓒ Ⓓ Ⓔ
15 Ⓐ Ⓑ Ⓒ Ⓓ Ⓔ		32 Ⓐ Ⓑ Ⓒ Ⓓ Ⓔ
16 Ⓐ Ⓑ Ⓒ Ⓓ Ⓔ		33 Ⓐ Ⓑ Ⓒ Ⓓ Ⓔ
17 Ⓐ Ⓑ Ⓒ Ⓓ Ⓔ		34 Ⓐ Ⓑ Ⓒ Ⓓ Ⓔ

PART II

1. The primary function of a take-up pulley in a belt conveyor is to
    A) carry the belt on the return trip.
    B) track the belt.
    C) maintain proper belt tension
    D) change the direction of the belt

2. Which device is used to transfer power and rotary mechanical motion from one shaft to another?

    A) Bearing
    B) Lever
    C) Idler roller
    D) Gear
    E) Bushing

See Figure III-A-22 on Page 66

3. Which of the following circuits is shown in Figure III-A-22?

    A) Series circuit
    B) Parallel circuit
    C) Series, parallel circuit
    D) Solid state circuit
    E) None of the above

4. A circuit has two resistors of equal value in series. The voltage and current in the circuit are 20 volts and 2 amps respectively. What is the value of EACH resistor?

    A) 5 ohms
    B) 10 ohms
    C) 20 ohms

D) Not enough information given

5. What is the total net capacitance of two 60-farad capacitors connected in series?

    A) 30 farads
    B) 60 farads
    C) 90 farads
    D) 120 farads
    E) 360 farads

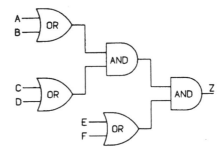

Figure 79-4-17B

6. Select the Boolean equation that matches the circuit diagram in Figure 79-4-17B.

    A) Z = AB+CD+EF
    B) Z z (A+B) (C+D) (E+F)
    C) Z = A+B+C+D+EF
    D) Z = ABCD(E+F)

7. If two 30-mH inductors are connected in series, what is the total net inductance of the combination?

    A) 15 mH
    B) 20 mH
    C) 30 mH
    D) 45 mH
    E) 60 mH

8.   In pure number 6 binary the
      decimal would be expressed as

      A) 001
      B) 011
      C) 110
      D) 111

**File Cabinet Picture
See Figure 75-25-1 on
Page 67**

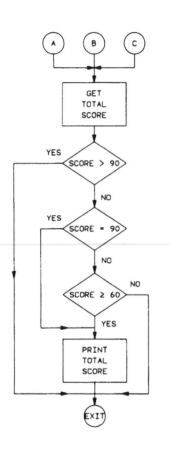

FIGURE 75-8-1 1

9.   In Figure 75-8-11, which of the
      following scores will be printed?

      A) All scores > 90 and < 60
      B) All scores < 90
      C) All scores ≤ 90 and ≥ 60
      D) All scores < 60

10.   Crowbars, light bulbs and vacuum
      bags are to be stored in the cabinet
      shown in Figure 75-25-1. Consid-
      ering the balance of weight, what
      would be the safest arrangement?

      A) Top Drawer - Crowbars
         Middle Drawer - Light Bulbs
         Bottom Drawer - Vacuum bags
      B) Top Drawer - Crowbars
         Middle Drawer - Vacuum bags
         Bottom Drawer - Light Bulbs
      C) Top Drawer - Vacuum Bags
         Middle Drawer - Crowbars
         Bottom Drawer - Light Bulbs
      D) Top Drawer - Vacuum Bags
         Middle Drawer - Light Bulbs
         Bottom Drawer - Crowbars
      E) Top Drawer - Light Bulbs
         Middle Drawer - Vacuum Bags
         Bottom Drawer - Crowbars

11.   Which is most appropriate for
      pulling a heavy load?

      A) Electric lift
      B) Fork lift
      C) Tow Conveyor
      D) Dolly
      E) Pallet truck

12. The electrical circuit term "open circuit" refers to a closed loop being opened. When an ohmmeter is connected into this type of circuit, one can expect the meter to

   A) Read infinity
   B) Read infinity and slowly return to ZERO
   C) Read ZERO
   D) Read ZERO and slowly return to infinity
   E) None of the above

13. Contaminants have caused bearings to fail prematurely. Which pair of the items listed below should be kept away from bearings?

   A) Dirt and oil
   B) Grease and water
   C) Oil and grease
   D) Dirt and moisture
   E) Water and oil

14. In order to operate a breast drill, which direction should you turn it?

   A) Clockwise
   B) Counterclockwise
   C) Up and down
   D) Back and forth
   E) Right, then left

15. Which is the correct tool for tightening or loosening a water pipe?

   A) Slip joint pliers
   B) Household pliers
   C) Monkey wrench
   D) Water pump pliers
   E) Pipe wrench

16. What is one purpose of a chuck key?

   A) Open doors
   B) Remove drill bits
   C) Remove screws
   D) Remove set screws
   E) Unlock chucks

17. When smoke is generated as a result of using a portable electric drill for cutting holes into a piece of angle iron, one should

   A) use a fire watch.
   B) cease the drilling operation.
   C) use an exhaust fan to remove smoke.
   D) use a prescribed coolant solution to reduce friction.
   E) call the Fire Department.

18. The primary purpose of soldering is to

   A) melt solder to a molten state.
   B) heat metal parts to the right temperature to be joined.
   C) join metal parts by melting the parts.
   D) harden metal.
   E) join metal parts.

19. Which of the following statements is correct of a soldering gun?

   A) Tip is not replaceable
   B) Cannot be used in cramped places
   C) Heats only when trigger is pressed
   D) Not rated by the number of watts they use
   E) Has no light

20. What unit of measurement is read on a dial torque wrench?

A) Pounds
B) Inches
C) Centimeters
D) Foot-pounds
E) Degrees

21. Which instrument is used to test insulation breakdown of a conductor?

A) Ohmmeter
B) Ammeter
C) Megger
D) Wheatstone bridge
E) Voltmeter

22. ½ of 1/4 =

A) 1/12
B) 1/8
C) 1/4
D) ½
E) 8

23. 2.6 - .5 =

A) 2.0
B) 2.1
C) 3.1
D) 3.3
E) None of the above

24. Simplify the following expression in terms of amps:

563×10^{-6}

A) 563,000,000 amps
B) 563,000 amps
C) .563 amps
D) .000563 amps
E) .000000563 amps

25. Solve the power equation

$P = I^2 R$ for R

A) R = EI
B) $R = I^2 P$
C) R = PI
D) $R = P/I^2$
E) R = E/I

26. The product of 3 kilo ohms times 3 micro ohms is

A) 6×10^{-9} ohms
B) 6×10^{-3} ohms
C) 9×10^{3} ohms
D) 9×10^{-6} ohms
E) 9×10^{-3} ohms

In sample question 25 below, select the statement which is most nearly correct according to the paragraph.

"Prior to 1870, a conveyor that made use of rollers was developed for transporting clay. This construction substituted rolling friction at the idler bearing points for the sliding friction of the slider bed. A primitive type of "roughing belt conveyor was developed about the same time for the handling of grain. This design was improved during the latter part of the century when the "roughing idler was developed."

27. According to the above paragraph, which of the following statements is most nearly correct?

A) The "roughing belt conveyor was developed about 1870 to handle clay and grain.

B) Rolling friction construction was replaced by sliding friction construction prior to 1870.

C) In the late nineteenth century, conveyors were improved with the development of the "roughing idler.

D) The "roughing idler, a significant design improvement for conveyors, was developed in the early nineteenth century.

E) Conveyor belts were invented and developed in the 1800's.

For sample question 28 below, select from the drawings of objects on the right labeled A, B, C, and D, the one that would have the TOP, FRONT, and RIGHT views shown in the drawing at the left

28.

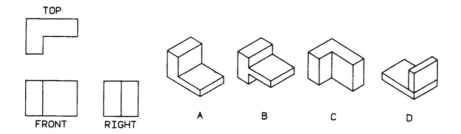

In sample question 29 below, there is, on the left, a drawing of a flat piece of paper and, on the right, four figures labeled A, B, C, and D. When the paper is bent on the dotted lines it will form one of the figures on the right. Decide which alternative can be formed from the flat piece.

29

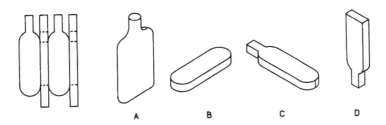

In each of the sample questions below, look at the symbols in the first two boxes. Something about the three symbols in the first box makes them alike; something about the two symbols in the other box with the question mark makes them alike. Look for some characteristic that is common to all symbols in the same box, yet makes them different from the symbols in the other box. Among the five answer choices, find the symbol that can best be substituted for the question mark, because it is <u>like</u> the symbols in the second box, and, for the same reason, different from those in the first box.

30.

USE DIAGRAM ON PAGE 72 QUESTION 32

In sample question 30 above, all the symbols in the first box are vertical lines. The second box has two lines, one broken and one solid. Their <u>likeness</u> to each other consists in their being horizontal; and their being horizontal makes them <u>different</u> from the vertical lines in the other box. The answer must be the only one of the five lettered choices that is a horizontal line, either broken or solid. NOTE: There is not supposed to be a series or progression in these symbol questions. If you look for a progression in the first box and the second box, you will be wasting time. Remember, look for a <u>likeness</u> within each box and a <u>difference</u> between the two boxes.

Now do sample questions 31 and 32.

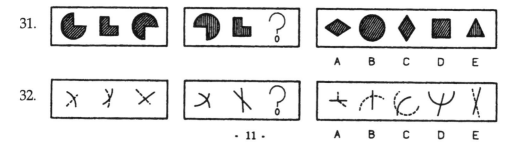

· 11 ·

33.   In Figure 3-8-6 below, what is the measurement of Dimension F? Drawing is not actual size.

A) 1 3/4 inches
B) 2 1/4 inches
C) 2 ½ inches
D) 3 3/4 inches
E) None of the above

Use Figure 3-8-6 on page 68

34.   In Figure 160-57 below, what is the current flow through R when:

   V = 50 volts
   R1 = 25 ohms
   R2 = 25 ohms
   R3 = 50 ohms
   R4 = 50 ohms
   R5 = 50 ohms

and the current through the entire
circuit totals one amp?

   A   0.5 amp
   B) 5.0 amps
   C) 5.0 milliamps
   D) 50.0 milliamps
   E) None of the above

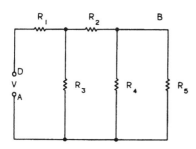

Figure 160-57

EXHIBIT B

The following positions use Test M/N 932:

Position Title	Register
Electronic Technician 8	M26
Electronic Technician 9	M27
Electronic Technician 10	M28

CORRECT ANSWERS TO
SAMPLE QUESTIONS

1.	C		18.	E
2.	D		19.	C
3.	A		20.	D
4.	A		21.	C
5.	A		22.	B
6.	B		23.	B
7.	D		24.	D
8.	C		25.	D
9.	C		26.	E
10.	E		27.	C
11.	E		28.	C
12.	A		29.	C
13.	D		30.	C
14.	A		31.	E
15.	E		32.	D
16.	B		33.	C
17.	D		34.	A

EXAM 933 - Measures 16 knowledge, skills, and abilities used by a variety of maintenance positions including Maintenance Mechanic and Overhaul Specialist.

Test M/N 933 covers the following Knowledge, Skills, and Abilities:

✔   *Knowledge of basic mechanics* refers to the theory of operation, terminology, usage, and characteristics of basic mechanical principles as they apply to such things as gears, pulleys, cams, pawls, power transmissions, linkages, fasteners, chains, sprockets, and belts; and including hoisting, rigging, roping, pneumatics, and hydraulic devices.

✔   *Knowledge of basic electricity* refers to the theory, terminology, usage, and characteristics of basic electrical principles such as ohm's Law, Kirchoff's Law, and magnetism, as they apply to such things as AC-DC circuitry and hardware, relays, switches, and circuit breakers.

✔   *Knowledge of basic electronics* refers to the theory, terminology, usage, and characteristics of basic electronic principles concerning such things as solid state devices, vacuum tubes, coils, capacitors, resistors, and basic logic circuitry.

✔   *Knowledge of safety procedures and equipment* refers to the knowledge of industrial hazards (e.g., mechanical, chemical, electrical, electronic) and procedures and techniques established to avoid injuries to self and others such as lock-out devices, protective clothing, and waste disposal techniques.

✔   *Knowledge of lubrication materials and procedures* refers to the terminology, characteristics, storage, preparation, disposal, and usage techniques involved with lubrication materials such as oils, greases, and other types of lubricants.

✔   *Ability to perform basic mathematical computations* refers to the ability to perform basic calculations such as addition, subtraction, multiplication and division with whole numbers, fractions and decimals.

✔   *Ability to perform more complex mathematics* refers to the ability to perform calculations such as basic geometry, scientific notation, and number conversions, as applied to mechanical, electrical and electronic applications.

✔   *Ability to apply theoretical knowledge to practical applications* refers to mechanical, electrical and electronic maintenance applications such as inspection, troubleshooting equipment repair and modification, preventive maintenance, and installation of electrical equipment.

✔   *Ability to detect patterns* refers to the ability to observe and analyze qualitative factors such as number progressions, spatial relationships, and auditory and visual patterns. This includes combining information and determining how a given set of numbers, objects, or sounds are related to each other.

✔   *Ability to use written reference materials* refers to the ability to locate, read, and comprehend text material such as handbooks, manuals, bulletins, directives, checklists and route sheets.

✔   *Ability to follow instructions* refers to the ability to comprehend and execute written and oral instructions such as work orders, checklists, route sheets, and verbal directions and instructions.

✔   *Ability to use hand tools* refers to knowledge of, and proficiency with, various hand tools. This ability involves the safe and efficient use and maintenance of such tools as screwdrivers, wrenches, hammers, pliers, chisels, punches, taps, dies, rules, gauges, and alignment tools.

✔   *Ability to use technical drawings* refers to the ability to react and comprehend technical materials such as diagrams, schematics, flow charts, and blueprints.

✔   *Ability to use test equipment* refers to the knowledge of, and proficiency with, various mechanical, electrical and electronic test equipment such as VOMS, oscilloscopes, circuit tracers, amprobes, and tachometers.

✔   *Ability to solder* refers to the knowledge of, and the ability to safely and effectively apply, the appropriate soldering techniques.

The sample exam that follows illustrates the types of questions that will be used in Test M/N 933. The samples will also show how the questions in the test are to be answered. Job descriptions for these occupations are included in Chapter Nine.

UNITED STATES POSTAL SERVICE

SAMPLE QUESTIONS - TEST M/N 933

The purpose of this booklet is to illustrate the types of questions that will be used in Test M/M 933. The samples will also show how the questions in the test are to be answered.

Test M/N 933 measures 16 Knowledge, Skills, and Abilities (KSAs) used by a variety of maintenance positions. Exhibit A lists the actual KSAs that are measured, and Exhibit B lists the positions that use this examination. However, not all KSAs that are measured in this test are scored for every position listed. The qualification standard for each position lists the KSAs required for the position. Only those questions that measure KSAs required for the position(s) for which you are applying will be scored for the position(s).

The suggested answers to each question are lettered A, B, C, etc. Select the BEST answer and make a heavy pencil mark in the corresponding space on the Sample Answer Sheet. Each mark must be dense black. Each mark must cover more than half the space and must not extend into neighboring spaces. If the answer to Sample 1 is B, you would mark the Sample Answer Sheet like this:

After recording your answers, compare them with those in the Correct Answers to Sample Questions. If they do not agree, carefully re-read the questions that were missed to get a clear understanding of what each question is asking.

During the test, directions for answering questions in Part I will be given orally, either by a cassette tape or by the examiner. You are to listen closely to the directions and follow them. To practice for this part of the test you might have a friend read the direction to you while you mark your answers on the Sample Answer Sheet. Directions for answering questions in Part II will be completely described in the test booklet.

STUDY CAREFULLY BEFORE YOU GO TO THE EXAMINATION ROOM

PART I

In Part I of the test, you will be told to follow directions by writing in a test booklet and then on an answer sheet. The test booklet will have lines of material like the following five samples:

SAMPLE   1.   5 _____

SAMPLE   2.   1 6 4 3 7

SAMPLE   3.   D B A E C

SAMPLE   4.   (8__) (5__) (2__) (9__) (10__)

SAMPLE   5   (7__) [6__] (1__) [12__]

To practice this test, have someone read the instructions on the **next page** to you and you follow the instructions. When they tell you to darken the space on the Sample Answer Sheet, use the one on this page.

```
                    SAMPLE ANSWER SHEET
  1  Ⓐ Ⓑ Ⓒ Ⓓ Ⓔ      5  Ⓐ Ⓑ Ⓒ Ⓓ Ⓔ      9  Ⓐ Ⓑ Ⓒ Ⓓ Ⓔ
  2  Ⓐ Ⓑ Ⓒ Ⓓ Ⓔ      6  Ⓐ Ⓑ Ⓒ Ⓓ Ⓔ     10  Ⓐ Ⓑ Ⓒ Ⓓ Ⓔ
  3  Ⓐ Ⓑ Ⓒ Ⓓ Ⓔ      7  Ⓐ Ⓑ Ⓒ Ⓓ Ⓔ     11  Ⓐ Ⓑ Ⓒ Ⓓ Ⓔ
  4  Ⓐ Ⓑ Ⓒ Ⓓ Ⓔ      8  Ⓐ Ⓑ Ⓒ Ⓓ Ⓔ     12  Ⓐ Ⓑ Ⓒ Ⓓ Ⓔ
```

<u>Instructions to be read</u> (the words in parentheses should not be read aloud).

You are to follow the instructions that I shall read to you. I cannot repeat them.

Look at the samples. Sample 1 has a number and a line beside it. On the line write an A. (Pause 2 seconds.) Now on the Sample Answer Sheet, find number 5 (pause 2 seconds) and darken the space for the letter you just wrote on the line. (Pause 2 seconds.)

Look at Sample 2. (Pause slightly.) Draw a line under the third number. (Pause 2 seconds.) Now look on the Sample Answer Sheet, find the number under which you just drew a line and darken space B as in baker for that number. (Pause 5 seconds.)

Look at Sample 3. (Pause slightly.) Draw a line under the third letter in the line. (Pause 2 seconds.) Now on your Sample Answer Sheet, find number 9 (pause 2 seconds) and darken the space for the letter under which you drew a line. (Pause 5 seconds.)

Look at the five circles in Sample 4. (Pause slightly.) Each circle has a number and a line in it. write D as in dog on the blank in the last circle. (Pause 2 seconds.) Now on the Sample Answer Sheet, darken the space for the number-letter combination that is in the circle you just wrote in. (Pause 5 seconds.)

Look at Sample 5. (Pause slightly.) There are two circles and two boxes of different sizes with numbers in them. (Pause slightly.) If 4 is more than 2 and if 5 is less than 3, write A in the smaller circle. (Pause slightly.) Otherwise write C in the larger box. (Pause 2 seconds.) Now on the Sample Answer Sheet, darken the space for the number-letter combination in the circle or box in which you just wrote. (Pause 5 seconds.)

Now look at the Sample Answer Sheet. (Pause slightly.) You should have darkened spaces 4B, 5A, 9A, 10D, and 12C on the Sample Answer Sheet. (If the person preparing to take the examination made any mistakes, try to help him or her understand why the mistakes are wrong.)

SAMPLE ANSWER QUESTIONS

1 Ⓐ Ⓑ Ⓒ Ⓓ Ⓔ   18 Ⓐ Ⓑ Ⓒ Ⓓ Ⓔ
2 Ⓐ Ⓑ Ⓒ Ⓓ Ⓔ   19 Ⓐ Ⓑ Ⓒ Ⓓ Ⓔ
3 Ⓐ Ⓑ Ⓒ Ⓓ Ⓔ   20 Ⓐ Ⓑ Ⓒ Ⓓ Ⓔ
4 Ⓐ Ⓑ Ⓒ Ⓓ Ⓔ   21 Ⓐ Ⓑ Ⓒ Ⓓ Ⓔ
5 Ⓐ Ⓑ Ⓒ Ⓓ Ⓔ   22 Ⓐ Ⓑ Ⓒ Ⓓ Ⓔ
6 Ⓐ Ⓑ Ⓒ Ⓓ Ⓔ   23 Ⓐ Ⓑ Ⓒ Ⓓ Ⓔ
7 Ⓐ Ⓑ Ⓒ Ⓓ Ⓔ   24 Ⓐ Ⓑ Ⓒ Ⓓ Ⓔ
8 Ⓐ Ⓑ Ⓒ Ⓓ Ⓔ   25 Ⓐ Ⓑ Ⓒ Ⓓ Ⓔ
9 Ⓐ Ⓑ Ⓒ Ⓓ Ⓔ   26 Ⓐ Ⓑ Ⓒ Ⓓ Ⓔ
10 Ⓐ Ⓑ Ⓒ Ⓓ Ⓔ   27 Ⓐ Ⓑ Ⓒ Ⓓ Ⓔ
11 Ⓐ Ⓑ Ⓒ Ⓓ Ⓔ   28 Ⓐ Ⓑ Ⓒ Ⓓ Ⓔ
12 Ⓐ Ⓑ Ⓒ Ⓓ Ⓔ   29 Ⓐ Ⓑ Ⓒ Ⓓ Ⓔ
13 Ⓐ Ⓑ Ⓒ Ⓓ Ⓔ   30 Ⓐ Ⓑ Ⓒ Ⓓ Ⓔ
14 Ⓐ Ⓑ Ⓒ Ⓓ Ⓔ   31 Ⓐ Ⓑ Ⓒ Ⓓ Ⓔ
15 Ⓐ Ⓑ Ⓒ Ⓓ Ⓔ   32 Ⓐ Ⓑ Ⓒ Ⓓ Ⓔ
16 Ⓐ Ⓑ Ⓒ Ⓓ Ⓔ   33 Ⓐ Ⓑ Ⓒ Ⓓ Ⓔ
17 Ⓐ Ⓑ Ⓒ Ⓓ Ⓔ   34 Ⓐ Ⓑ Ⓒ Ⓓ Ⓔ

PART II

1. The primary function of a take-up pulley in a belt conveyor is to

    A) carry the belt on the return trip.
    B) track the belt.
    C) maintain proper belt tension.
    D) change the direction of the belt.
    E) regulate the speed of the belt.

2. Which device is used to transfer power and rotary mechanical motion from one shaft to another?

    A) Bearing
    B) Lever
    C) Idler roller
    D) Gear
    E) Bushing

3. What special care is required in the storage of hard steel roller bearings? They should be

    A) cleaned and spun dry with compressed air.
    B) oiled once a month.
    C) stored in a humid place.
    D) wrapped in oiled paper.
    E) stored at temperatures below 90 degrees Fahrenheit.

4. Which is the correct method to lubricate a roller chain?

    A) Use brush to apply lubricant while chain is in motion
    B) Use squirt can to apply lubricant while chain is in motion
    C) Use brush to apply lubricant while chain is not in motion
    D) Soak chain in pan of lubricant and hang to allow excess to drain
    E) Chains do not need lubrication

5. A circuit has two resistors of equal value in series. The voltage and current in the circuit are 20 volts and 2 amps respectively. What is the value of EACH resistor?

    A) 5 ohms
    B) 10 ohms
    C) 15 ohms
    D) 20 ohms
    E) Not enough given

See Figure III-A-22 on Page 66

6. Which of the following circuits is shown in Figure III-A-22?

    A) Series circuit
    B) Parallel circuit
    C) Series, parallel circuit
    D) Solid state circuit
    E) None of the above

7. What is the total net capacitance of two 60 farad capacitors connected in series?

    A) 30 F
    B) 60 F
    C) 90 F
    D) 120 F
    E) 360 F

8. If two 30 mH inductors are connected in series, what is the total net inductance of the combination?

    A) 15 mH
    B) 20 mH
    C) 30 mH
    D) 45 mH
    E) 60 mH

**File Cabinet Picture
See Figure 75-25-1 on
Page 67**

9. Crowbars, light bulbs and vacuum bags are to be stored in the cabinet shown in Figure 75-25-1. Considering the balance of weight, what would be the safest arrangement?

   A) Top Drawer - Crowbars
      Middle Drawer - Light Bulbs
      Bottom Drawer - Vacuum bags
   B) Top Drawer - Crowbars
      Middle Drawer - Vacuum bags
      Bottom Drawer - Light Bulbs
   C) Top Drawer - Vacuum Bags
      Middle Drawer - Crowbars
      Bottom Drawer - Light Bulbs
   D) Top Drawer - Vacuum Bags
      Middle Drawer - Light Bulbs
      Bottom Drawer - Crowbars
   E) Top Drawer - Light Bulbs
      Middle Drawer - Vacuum Bags
      Bottom Drawer - Crowbars

10. Contaminants have caused bearings to fail prematurely. Which pair of the items listed below should be kept away from bearings?

    A) Dirt and oil
    B) Grease and water
    C) Oil and grease
    D) Dirt and moisture
    E) Water and oil

11. The electrical circuit term "open circuit" refers to a closed loop being opened. When an ohmmeter is connected into this type of circuit, one can expect the meter to

    A) read infinity.
    B) read infinity and slowly return to ZERO.
    C) read ZERO.
    D) read ZERO and slowly return to infinity.
    E) None of the above

12. Which is most appropriate for pulling a heavy load?

    A) Electric lift
    B) Fork lift
    C) Tow conveyor
    D) Dolly
    E) Pallet truck

13. In order to operate a breast drill, which direction should you turn it?

    A) Clockwise
    B) Counterclockwise
    C) Up and down
    D) Back and forth
    E) Right, then left

14. Which is the correct tool for tightening or loosening a water pipe?

    A) Slip joint pliers
    B) Household pliers
    C) Monkey wrench
    D) water pump pliers
    E) Pipe wrench

15. What is one purpose of a chuck key?

    A) Open doors
    B) Remove drill bits
    C) Remove screws
    D) Remove set screws
    E) Unlock chucks

16. When smoke is generated as a result of using a portable electric drill for cutting holes into a piece of angle iron. One should

A) use a fire watch.
B) cease the drilling operation.
C) use an exhaust fan to remove smoke.
D) use a prescribed coolant solution to reduce friction.
E) call the Fire Department.

17. The primary purpose of soldering is to

A) melt solder to a molten state.
B) heat metal parts to the right temperature be joined.
C) join metal parts by melting the parts.
D) harden metal.
E) join metal carts.

18. Which of the following statements is correct concerning a soldering gun?

A) Tip is not replaceable
B) Cannot be used in cramped places
C) Heats only when trigger is pressed
D) Not rated by the number of watts it uses
E) Has no light

19. What unit of measurement is read on a dial torque wrench?

A) Pounds
B) Inches
C) Centimeters
D) Foot-pounds
E) Degrees

20. Which instrument is used to test insulation breakdown of a conductor?

A) Ohmmeter
B) Ammeter
C) Megger
D) Wheatstone bridge
E) Voltmeter

21. ½ of 1/4 =

A) 1/12
B) 1/8
C) 1/4
D) ½
E) 8

22. 2.6 - .5 =

A) 2.0
B) 2.1
C) 3.1
D) 3.3
E) None of the above

23. Solve the power equation

$P = I^2R$ for R

A) $R = EI$
B) $R = I^2P$
C) $R = PI$
D) $R = P/I^2$
E) $R = E/I$

24. The product of 3 kilo ohms times 3 micro ohms is

A) 6×10^{-9} ohms
B) 6×10^{-3} ohms
C) 9×10^{3} ohms
D) 9×10^{-6} ohms
E) 9×10^{-3} ohms

In sample question 25 below, select the statement which is most nearly correct according to the paragraph.

"Prior to 1870, a conveyor that made use of rollers was developed for transporting clay. This construction substituted rolling friction at the idler bearing points for the sliding friction of the slider bed. A primitive type of roughing belt conveyor was developed about the same time for the handling of grain. This design was improved during the latter part of the century when the roughing idler was developed."

25. According to the above paragraph, which of the following statements is most nearly correct?

    A) The troughing belt conveyor was developed about 1870 to handle clay and grain.

    B) Rolling friction construction was replaced by sliding friction construction prior to 1870.

    C) In the late nineteenth century, conveyors were improved with the development of the roughing idler.

    D) The roughing idler, a significant design improvement for conveyors, was developed in the early nineteenth century.

    E) Conveyor belts were invented and developed in the 1800's.

26. A small crane was used to <u>raise</u> the heavy part. <u>Raise</u> MOST nearly means

    A) lift
    B) drag
    C) drop
    D) deliver
    E) guide

27. <u>Short</u> MOST nearly means

    A) tall
    B) wide
    C) brief
    D) heavy
    E) dark

For sample question 28 below, select from the drawings of objects on the right labeled A, B, C, and D, the one that would have the TOP, FRONT, and RIGHT views shown in the drawing at the left

28.

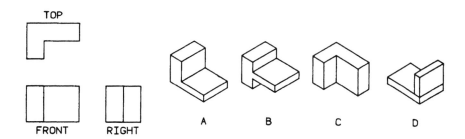

In sample question 29 below, there is, on the left, a drawing of a flat piece of paper and, on the right, four figures labeled A, B, C, and D. When the paper is bent on the dotted lines it will form one of the figures on the right. Decide which alternative can be formed from the flat piece.

29

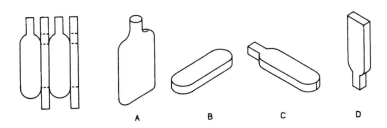

In each of the sample questions below, look at the symbols in the first two boxes. Something about the three symbols in the first box makes them alike; something about the two symbols in the other box with the question mark makes them alike. Look for some characteristic that is common to all symbols in the same box, yet makes them different from the symbols in the other box. Among the five answer choices, find the symbol that can best be substituted for the question mark, because it is like the symbols in the second box, and, for the same reason, different from those in the first box.

30.

USE DIAGRAM ON PAGE 72 QUESTION 32

In sample question 30 above, all the symbols in the first box are vertical lines. The second box has two lines, one broken and one solid. Their <u>likeness</u> to each other consists in their being horizontal; and their being horizontal makes them <u>different</u> from the vertical lines in the other box. The answer must be the only one of the five lettered choices that is a horizontal line, either broken or solid. NOTE: There is not supposed to be a series or progression in these symbol questions. If you look for a progression in the first box and the second box, you will be wasting time. Remember, look for a <u>likeness</u> within each box and a <u>difference</u> between the two bo xes.

Now do sample questions 31 and 32.

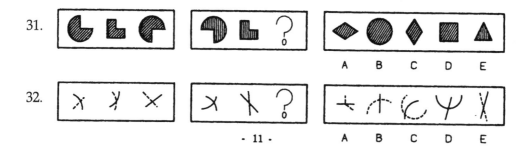

33. In Figure 3-8-6 below, what is the measurement of Dimension F? Drawing is not actual size.

    A) 1 3/4 inches
    B) 2 1/4 inches
    C) 2 ½ inches
    D) 3 3/4 inches
    E) None of the above

Use Figure 3-8-6 on page 68

34. In Figure 160-57 below, what is the current flow through R when:

    V = 50 volts
    R1 = 25 ohms
    R2 = 25 ohms

R3 = 50 ohms
R4 = 50 ohms
R5 = 50 ohms

and the current through the entire circuit totals one amp?

    A 0.5 amp
    B) 5.0 amps
    C) 5.0 milliamps
    D) 50.0 milliamps
    E) None of the above

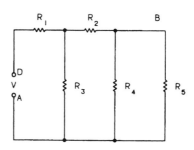

Figure 160-57

EXHIBIT B

The following positions use test M/N 933:

Position Title	Register Number
Maintenance Mechanic, MPE/06	M32
Maintenance Mechanic, MPE/07	M33
Overhaul Specialist	M34

CORRECT ANSWERS TO
SAMPLE QUESTIONS

1.	C		18.	C
2.	D		19.	D
3.	D		20.	C
4.	D		21.	B
5.	A		22.	B
6.	A		23.	D
7.	A		24.	E
8.	E		25.	C
9.	E		26.	A
10.	D		27.	C
11.	A		28.	C
12.	E		29.	C
13.	A		30.	C
14.	E		31.	E
15.	B		32.	D
16.	D		33.	C
17.	E		34.	A

AUTOMOTIVE MECHANIC EXAMINATION 943

The questions on the facing page are examples of the types of questions that will be used on Examination 943. Study these questions carefully. Each question has several suggested answers. You are to decide which one is the best answer.

On the Sample Answer Sheet below, find the answer space that is numbered the same as the question, then darken the space that is lettered the same as the answer you have selected. After you have answered all the questions, compare your answers with the correct ones provided.[1]

SAMPLE ANSWER SHEET

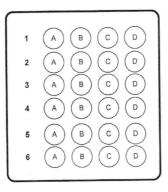

Sample Questions Examination 943 - Automotive Mechanic

1. A spongy brake pedal usually indicates:
a. worn shoes or pads
b. defective brake booster
c. brakes out of adjustment
d. air in the system

2. A battery load test determines if the:
a. voltage meets a minimum standard
b. amperage meets a minimum standard
c. charging system is defective
d. cold cranking amperes are sufficient

3. Oil pressure gauges may be of the
_____ or _____ type.
a. thermistor, primary
b. magnetic, bimetallic
c. secondary, property
d. cadmium, electrical

4. All of the following could cause tire wear if not within manufacturer's specs: EXCEPT:
a. steering axis inclination
b. toe-in
c. caster
d. camber

5. A hydro-boost system provides assisted power to the steering and which other system?
a. electrical
b. air-ride suspension
c. air conditioner
d. braking

6. No cranking and no lights when the key is turned to the START position may be caused by all the following EXCEPT a/an:
a. dead battery
b. open fusible link
c. burned-out headlight
d. open circuit

The correct answers to questions 1 through 6 are: 1d, 2a, 3b, 4c, 5d, and 6c.

---

[1] The Postal Service's Sample 94 Automotive Mechanic Examination, 10/2002

ACCOUNTING TECHNICIAN JUNIOR EXAMINATION 741

If you are scheduled to take United States Postal Service Test 741 (Accounting Technician, Junior), you need to know the following:[2]

1.   YOU ARE ALLOWED TO USE A CALCULATOR. YOU MAY BRING YOUR OWN IF YOU WISH TO DO SO. Quiet calculators performing only basic functions (addition, subtraction, multiplication, division, square root and percentage) will be permitted.

   Calculators NOT permitted are those requiring an electrical outlet or those which are programmable. Devices with an alphabetical and typewriter keyboard, a printer or tape, spell-check, thesaurus, address/appointment book, language translator, dictionary, checkers or anything technologically more advanced resembling computer features are NOT permitted. You will be prohibited from using them during the examination.

2.   The examination you are scheduled to take lasts 2 hours and 30 minutes, and is divided in seven sections testing applicants' abilities to perform the duties of a junior accountant.

3.   A sample of the type of questions you will have to answer is included in Pages 2 and 3. Please read carefully to familiarize yourself with the material included in the test.

SAMPLE QUESTIONS ON NEXT TWO PAGES

---

[2] The Postal Service's Sample 741 Accounting Technician, Junior Examination, 10/2001

Listed below are certain types of questions that will appear on the test. Work through the questions, and then check for the listed correct answer. There will be other types of questions on the test, so this is only a partial listing.

1. Each question consists of a series of numbers which progress in a definite order. Determine the pattern or trend in each sequence of numbers. Select the correct number, from the five alternatives, that would continue the series.

   5, __, 15,20,25

   A)   10
   B)   11
   C)   12
   D)   13
   E)   14

   10 is the correct answer.

2. Compare each set or line of information in the *LIST TO BE VERIFIED* with the corresponding set in the *CORRECT LIST*. For each line in the *LIST TO BE VERIFIED,* indicate which of the following alternatives is true:

   There is an error(s) in:

   A)   **One** column
   B)   **Two** columns
   C)   **Three** columns
   D)   **Four** columns
   E)   **None of the columns**

   CORRECT LIST
   June Ramplede
   1833
   253-05-0031
   683-10

   LIST TO BE VERIFIED

Name	*Identifying Member*	*Resident City Code*	*Location Number*
Jane Ramplede	1833	253-05-0031	683-10

   The correct answer is A. There is an error in one column, the Name column.

3. Find the correct space in each listing for the name or code in italics on the first line of each question so that it will be in alphabetical and/or numerical order with the others.

    02059625

    A) →
            02059824

    B) →
            02059913

    C) →
            02064623

    D) →
            02069102

    E) →

    The correct answer is A.

4. 25.4 + 69.2 =

    A)   84.6
    B)   94.2
    C)   94.6
    D)   96.8
    E)   None of the above

    C) 94.6 is the correct answer.

5. Look at the numbers below. Circle the second number from the left. Add 3 to that number. What is the resulting answer?

    2 5 7 1 4 7

    A)   7
    B)   8
    C)   9
    D)   10
    E)   11

    B) 8 is the correct answer

Chapter Five
The 473, 473-C, & 473-E Postal Exams

This chapter includes a study guide with sample test questions for the 473, 473-C, and 473-E Postal Exams. You will also find helpful test taking tips and strategies that you can use for the practice and official exams.

The Postal Service hires workers for major entry-level mail handling jobs from applicants who successfully pass the 473 exam with a score of 70 or higher. Applicants are required to take a 90-minute unproctored assessment online and a 90-minute written proctored exam within fourteen days of applying. Review the hiring process in Chapter Two for complete details. Applicants who pass the exam are placed on the hiring register according to score. The highest scoring applicants will be called for an interview, medical screening, and drug test. Disabled veterans who pass the exam are placed at the top of the register by law, ahead of all other applicants who took the exam. The higher your score, the better chance you have of being called for an interview and hired.

In addition to exam results, the Postal Service will review your employment history, education, military service if applicable, and complete a background check.

CAUTION
You don't have to pay anyone to take a postal exam. Exams are administered at no cost to the applicant. Locate exam announcements for your area online, or at local, state, and federal buildings. Review the Postal Service's recruiting process and explore occupations on the following Web site:

www.postalwork.net/

ENTRY LEVEL JOBS COVERED BY THE 473 EXAM

City and Rural Carrier   Mail delivery and collection in the city and suburban areas by foot or vehicle. Must be able to carry 35 pound mail bags and containers or parcels weighing up to 70 pounds. Mail carriers work standing, reaching, and walking most of their workday.

Mail Processing Clerk   Sorts mail manually or by operating and monitoring automated equipment. Clerks transport processed mail in the work area, and bundle and collate mail as necessary. Heavy lifting of mail and containers may be required.

Mail Handler   Responsible for transporting, unloading and loading mail containers and equipment in their facility. They frequently carry equipment and packages that weigh 70 pounds or less and push heavy wheeled containers.

Sales, Services, and Distribution Associate   Responsible for retail sales, customer support and mail distribution. All associates must also complete on-the-job training.

The **473 Major Entry Level Jobs Exam** is also referred to as the 473 Battery Exam. This exam measures an applicant's general aptitude and personal characteristics, not factual knowledge. The main difference between the 473 and 473-C exam is the target audience. The 473-C exam is announced primarily when the Postal Service is recruiting large numbers of City Letter Carriers, and the 473 exam is used to cover all of the job categories listed above. The two exams are essentially the same. The 473-E exam incorporates the new online assessment.

Review this chapter to improve your test scores and to become familiar with the test taking process and strategies, application forms, answer sheets, and sample questions. The 473 examination and completion of forms will require approximately two hours and fifteen minutes, online and proctored sessions combined..

EXAM CONTENT

The five sections of the test are listed in Table 5-1 on page 105. Part D is now completed online when you first apply. Parts A through C are proctored exams administered at testing facilities in your area. You will be allowed to work only on one section of the test at a time. If you finish a part early you aren't permitted to proceed to the next part or to return to a part that you previously completed. The computer explains each part in turn and you must follow the instructions.

Table 5-1 Entry-level Battery 473			
Test Unit	**# of Questions**	**Time Allowed**	**Covered Subjects**
Part A Address Checking	60	11 min.	Determine if two addresses are identical.
Part B Forms Completion	30	15 min.	Information identification for completing forms correctly.
Part C Section 1 - Coding	36	6 min.	Using proper code to assign to addresses.
Part C Section 3 - Memory	36	7 min.	Memorize assigned codes for addresses.
Part D Inventory of Personal Experience and Characteristics	236	90 min.	Assess applicant's experience and characteristics related to the job. (Online Assessment)

Address Cross Comparison (Part A)

Part A includes 60 questions, and you have 11 minutes to complete this section. You will be tested on how fast and accurately you can compare two address lists. Postal workers must be able to differentiate between two addresses to determine if they are the same or different destinations. Address differences include different spelling or transposed numbers. The questions are multiple choice.

- A is selected if there are no errors.
- B is selected if only the addresses are different.
- C is selected if only the Zip Codes are different.
- D is selected if both the address and Zip Code are different.

Forms Completion (Part B)

Part B includes 30 questions, and you will have 15 minutes to complete this section. You will be provided with various sample forms and asked questions about what is to be entered on the form. For example, you might be given a form with 9 blocks, and block 5 may be the Zip code block. A possible question would be where you would enter the Zip code. The answer would be "block 5." You could also be asked what type of data goes in a specified box such as a number, check mark or name. All 30 questions are multiple choice A, B, C, or D.

Coding (Part C Section 1)

The coding section includes 36 questions, and you have six minutes to complete this section. You will be given four delivery routes, A through D, with street addresses. The questions list an address and you have to assign the correct delivery route for the address. The delivery routes will be given to you for the Coding exam and you will have to memorize the routes for the Memory section.

Memory (Part C Section 2)

The memory section includes 36 questions that are similar to the coding section questions. You have to select the correct delivery route, A, B, C, or D, without looking at the chart. You will be given time to memorize the addresses and routes before the exam starts.

Personal Characteristics and Experience (Part D)

This section takes 90 minutes and is completed online when you first apply. The Postal Service evaluates your personal experience, characteristics and tendencies. For example, you will be asked your likes and dislikes and whether you have experience in certain areas. You really can't prepare for this section; it's your personal profile. If you answer the questions honestly the Postal Service will be able to identify the job that is best suited to your characteristics. The answers are multiple choice. The question *"Do you like to work in groups?"* would have the answers (A) Strongly Agree, (B) Agree, (C), Disagree, (D) Strongly Disagree. A question similar to *"Are you willing to work rotating shifts?"* would have the answers (A) Very Often, (B) Often, (C) Sometimes, (D) Rarely. We do include some helpful hints on how to prepare for this section later in this chapter.

Exam Process

All exams are multiple choice, and the answers are typically A, B, C or D. However, in Part D there may be up to seven answers, A through G, to choose from. The test is entirely administered and timed by a computer and all the testing instructions are provided by the computer. Prior to starting the exam you will be guided through several practice and instruction screens to familiarize you with the testing process and use of the computer. Several practice exams are provided. The following example shows the typical answer grid that we use throughout this study guide.

Sample Answer Grid	
1	Ⓐ Ⓑ Ⓒ Ⓓ
2	Ⓐ Ⓑ Ⓒ Ⓓ
3	Ⓐ Ⓑ Ⓒ Ⓓ
4	Ⓐ Ⓑ Ⓒ Ⓓ

GENERAL INFORMATION

All hiring for the Postal Service is decentralized. When you apply for a postal job in any city you are applying only for a particular job vacancy. Your exam results can be used to apply for other job applications for a set time period as long as you have your Exam History Code that the Postal Service sends you after passing a test. The applicants with the highest grades are called for an interview. You have to apply for each job opening that you wish to be considered for. If you want to be considered for jobs in other areas you have to apply for jobs in that area.

All postal jobs — just like all federal Civil Service jobs — are highly competitive and you have to complete a considerable amount of paperwork including writing detailed work experience descriptions back at least 10 years, or to age 16 if you are a recent high school graduate.

EXAM OVERVIEW

The Postal Service will e-mail you a scheduling notice shortly after registering, applying, and completing your online assessment. The notice will specify the exam locations, various times, and dates available along with a link to the Assessment Introduction Package. Select the location, date and time that best suits your needs. The Assessment Introduction Package provides general test information and several sample test questions for each part of the exam.

The Assessment Introduction Package instructs you to bring the following items with you to the exam:

- Your login ID and Password (Login ID and Password for your assessment account. These are set up when you take the online unproctored Section D assessment)
- A state or federal picture ID (Generally your photo driver's license, passport, U.S. Military ID, etc.)
- Arrive at least 15 minutes early. (If you are more than 15 minutes late you can't take the exam)

The items listed above are **REQUIRED**. If you neglect to bring a valid photo ID or your user ID and password, or arrive over 15 minutes, late you will not be allowed to take the exam .

The examiner will provide you with disposable ear plugs and assist you with logging in to start the test. The examiner will not have access to any information related to your assessment results or your next step. You will receive an e-mail message with instructions on how to access your test results. You can also check your assessment results as part of your candidate profile in eCareer after your exam is complete. Return to www.usps.com.employment to log into eCareer and review your assessment results.[1]

TEST-TAKING STRATEGIES

The following strategies will help you improve your grades and complete more answers on the timed exams. Use these techniques on the practice tests in this book and when you take your actual Postal Service exam. If you practice these techniques now, when you take the postal exam they will become second nature.

> ➤   Get plenty of rest the night before the exam.

> ➤   Eliminate the answers in multiple choice questions that make no sense at all. You can often eliminate half of the answers through this method. If you have to guess an answer, you improve your chances through the process of elimination.

> ➤   You will be penalized for guessing on Part A, Address Checking, and Part C, Coding and Memory, due to the methods that the Postal Service uses to grade these sections. It is also unwise to guess or try to manipulate your answers for Section D, Personal Characteristics. Guessing on Part B, Forms Checking, will not adversely effect your scores.

> ➤   Don't forget your eyeglasses, hearing aid or anything else that you may need for the exam. Personal items such as cell phones, pagers, and PDAs are not allowed in the testing room.

> ➤   Review the directions to the testing facility and arrive early. You don't need the additional stress of getting lost on the way to the exam and arriving late. Arriving early will also give you time to get familiar with the testing facility. You can locate directions to the testing site on any of the Internet search engine mapping sites such the one at http://Yahoo.com.

> ➤   The test will take up to 90 minutes including initial introductions and the time it takes to complete the computer familiarization steps. Breaks are not permitted. Take care of personal needs before the test starts, and limit your fluid intake.

---

[1] Excerpted from "Assessment Information Package - Exam 473, Copyright © 2008 U.S. Postal Service"

➤ Be skeptical when an answer includes the words like, "always, never, all, none, generally," or "only." These words can be a trap. Only select an answer with these words in it if you are absolutely sure it is the right answer.

➤ If two answers have opposite meanings, take your time and look closer. Many times one of the two is correct.

➤ Make sure, when you select your answer to a specific question, that it registered on the screen. Sometimes going between the selected answer and enter keys the answer didn't register and I had to go back and reselect the answer before proceeding.

➤ One word can dramatically change the meaning of a sentence. Read each question word-for-word before answering.

➤ Don't dwell on the exam to the point that it upsets you. Answer the questions that you know first. If you have problems with a question, skip it and go to the next test question. You can mark a question for review and return to it later if time permits. After you complete the section, you can return to the unanswered questions you marked for review and give them more thought.

✎ **One word of caution**. Once you finish a section and are directed to go on to the next part, you can't go back to previously completed sections. You can go back only within the current section that you are working on if the time isn't up.

➤ Focus on one question at a time. Don't let your mind wander back to questions you skipped or to other sections. If you stay focused on each question you will be able to concentrate better on the exam.

> If you don't attend your scheduled exam appointment, you are not permitted to reschedule. An incomplete test result will be recorded for the job vacancy that you applied for. You can reschedule if you contact the assessment center no later than 24 hours before your scheduled exam time.

ADDRESS CHECKING - PART A

Part A includes 60 questions and you have 11 minutes to complete this section. You will be tested on how fast and accurately you can compare two lists. Postal workers must be able to differentiate between two addresses to determine if they are the same or different destinations. Address differences include different spelling or transposed numbers. The questions are multiple choice.

Questions include an address with street or P.O. box, city, and state in the first column of each list and a ZIP code in the second column. The example below shows the address on the left and the Zip code on the right in each list. You will compare the *Correct List* on the left to the *List to be Checked* on the right. You are required to determine if the address to be checked is exactly the same or different as the address and Zip code on the *Correct List*. You must determine if the address and Zip code is exactly the same or different including the numbers, punctuation, capitalization, and spelling. You will make your selections from the list below:

- A is selected if there are no errors, everything is exactly alike.
- B is selected if only the addresses are different.
- C is selected if only the Zip codes are different.
- D is selected if both the address and Zip code are different.

Prior to starting the actual exam you will be given two sample exercises of several questions on each to familiarize you with the process. This introduces you to what is expected on the exam. Complete the four sample questions that follow to better understand the process.

| A. No Errors | B. Address Only | C. ZIP Code Only | D. Both |

Correct List			List to be Checked		
#	Address	Zip Code		Address	Zip Code
S1.	1915 Park Place Fairview, TX	79411		1915 Park Place Fairview, TX	79141
S2.	401 McAuthur Drive Benton, NC	27514-1132		401 McAuther Drive Benton, NC	27514-1132
S3.	6915 Amber Way Pittsburgh, PA	15129-0005		6915 Amber Way Pittsburgh, PA	15129-0005
S4.	19150 First Street Kalamazoo, MI	49007-2334		19105 First Street Kalamizoo, MI	49070-2344

Sample Answer Grid	
S1	Ⓐ Ⓑ Ⓒ Ⓓ
S2	Ⓐ Ⓑ Ⓒ Ⓓ
S3	Ⓐ Ⓑ Ⓒ Ⓓ
S4	Ⓐ Ⓑ Ⓒ Ⓓ

Question S1

You will discover that the street, city and state are identical. However, the ZIP code is different. The third and fourth digits in the Zip code on the *List to be Checked* are reversed. Mark answer **"C"** for Zip Code Only.

Question S2

You will find the addresses have different spellings. McAuthur is spelled McAuther on the *List to be Checked*. The Zip Codes are identical. You will mark **"B"** on the sample answer sheet.

Question S3

The address and Zip Code of both lists are identical. Mark **"A"** on the answer sheet.

Question S4

You will find the street address and Zip Code numbers are different. The *Correct List* street number is 19150 and the list to be corrected street number is 19105. The last two digits of the first five Zip Code numbers are reversed. Also, the Zip Code's last 4 digits are not the same and the name Kalamazoo is misspelled. In this case you would mark **"D"** for both.

Before we start the actual practice exams for address checking there are a number of techniques you can use to improve your score and to improve your efficiency so that you will have more time to devote to the exam.

> ***Time is critical***. You will have 11 minutes to complete 60 questions. That's only 11 seconds per question. The more you practice and prepare for the exam the more questions you will be able to answer and the greater chance you have of earning a higher score.

Lets take another look at the four sample questions on the next page. Notice that I underlined the errors. When you start the sample questions and during the test, concentrate on the address first and then move on to the Zip code for each question. You can mark differences on the exam booklet for Part A as stated in the exam booklet on the bottom of page one. If you find an error in the address, mark it and move on to the Zip code and do the same. Once you find an error in either the address or Zip code, don't look for additional errors. All you need to do is find one and you don't want to waste the precious time you have. You will notice that question S4 on the next page has two errors in the address. Stop after you find the first one, mark it and move on to the Zip code.

Another helpful technique is to memorize the four potential answers now so that you won't waste time searching for the correct answer for each question during the exam. Memorize the answers NOW, before you take the exam.

A. No Errors	B. Address Only	C. ZIP Code Only	D. Both

I try to think of things in what I perceive to be logical order. When I look at the answers it makes sense that **(A)** equals **No Errors**, **(B)** is next and the first column of the *list to be corrected* is the address so I can remember that the answer for "Address Only" **(B)** is the first incorrect answer and it is in the first column of the list to be corrected. Then since the second column in the list to be corrected is the ZIP code, if only the Zip code is incorrect I would mark **(C).** Finally, if both the address and Zip code are incorrect I mark **(D).** To me this is logical. However we all have our own reality, and you must design a scenario that makes sense to you.

Others use acronyms to remember lists. In this case you can take the first letter of each of the four answers, **NAZB** and memorize this new word.

N = No Errors = **Answer A**
A = Address Only = **Answer B**
Z = Zip Code Only = **Answer C**
B = Both = **Answer D**

Correct List			List to be Checked	
#	**Address**	**Zip Code**	**Address**	**Zip Code**
S1.	1915 Park Place Fairview, TX	79411	1915 Park Place Fairview, TX	79141
S2.	401 McAuthur Drive Benton, NC	27514-1132	401 McAuther Drive Benton, NC	27514-1132
S3.	6915 Amber Way Pittsburgh, PA	15129-0005	6915 Amber Way Pittsburgh, PA	15129-0005
S4.	19150 First Street Kalamazoo, MI	49007-2334	19105 First Street Kalamizoo, MI	49070-2344

With practice you should be able to complete the 60 questions in the time allotted. If you finish early, go back and review the questions that you found to be alike. You can easily identify them because you won't have any marks on them. Check these first to see if you missed something, then go on to others if time permits. If you do find that you have to change an answer, be sure to erase the incorrect answer completely. Otherwise the scanner used to grade your exam may not be able to grade that question.

It is best not to guess on answers in this section due to the way it is scored. The Postal Service adds the number of questions that you got right and then subtracts one third of the questions you got wrong. Each of the four exam parts is scored differently.

The practice exams for Part A start on the next page. The answer sheet is on the page directly following this practice exam. For your convenience you can copy the answer sheets so that your answer sheet will be next to the exam questions that you are working on. **Be sure to time yourself for this section.** The more you practice the better you score will be. Time this practice exam for 11 minutes.

— **Answer Sheet page 149, Answer Key page 153** —

PART A PRACTICE EXAM 1 (Address Checking)

A. No Errors	B. Address Only	C. ZIP Code Only	D. Both

#	Address	ZIP	Address	ZIP
1	P.O. Box 1243￼Aikron, OH	44326-3452	P.O. Box 1243￼Aikron, OH	44362-2352
2	6000 Buford Dr￼Houston, TX	77006-0001	6000 Buford Dr￼Houston, TX	77006-0001
3	505 SE 35ᵗʰ St.￼Portland, OR	97211-0124	505 SE 53ʳᵈ St.￼Portland, OR	92711-0124
4	5990 Lascolinas Circle￼Lake Worth, FL	33463	5990 Lascolinas Circle￼Lake Worth, FL	33463
5	P.O. Box 5478￼Hollister, FL	32147-7564	P.O. Box 5487￼Hollister, FL	32147-7584
6	1767 Timber Road￼Vista, CA	92080	1766 Timber Road￼Vista, CA	92080
7	3030 Front Street￼Raleigh, NC	27610	3030 Front Street￼Raleigh, NC	27610
8	P.O. Box 10239￼Camp Lejeune, NC	28547-0072	P.O. Box 12390￼Camp Lejeune, NC	28547-0072
9	102 Madera Drive￼Eatonville, WA	98328-4461	102 Midera Drive￼Eatonille, WA	98328-6441
10	81000 Darting Manor Dr.￼Laurel, MD	29723	81000 Darting Manor Dr.￼Laurel, MD	29723
11	200 Rock Chain Drive￼Eagle River, AK	99576	200 Rock Cliff Drive￼Eagle River, AK	99516
12	206 Chancelor Street￼Suffolk, VA	23434-9802	206 Chancelor Street￼Sufolk, VA	24343-9802
13	1015 23ʳᵈ Street￼Markham, IL	60427-3772	1015 23ʳᵈ Street￼Markham, IL	80427-3772
14	900 School Brook Road￼Socorro, NM	87801-0212	900 School Brook Ave.￼Socorro, NM	87801-0121
15	4423 Potter Ave., Apt 23￼Fort Wayne, IN	46835	4423 Potter Ave., Apt 23￼Fort Wayne, IN	46835
16	1509 Meadow View Drive￼Dallas, TX	75222	1509 Meadow View Drive￼Fort Worth, TX	75222
17	P.O. Box 1243￼Penn Hills, PA	15255-4432	P.O. Box 12433￼Penn Hills, PA	15255-4432
18	3445 Sumpter Avenue￼Lisbon, IA	52253	3445 Sumpter Avenue￼Lisbon, IA	52553
19	P.O. Box 666￼Ord, NE	68862	P.O. Box 666￼Ord, NE	68662
20	1062 Amherst Street￼Moon Township, PA	15108-2601	1062 Amherst Ave.￼Moon Township, PA	15108-2601

A. No Errors	B. Address Only	C. ZIP Code Only	D. Both

#	Address	ZIP	Address	ZIP
21	2414 Easton Road Houston, TX	77003-8791	2414 Easton Road Houston, TX	77003-8791
22	4014 E. Belmont Chicago, IL	60614-0201	4014 E. Boumont Chicago, IL	60614-0201
23	5235 Westminster Place Portland, OR	97311-7904	5235 Westminster Place Portland, OR	97113 -7904
24	1 001 Highland Avenue Needham, MA	02494	1001 Highland Place Needham, MA	04294
25	P.O. Box 1904 Hempfield, FL	32107-7543	P.O. Box 1904 Hempfield, FL	32107-7543
26	878 N 41 2nd Street Tacoma, WA	98418-2194	878 N 41 2nd Street Tacoma, WA	98418-2004
27	143 North Avenue Outreach, NC	27310	143 South Avenue Outreach, NC	27310
28	P.O. Box 432 Pendalton, SC	29708-1092	P.O. Box 325 Pendalton, SC	29709-1092
29	987 Fifth Avenue Delray, WA	97318-4298	987 Forbes Avenue Delray, WA	97318-4298
30	1208 Elm Street South Park, PA	15244-2787	1208 Elm Street South Park, PA	15244-2787
31	4520 River Road Eagles Nest, AK	99326	4520 River Road Eagles Nest, AK	99326
32	1309 Chambers Lane Wilton, VA	24389-8276	1390 Chambers Lane Wilton, VA	24389-8276
33	P.O. Box 1998 Willshier, IN	70398-0989	P.O. Box 1998 Willshier, IN	70399-0989
34	1902 Stanley Road Saddlebrook, TX	71342-0853	1902 Stanley Road Saddlebrook, TX	71344-0835
35	116 East 9th St. Torrington, CT	06790-2314	116 West 9th St. Torrington, CT	06791-2314
36	142 Midland Drive Dallas, TX	75122-2134	142 Midway Drive Dallas, TX	75122-2134
37	P.O. Box 232 Hershey, PA	18752-2790	P.O. Box 322 Hershey, PA	18752-2790
38	7675 Sharon Street Trusville, AL	35173-8312	7675 Sharon Street Trusville, AL	53573-8312
39	P.O. Box 1546 Erie, PA	16842-1978	P.O. Box 1546 Erie, PA	16842-1978
40	150 Mission Avenue Godfrey, VA	22689	160 Mission Avenue Godfrey, VA	22589

A. No Errors	B. Address Only	C. ZIP Code Only	D. Both

#	Address	ZIP	Address	ZIP
41	52 Saratoga Street Gloversville, NY	12078	52 Saratoga Street Gloversville, NY	12068-2310
42	244 North Adams Ave Eldridge, IL	61534-2101	244 South Adams Ave Eldridge, IL	61534-2101
43	6543 Marcie St. Labrook, LA	70013-2345	6543 Marty St. Labrook, LA	70113-2345
44	P.O. Box 1567 Falstaff, AZ	85287-9436	P.O. Box 1567 Falstaff, AZ	85287-9436
45	348 Park Place Harlenton, NY	12044-2107	348 Park Place Harlenton, NY	12045-2107
46	1414 16th St., Apt. 345 Tacoma, WA	98433-2224	1414 17th St., Apt. 345 Tacoma, WA	98433-2224
47	78 Lake Rd. Woodbury, NY	11779-0124	78 Lakefront Rd. Woodbury, NY	11799-0124
48	P.O. Box 1990 Randolph, NC	28649-9089	P.O. Box 1990 Randolph, NC	28649-9089
49	987 Atlantic Ave. Ocean City, NY	07200-0989	987 Atlantic Ave. Ocean City, NY	07201-0989
50	229 Westover Terrace Oklahoma, City, OK	74022-1524	229 Westover Place Oklahoma, City, OK	74022-1524
51	5120 Trenton Blvd. Wilkinsburg, PA	15219-0236	5120 Trenton Blvd. Wilkinsburg, PA	15219-0236
52	145 River Rd. Pittsburgh, PA	15222-3245	144 River Rd. Pittsburgh, PA	15221-3245
53	Manor Hall East, #456 York, PA	17404-5645	Manor Hall East, #456 York, PA	17440-5645
54	4545 S. Beacon Chicago, IL	60676-4253	4545 N. Beacon Chicago, IL	60676-4253
55	1990 Westend Dr. Boston, MA	10846-9056	1990 Westward Dr. Boston, MA	10845-9056
56	124 South Park Ave. Sandford, FL	33354-0967	124 South Park Ave. Sandford, FL	33354-0967
57	P.O. Box 1987 Seaward, LA	70124	P.O. Box 1987 Seaward, LA	70224
58	653 Northwood St. Trenton, MI	46798-2354	653 Northview St. Trenton, MI	46798-2354
59	P.O. Box 516 Chicago, IL	60654-9176	P.O. Box 515 Chicago, IL	60654-9176
60	1911 Macie St. Bradbury, NY	11687-7658	1911 Macie St. Bradbury, NY	11687-7658

FORMS CHECKING - PART B

This section includes 30 questions that have to be completed in 15 minutes. There will be six questions for each of five different forms on the exam. Before starting the actual test the examiners will give you a two-minute exercise with several questions that you will answer. These questions are not graded. After the introductory exercise you will start the actual exam.

Refer to the Domestic Return Receipt form on the next page to answer the first two sample questions for practice and use the same for the first six questions of the timed exam.

Sample Questions

S1. Where do you enter the sender's address on this form?
A. Box 3 (Front)
B. Box 10 (Back)
C. Box 3 and 10
C. None of the above

ANSWER: The sender's address is entered in Box 10 and the correct answer is B.

S2. The letter will be sent certified. Each certified letter has an article number. What two blocks must be filled out to designate a certified mailing?
A. Box 1 and 2
B. Box 10 and 1
C. Box 4 and 5
D. Box 3 only

ANSWER: The correct answer is C. Questions can be tricky if you read more into the question than what is presented. In this example, all certified mailings are assigned an article number that is listed in block 4 and you would check the certified box in block 5. Even though the remainder of the form must be filled out before it can be processed, the question is only asking about what must be filled out to designate a certified mailing. Focus on what they give you in the question, the known facts.

PRACTICE EXAM PART B

Use the **Domestic Return Receipt** form on the next page for the first 6 questions of the exam. You have 15 minutes for the 30 questions or 30 second per question. Set your timer for three minutes for each six question segment. The questions are on the opposite page so that you can easily refer to the forms as needed. Take a few seconds after you set the timer to familiarize yourself with the form. Copy the answer sheet in the back of this section and have the answer sheet next to the questions so you can easily mark your answers and not lose time.

— Answer Sheet page 149, Answer Key page 153 —

DOMESTIC RETURN RECEIPT (Back)

SENDER INSTRUCTIONS

Print your name, address, and ZIP Code
in the space provided.

- Complete items 1,2,3, and 4 on the
  reverse.
- Attach to front of article if space
  permits, otherwise affix to back of
  article.
- Endorse article "Return Receipt
  Requested" adjacent to number.

RETURN

TO ➡

Print Sender's name, address, and ZIP Code in the space below.

10. _____

_____

_____

DOMESTIC RETURN RECEIPT (Front)

● **SENDER:** Compare items 1 and 2 when additional services are desired, and complete 3 and 4.
Put your address in the "RETURN TO" Space on the reverse side. Failure to do this will prevent this card
from being returned to you. The return receipt fee will provide you the name of the person delivered to and
the date of delivery. For additional fees the following services are available. Consult postmaster for fees and
check box(es) for additional service(s) requested.

1. ☐ Show to whom delivered, date, and addresses's address.   **2.** ☐ Restricted Delivery
↑ *(Extra charge)* ↑   ↑ *(Extra charge)* ↑

3. Article Addressed to:	**4.** Article Number:
	5. Type of Service: ☐ Registered ☐ Insured ☐ Certified ☐ COD ☐ Express Mail
	Always obtain signature of addresses or agent and <u>DATE DELIVERED</u>.
6. Signature - Addressee	9. Addressee's Address *(ONLY if requested and fee paid)*
7. Signature - Agent	
8. Date of Delivery	

Start section 1 of your timed exercise, set your timer for 3 minutes. There are five sections with 6 questions each.

1. Where would you enter the article number for a certified mailing on this form?

    A. Box 10
    B. Box 4
    C. Box 3 and 9
    D. Box 3 only

2. The person sending a certified letter wants to receive the return receipt at his home address. Where does he put his return address?

    A. Box 3
    B. Box 9
    C. Box 10
    D. The article number in Box 4 and signs in Box 7

3. Which of these would indicate restricted delivery?

    A. Box 5
    B. Box 2
    C. A signature in Box 7 and Box check mark in Box 1
    D. Box 1, 3, and 7

4. Which of these could be a correct answer for Box 8?

    A. A check mark
    B. Article number
    C. Signature
    D. March 15, 2005

5. Which one of the following could be the correct entry for Box 5?

    A. Your initials
    B. 4/19/2005
    C. A check mark
    D. None of the above

6. Which of the following should have a name entered?

    A. Box 1
    B. Box 4
    C. Box 6
    D. Box 2

Practice Exam - Section 2 of Part B

#	
Authorization to Hold Mail	

Authorization to Hold Mail

Postmaster - Please hold mail for:

1. Name(s)

2. Address

3a. Begin Holding Mail (Date) | **3b.** Resume Delivery (Date)

4. ☐ **Option A**

I will pick up all accumulated mail when I return and understand that mail delivery will not resume   until I do. (This is suggested if your return date may change or if no one will be at home to receive   mail)

5. ☐ **Option B**

Please deliver all accumulated mail and resume normal delivery on the ending date shown above.

6. Customer Signature

For Post Office Use Only

7. Date Received

8a. Clerk | **8b.** Bin Number

9a. Carrier | **9b.** Route Number

Customer Option A Only

Carrier: Accumulated mail has been picked up:

10a. Resume delivery on (date) _____

10b. By: _____

Start section 2 of your timed exercise, questions 7 through 12. Set your timer for 3 minutes. There are five sections with 6 questions each.

7. Joe Smith and Bob Barker live at the same address. Bob is going on an extended vacation and will be away for two months. Joe is not leaving and wants his mail to continue. What name(s) should you enter in Box 1?

    A. Joe Smith
    B. Joe Smith and Bob Barker
    C. Bob Barker
    D. The postmaster's name

8. If you check Option B, which of the following statements is correct?

    A. The person will pick up his accumulated mail when he returns.
    B. Your mail carrier will deliver your mail when you return after you contact the Post Office.
    C. Your mail carrier will restart delivery on a predetermined date.
    D. None of the above

9. What fields would the customer complete on this form?

    A. Blocks 1, 2, 3a, and 6 only
    B. Blocks 1 through 6 only
    C. Blocks 7 through 10b
    D. All of the above

10. Which of the selections specify the date to start holding mail?

    A. Box 3b
    B. Box 7
    C. Box 3a
    D. Line 10a

11. What would be a correct entry for line 10a?

    A. Jay W. Brook
    B. A check mark
    C. June 1, 2005
    D. 13547

12. Postal Clerk Jim McKee accepted Jeff Brown's Authorization to Hold Mail. Jeff's carrier is Janet Ward. What box is Jim McKee's name entered in?

    A. Box 1
    B. Box 9a
    C. Box 1 and 6
    D. None of the above

Practice Exam - Section 3 of Part B

Certificate of Bulk Mailing

MAILER: Prepare this statement in ink. Affix meter stamp or uncanceled postage stamps covering the fee in the block to the right. Present for certification.

7. Meter stamp or postage (uncanceled) stamps in payment of fee to be affixed here and canceled by postmarking, including date.

Fee for Certification

1. Up to 1,000 pieces (1 certificate for total number)

2. For each additional 1,000 pieces, or fraction

3. Duplicate Copy

USE CURRENT RATE CHART

4a. Number of identical Pieces	4.b Class of Mail	4c. Postage on Each	4d. Number of Pieces to the Pound	4e. Total Number of Pounds	4f. Total Postage Paid	4g. Fee Paid

5a. Mailed For	5b. Mailed By

Postmaster's Certificate

6. It is hereby certified that the above-described mailing has been received and number of pieces and postage verified.

_____
(Postmaster or Designee)

Start section 3 of your timed exercise, questions 13 through 18. Set your timer for three minutes. There are five sections with six questions each.

13. ACME Int'l is mailing its annual catalog under the bulk mail rates program. The company hired Abbott Services to pick up the bulk mailing of 1,000 pounds that included 5,000 individual pieces of first class mail. What figure would be placed in block 4d?

   A. 1000
   B. 5
   C. 5000
   D. ZERO

14. Using the same example as question 13, what would be entered on Line 5a and 5b?

   A. 5a "Postmaster" and 5b "Abbott Services"
   B. 5a "Cost Reduction" and 5a "ACME Int'l"
   C. 5a "ACME Int'l" and 5b "Abbott Services"
   D. None of the above

15. Can a Designee sign this form for the Postmaster?

   A. Yes
   B. No
   C. Never
   D. Only in block 5b

16. What could be the class of mail entered in block 4b?

   A. First
   B. 15th
   C. No Class
   D. None of the above

17. The mailer has 15 identical pieces for this mailing. Where would you enter this information?

   A. Box 4e
   B. No identical pieces can be added
   C. Box 4a
   D. In the remarks in Box 6

18. Where do you attach the meter stamp or postage on this form?

   A. You affix postage to each piece of mail, not to the Certificate of Bulk Mailing..
   B. To the back of the certificate
   C. In Box 7
   D. In Box 6

Practice Exam - Section 4 of Part B

Bar Code	EXPRESS MAIL			Mailing Label

ORIGIN (POSTAL USE ONLY)

PO ZIP Code 1a.	Day of Delivery 1b. ☐ Next ☐ Second	Flat Rate Envelope 1c. ☐
Date In 2d.	2b. ☐ 12 noon ☐ 3 PM	Postage 2c. $
Time In 3a. ☐ AM ☐ PM	Military 3b. ☐ 2ⁿᵈ Day ☐ 3ʳᵈ Day	Return Receipt Fee 3c.
Weight 4a. Lbs. Ozs.	Int'l Alpha Country Code 4b.	COD Fee 4c.	Insurance Fee
No Delivery 5a. ☐ Wknd ☐ Holiday	Acceptance Clerk Initials 5b.	Total Postage & Fees 5c. $

CUSTOMER USE ONLY

Method of Payment

7a. Express Mail Corp Acct. No.

8a. from: (PLEASE PRINT)   PHONE :_____

DELIVERY (POSTAL USE ONLY)

Delivery Attempt 1d. Mo. Day	Time 1e. ☐ AM ☐ PM	Employee Signature 1f.
Delivery Attempt 2d. Mo. Day	Time 2e. ☐ AM ☐ PM	Employee Signature 2f.
Delivery Attempt 3d. Mo. Day	Time 3e. ☐ AM ☐ PM	Employee Signature 3f.

CUSTOMER USE ONLY
6. ☐ WAIVER OF SIGNATURE

_____
Customer Signature

NO DELIVERY ☐ Weekend ☐ Holiday

Federal Agency Acct. No.

7b. Or Postal Service Acct. No.

8b. TO: (PLEASE PRINT)   PHONE: _____

☐☐☐☐☐ + ☐☐☐☐
zip + 4

Start section 4 of your timed exercise, questions 19 through 24. Set your timer for three minutes. There are five sections with six questions each.

19. Which of the following answers could be a correct entry for Box 1d?

   A. $18.65
   B. 12 Noon
   C. 6/15
   D. 6/15/05

20. Joe Smith dropped a Flat Rate Express Mail package at the Post Office at 11:00 AM on 8/11/05. The postal clerk informed Joe that his package would be delivered by noon the next day. How would the clerk note this on the form?

   A. Write the date 8/12/05 in Box 1d and the time in 1e.
   B. Check "Noon" in Box 2b and "Next" in Box 1b
   C. Write the date 8/12/05 in 3c
   D. None of the above

21. The customer requests no weekend delivery and "Waiver of Signature." How does the customer select these options?

   A. Signs Box 6
   C. Checks "Waiver of Signature in Box 6
   B. Customer signs his name and checks "Waiver of Signature" and "Weekend" in Box 6.
   D. None of the above

22. The mail carrier was unable to make delivery on his first attempt on 8/12/05 because the customer was not home. The carrier (employee) did not leave the package. Where does the carrier sign this form?

   A. Box 6
   B. Box 1f
   C. Box 2f and 3f
   D. None of the above

23. The clerk weighed the Express Mail package and advised the customer that the package would cost $17.95 to mail overnight. Where does the clerk initial the mailing label and enter the package weight?

   A. Initial in Box1f and weight in Box 2c
   B. Initial in Box 5b and weight in Box 4a
   C. Enter $17.95 in Box 2c and Initial in Box 6
   D. No initials or weight is required on this form

24. Where would you enter the recipient's ZIP code on this form?

   A. Box 8a
   B. Box 4c
   C. Box 8b
   D. Zip code not required

Practice Exam - Section 5 of Part B

Application for Post Office Box or Caller Service			
Customers: Complete white boxes		Post Office: Complete shaded boxes	
1a. Name(s) to which box number(s) is (are) assigned			1b. Box or Caller Number _____ through _____
2a. Name of person applying, Title (if representing an organization), and name of organization *(if different from name in Box 1a above)*			2b. Will this box be used for: ☐ Personal use ☐ Business use
3a. Address *(number, street, apt. no., city, state, Zip Code)*. When address changes, cross out address here and put new address on back.			3b. Telephone number *(Include area code)*
4a. Data application received	4b. Box size needed	4c. ID and physical address verified by *(initials)*	4d. Dates of service _____ through _____
5a. Two types of identification are required. One must contain a photograph of the addressee(s). Social security cards, credit cards, and birth certificates are unacceptable as identification. Write in identifying information. Subject to verification.		5b. Eligibility for Carrier Delivery ☐ City ☐ Rural ☐ HCR ☐ None	5c. Service Assigned ☐ Box ☐ Caller ☐ Reserve #
		6. List name(s) of minors or names of others **receiving mail** in individual box. Other persons must present two forms of valid ID. If applicant is a firm, name each member **receiving mail**. Each member must have verifiable ID upon request. *(Continue on reverse side)*	
WARNING: *The furnishing of false or misleading information on this form or omission of information may result in criminal sanctions (including fines and imprisonment) and/or civil sanctions (including multiple damages and civil penalties) (18U.S.C. 1001)*		7. Signature of applicant (Same as item 3). I agree to comply with all Postal rules regarding Post Office box or caller services.	

Start section 5 of your timed exercises, questions 25 through 30. Set your timer for three minutes. This is the last set of six questions.

25. David Jones is applying to open a post office box in Canton, Ohio. He has his driver's license photo ID and his Social Security card for identification. Will the Postal Service process his request?

   A. The clerk will accept his application and attach photocopies of his photo ID and Social Security Card to the application.
   B. Yes; however, the customer must also supply a certified copy of his birth certificate within 15 business days.
   C. No
   D. None of the above

26. What boxes on this form must the customer fill out?

   A. Box 1a, 1b, 2a, 2b, 3a, 6, and 7
   B. All but 1b, 4a, 4b, 4c, 4d, 5a, 5b, and 5c
   C. Box 1a, 3a, 2b, 6 and 7
   D. All of the above

27. What is required to be verified by the postal clerk prior to accepting your application?

   A. That you are a U.S. citizen
   B. You are eligible for carrier delivery
   C. Two forms of ID, one being a photo ID
   D. Your age

28. What would a correct entry be for Box 3a?

   A. Your name
   B. Names of all using the Post Office Box
   C. 324 Main St., Oil City, PA 15434
   D. (123) 456-7890

29. What would a correct entry be for Box 6?

   A. 1878 Forbes Ave., Fargo, ID 25678
   B. Bob Evans and Elizabeth Tyler
   C. Your signature
   D. None of the above

30. Jane Mansfield has two small children and an invalid parent that lives with her. Where does Jane list the names of others in her household who will use this box?

   A. Box 5a
   B. Nowhere; only the primary box holder's name goes on this form.
   C. All must sign box 7
   D. Box 6

CODING AND MEMORY - PART C
Coding Section

The coding and memory sections both use the same "Coding Guide." You have to assign a given address to the proper delivery route for 36 questions in six minutes for the coding section. The coding section is open book and you will refer to the Coding Guide while answering your questions. The Memory Section of Part C requires you to remember the coding guide you used in the Coding Section and assign delivery routes without looking at the guide.

CODING GUIDE	
Address Range	**Delivery Route**
400 – 499 Amherst Ave 101 – 190 Canton St. 1 – 29 Sutton Way	A
500 – 799 Amherst Ave 30 – 199 Sutton Way	B
2500 – 2699 University Blvd. 191 – 299 Canton St. 5 – 25 Rural Route 5	C
All mail that does not fall in one of the address ranges listed above.	D

Address Range - The Coding Guide is divided into two columns. The first column is the Address Ranges for each route. If you look at the first address range of Route A notice that all addresses from 400 through 499 Amherst Avenue are included in route A. Route B picks up the remaining Amherst Avenue addresses from 500 to 799.

Delivery Route - Each delivery route has multiple addresses assigned to that carrier. Route B includes the addresses from 500 to 799 Amherst Avenue and from 30 to 199 Sutton Way. For example, if a letter was addressed 101 Sutton Way you would select Route B for the answer.

Delivery Route D includes all addresses not assigned to a specific route. If you are given the address 332 Canton St. or 1905 Fifth Avenue you would select Delivery Route D as your answer. These addresses are not included in routes A, B, or C.

Sample Questions

	Address	Delivery Route			
1.	425 Amherst Ave.	A	B	C	D
2.	202 Sutton Way	A	B	C	D
3.	277 Canton St.	A	B	C	D
4.	10 Rural Route 6	A	B	C	D
5.	67 Sutton Way	A	B	C	D
6.	2601 University Blvd.	A	B	C	D

You are permitted to look at the Coding Guide while answering the Coding questions in this section. Use the sample answer sheet for the practice exams. Note that the Delivery Routes are listed A through D to the right of the questions in the exam booklet. Don't get confused during the exam and mark your answers in the exam booklet. **ONLY MARK YOUR ANSWERS ON THE ANSWER SHEET.** If you neglect to use the answer sheet your answers will not be graded.

Sample Question Answers

Question 1 – The address 425 Amherst Ave. Is in the address range as noted on the Coding Guide for Delivery Route A. You would darken answer A on the answer sheet. Remember to NOT put your answers in the exam booklet. Place your answer sheet next to the questions and darken the answer **"A"** on the answer sheet.

CAUTION: When you get to the memory section this will be even more critical. Note the spelling for the street address in this question. It is spelled "Amherst Ave." You will run into answers that are very similar to the street address. For example Amherst can also be spelled "Amhurst." Look at the entire address. If the street address in question 1 would have been spelled "Amhurst" the answer would have been D, not A.

Question 2 – Sutton Way is located in range A and B for street numbers from 1-199. The address in question two is 202 Sutton Way which is beyond the range of either route A or B. The answer is **"D"** (all mail that does not fall in one of the address ranges listed in A, B or C)

Question 3 – The answer for this question would be **"C."** You will find the address range from 191 - 299 Canton St. In Route C.

Question 4 – You will find a Rural Route in Route C. However, it is Rural Route 5, not Route 6. The correct answer is **"D"** (all mail that does not fall in one of the address ranges listed in A, B or C).

Question 5 – The correct answer is **"B."** 67 Sutton Way is in the address range of 30 - 199 Sutton Way in Route B.

Question 6 – 2601 University Blvd is listed in Route C and the address range is 2500 - 2699. Therefore, the correct answer is **"C."**

The Coding practice exam follows. You will have six minutes to complete this section. Copy the answer sheet in the back of this section and place it next to your book. Time the exam to see how many question you can answer in the time allotted. The Coding Guide was repeated on this page and on page 132 so that the questions would be next to the Coding Guide. You are permitted to use the Coding Guide for this section.

PART C
Coding Section Practice Exam
36 Questions

CODING GUIDE	
Address Range	**Delivery Route**
400 – 499 Amherst Ave 101 – 190 Canton St. 1 – 29 Sutton Way	A
500 – 799 Amherst Ave 30 – 199 Sutton Way	B
2500 – 2699 University Blvd. 191 – 299 Canton St. 5 – 25 Rural Route 5	C
All mail that does not fall in one of the address ranges listed above.	D

— Answer Sheet page 150, Answer Key page 154 —

CODING EXAM PRACTICE QUESTIONS

START TIME: _____

	Address	Delivery Route			
1.	20 Rural Route 5	A	B	C	D
2.	104 Sutton Way	A	B	C	D
3.	401 Amhurst Ave.	A	B	C	D
4.	1901 University Blvd.	A	B	C	D
5.	587 Amherst Ave.	A	B	C	D
6.	4 Sutton Way	A	B	C	D
7.	2601 Universal Blvd.	A	B	C	D
8.	197 Canton St.	A	B	C	D
9.	145 Sutton Way	A	B	C	D
10.	188 Canton St.	A	B	C	D
11.	401 Amherst Ave.	A	B	C	D
12.	2599 University Blvd.	A	B	C	D
13.	199 Sutton Way	A	B	C	D
14.	399 Canton St.	A	B	C	D
15.	634 Amherst Ave.	A	B	C	D
16.	189 Canton St.	A	B	C	D
17.	2499 University Blvd.	A	B	C	D
18.	2589 University Blvd.	A	B	C	D

TURN PAGE
TO CONTINUE

CONTINUE EXAM

CODING GUIDE	
Address Range	**Delivery Route**
400 – 499 Amherst Ave 101 – 190 Canton St. 1 – 29 Sutton Way	A
500 – 799 Amherst Ave 30 – 199 Sutton Way	B
2500 – 2699 University Blvd. 191 – 299 Canton St. 5 – 25 Rural Route 5	C
All mail that does not fall in one of the address ranges listed above.	D

CONTINUE EXAM

	Address	Delivery Route			
19.	3 Sutton way	A	B	C	D
20.	118 Sutton Way	A	B	C	D
21.	301 Canton St.	A	B	C	D
22.	24 Rural Route 5	A	B	C	D
23.	489 Amherst Ave.	A	B	C	D
24.	2601 Universal Blvd.	A	B	C	D
25.	597 Amherst Ave.	A	B	C	D
26.	19 Rural Route 5	A	B	C	D
27.	264 Canton St.	A	B	C	D
28.	127 Canton St.	A	B	C	D
29.	29 Sutton Way	A	B	C	D
30.	125 Rural Route 5	A	B	C	D
31.	616 Amherst Ave.	A	B	C	D
32.	2695 University Blvd.	A	B	C	D
33.	114 Sutton Way	A	B	C	D
34.	3 Sutton Way	A	B	C	D
35.	29 Rural Route 5	A	B	C	D
36.	201 Canton St.	A	B	C	D

STOP

Record Time Here: _____ Minutes
(You are limited to 6 minutes)

CODING AND MEMORY - PART C
Memory Section

Now that you completed the initial coding section, it's time to work on Part C, Section 2, memorization. You will use the same coding guide that was used in the previous section, and during the actual exam you will be given a short practice section as noted below:

Exam Schedule

- For the first section the examiners will give you three minutes to memorize the Coding Guide. Following this session you will be given 90 seconds to answer eight practice questions without the aide of the Coding Guide. You have to answer the questions from memory.
- Immediately following the practice session the examiners will allow you to study the same Coding Guide for another five minutes before taking the actual 36-question test. You will be allowed seven minutes after the study period to complete the 36 questions without the aide of the Coding Guide. You must answer the questions from memory. The questions for this section are numbered 37 to 72 because the exam for part C includes the first 36 questions that you answered in Section 1 of Part C.

The questions for the memory section are similar to the questions from the previous section. The only difference between the two sections is that in Section One you are allowed to view the Coding Guide while taking the exam. In Section Two you must answer questions 37 - 72 from memory. This is considered by many to be the hardest part of the exam. However, there are techniques that you can use to help you through this section and improve your scores.

Memorization Techniques

Efficient Utilization of Time

You have several study and practice sessions prior to the memory exam. You have an initial two-minute study period in the previous Coding Section along with a 90-second practice exam. **Remember that the same coding guide is used for both the coding and memory sections.** In the memory section you have a three minute study period and then a five-minute study period prior to the 36-question exam. All these pre-exam exercises are to familiarize you with the memorization section. This study guide provides sufficient familiarization so that you can put these sessions to much better use.

I suggest that you use the entire time to study and memorize the Coding Guide. This will give you over 11 minutes to memorize the guide.

If you decide to use the time as suggested above, be sure to at least mark the sample questions associated with the two pre-exam exercises so that test monitors won't stop you to explain the process. Just mark them randomly when told to and then continue studying the Coding Guide.

Number Sequence and Address Ranges

Several memory techniques were discussed earlier in Part A for address checking. The techniques listed here will help you memorize the address ranges and delivery routes in any coding guide.

CODING GUIDE	
Address Range	**Delivery Route**
400 – 499 Amherst Ave 101 – 190 Canton St. 1 – 29 Sutton Way	A
500 – 799 Amherst Ave 30 – 199 Sutton Way	B
2500 – 2699 University Blvd. 191 – 299 Canton St. 5 – 25 Rural Route 5	C
All mail that does not fall in one of the address ranges listed above.	D

The goal is to simplify the Coding Guide to manageable bits that you can recall easily. To do this you have to rearrange the information into a condensed and logical order that you can recall during the exam. To master this technique you need to practice on this Coding Guide and then go on to take the memory test.

Look at the Coding Guide. You will notice that street addresses repeat in the various routes. For example, Amherst Ave. is listed in Route A and B, Sutton Way repeats in A and B, and Canton St. repeats in A and C. Rural Route 5 and University Blvd. are only in route C. The goal is to put these streets into an order and number sequence that you can remember and do it within the allotted time.

Notice that most of the address ranges run sequentially. Amherst Ave runs from 400 - 499 in Route A and from 500 - 799 in Route B. Canton St., runs from 101 - 190 in Route A and from 191 - 299 in Route C. Two addresses, University Blvd., and Rural Route 5, are only in Delivery Route C. Rewrite the addresses and routes as follows:

- Amherst Ave. 400 - 499A - 799B
- Canton St. 101 - 190A - 299C
- Sutton Way 1 - 29A - 199B
- University Blvd. 2500 - 2699C
- Rural Route 5 - 25C

Remember one key fact. **The second sequential range is actually one count higher than the highest count for that street**. For example, Amherst is listed as "Amherst Ave. 400 - 499A - 799B." Route A runs from 400 - 499, add (1) to 499 and that equals 500. Therefore, Route B Amherst Ave. addresses run from 500 to 799. You only have to remember three numbers with this technique as long as you remember that the second range starts at the very next number in the first range –500 in this example.

Most exams have sequential routes. If you run into a Coding Guide that has non-sequential street addresses, you will have to add the complete second address range to the quick reference memory chart. If the B Route for Amherst Ave. was 601 - 799, you would write the line as "Amherst Ave. 400 - 499A - 601 -799B."

Here are several other techniques that will help you remember the revised lists. You may also have your own memory methods that you use to recall key information. Find out what works best for you and use them to your benefit.

- Reorder the list and use an acronym to recall the list. An acronym is an abbreviation that you can easily recall to start the process. An acronym example would be "IRS," which stands for "Internal Revenue Service." look at the list to see what abbreviation you can devise to help you remember the list. I reorganized the original list to the following:

  - **C**anton St. 101 - 190A - 299C
  - **A**mherst Ave. 400 - 499A - 799B
  - **R**ural Route 5 - 25C
  - **U**niversity Blvd. 2500 - 2699C
  - **S**utton Way 1 - 29A - 199B

The acronym that I came up with is **CARUS**. Write it out in a horizontal line on your test guide just as a memory jogger. You may not have time to write your entire list down, but this can help.

C = Canton St. 101 - 190A - 299C
A = Amherst Ave. 400 - 499A - 799B
R = Rural Route 5 - 25C
U = University Blvd. 2500 - 2699C
S = Sutton Way 1 - 29A - 199B

Now let's go a little further with this and use other memory joggers to help you memorize the list. Now that you have the list rewritten and reordered, how do you remember the address ranges?

1. Use associations to remember what is on the list. First, write down the acronym on your test booklet. You have to remember that C = Canton St. Now the routes associated with Canton St. are A and C. C is the first letter of the CARUS in your mind. Let it also equal A for Route A and now the second route will be C for the C in Canton, whatever makes sense to you. Now you know that C = Canton St., and that Canton St. is in Routes A and C. If words don't come to you, just take the first letter of each street in whatever order makes sense to you.

2. Look at the numbers 101-299 for Canton St. next. Where does the route separate? For C = Canton St. subtract 109 and that is where the split is. You can also just remember the three numbers. Coincidentally, 109 is the first two digits of 101 and the last digit of 299. Say it over several times in your head C = Canton St. = 101 - 190A - 299C. You already know that the second route starts at 191, one count up from 190.

3. I believe the easiest way to remember the address ranges and routes is to remember the entire string. Use the acronym to jog your memory and then say C = Canton St. = 101 - 190A - 299C. Close your eyes for a second and visualize the street, numbers and routes. With the acronym **CARUS** and visualization, you should be able to remember this short list in the time offered especially if you use all of the study periods, as recommended, to your advantage.

4. Many who take the exam try to streamline the amount of information to memorize even further by abbreviating the street names. Recall our discussion earlier when you had several street names with different spellings such as "Amherst" and "Amhurst." The actual exam will also include different designators and instead of using "Sutton Way" on a question it may read "Sutton Terrace." Therefore, if you only remembered "Sut" or "Sutton" you would not know what the correct answer was for that question.

5. You may be allowed to make notes on the exam booklet during the memory test. If allowed, you can write the acronym that you devise in the booklet and quickly note the street names and ranges. However, you need to practice before attempting this, otherwise you may take too much time and not finish the exam.

PART C
Coding Memory Section Practice Exam

You will be given five minutes to study the Coding Guide. Turn to page 35 and study the Coding Guide for <u>five minutes</u>. (Time this exercise.) We will use the same Coding Guide as the one used in the previous section that they do in the actual exam. A second practice exam follows this one using a different Coding Guide to give you more practice with this section.

If you don't have someone to time you, enter your start time below, and when you finish write down the stop time. Determine the total time used for the exam. Place a copy of the answer sheet next to your book for this section.

— **Answer Sheet page 150, Answer Key page 154** —

START TIME _____

	Address	Delivery Route			
37.	22 Sutton Way	A	B	C	D
38.	27 Rural Route 5	A	B	C	D
39.	534 Amherst Ave.	A	B	C	D
40.	2601 University Blvd.	A	B	C	D
41.	189 Canton St.	A	B	C	D
42.	34 Sutton Way	A	B	C	D
43.	2701 Universal Blvd.	A	B	C	D
44.	1924 Rural Route 5	A	B	C	D
45.	299 Canyon St.	A	B	C	D
46.	168 Canton St.	A	B	C	D
47.	521 Amherst Ave.	A	B	C	D
48.	189 Sutton Way.	A	B	C	D
49.	199 Sutton Place	A	B	C	D
50.	2599 University Blvd.	A	B	C	D
51.	2501 University Blvd.	A	B	C	D
52.	29 Sutton Way	A	B	C	D
53.	45 Sutton Way.	A	B	C	D
54.	35 Rural Route 5	A	B	C	D

CONTINUE EXAM

	Address	Delivery Route			
55.	19 Sutton Way	A	B	C	D
56.	31 Sutton Way	A	B	C	D
57.	205 Canton St.	A	B	C	D
58.	2691 University Blvd.	A	B	C	D
59.	432 Amherst Ave.	A	B	C	D
60.	801 Amherst Ave.	A	B	C	D
61.	151 Canton St.	A	B	C	D
62.	45 Sexton Way	A	B	C	D
63.	19 Rural Route 5	A	B	C	D
64.	619 Amherst Ave.	A	B	C	D
65.	107 Sutton Way	A	B	C	D
66.	140 Canton St.	A	B	C	D
67.	435 Fifth Ave.	A	B	C	D
68.	1500 University Blvd.	A	B	C	D
69.	122 Sutton Way	A	B	C	D
70.	35 Smithton Place	A	B	C	D
71.	578 Amherst Ave.	A	B	C	D
72.	149 Canton St.	A	B	C	D

STOP

Record Time Here: _____ Minutes

(You are limited to 7 minutes)

The memory section is considered by many to be the most difficult. Therefore, we included several practice exams. Before going on to the next memory practice exam review pages 134 to 138. Experiment with the memory techniques offered in this study guide or use your own unique methods to memorize the following new Coding Guide.

PART C
Coding Memory Section Practice Exam 2

You will be given five minutes to study this new Coding Guide. (Time this exercise.) If you don't have someone to time you, enter your start time below and when you finish write down the stop time. Determine the total time used for the exam. Remember, in the actual exam you only have seven minutes to complete this section. Place a copy of the answer sheet next to your book for this section.

START TIME _____

CODING GUIDE	
Address Range	**Delivery Route**
1891 – 3100 Eagle LN 25 – 40 Amberwood Hwy 200 – 499 Lemington CT	A
3101 – 3800 Eagle LN 500 – 799 Lemington CT	B
620 - 800 Trent Pkwy 6000 – 10000 Bedford Ave. 41 – 100 Amberwood Hwy	C
All mail that does not fall in one of the address ranges listed above.	D

STOP TIME _____

You are given 5 minutes to memorize
this Coding Guide before starting the next practice exam.

START TIME _____

7 Minutes to Complete Practice Memory Exam 2

— **Answer Sheet page 150, Answer Key page 154** —

	Address	Delivery Route			
37.	50 Amberwood Hwy	A	B	C	D
38.	3199 Eagle LN	A	B	C	D
39.	199 Lemington CT	A	B	C	D
40.	621 Trent Pkwy	A	B	C	D
41.	7067 Bedford Ave.	A	B	C	D
42.	1955 Eagle LN	A	B	C	D
43.	99 Amberwood Hwy	A	B	C	D
44.	501 Lemington CT	A	B	C	D
45.	899 Trent Pkwy	A	B	C	D
46.	3788 Eagle LN	A	B	C	D
47.	25 Amberwood Hwy	A	B	C	D
48.	800 Lexington CT	A	B	C	D
49.	2205 Eagle LN	A	B	C	D
50.	719 Trent Pkwy	A	B	C	D
51.	125 Amberwood Hwy	A	B	C	D
52.	6099 Bedford Ave.	A	B	C	D
53.	700 Lemington CT	A	B	C	D
54.	1898 Eagle LN	A	B	C	D

Continued on next page

CONTINUE EXAM

	Address	Delivery Route			
55.	9989 Bedford Ave.	A	B	C	D
56.	701 Lemington CT	A	B	C	D
57.	43 Amberwood Hwy	A	B	C	D
58.	2901 Eagle LN	A	B	C	D
59.	799 Trent Pkwy	A	B	C	D
60.	7001 Bedford Ave.	A	B	C	D
61.	29 Amberwood Hwy	A	B	C	D
62.	278 Lemington CT	A	B	C	D
63.	3201 Eagle LN	A	B	C	D
64.	619 Amherst Ave	A	B	C	D
65.	654 Trent Pkwy	A	B	C	D
66.	30 Amberwood Hwy	A	B	C	D
67.	775 Lemington CT	A	B	C	D
68.	2677 Eagle LN	A	B	C	D
69.	8888 Bedford Ave.	A	B	C	D
70.	700 Trent Pkwy	A	B	C	D
71.	199 Amberwood Hwy	A	B	C	D
72.	4102 Eagle LN	A	B	C	D

STOP

Record Time Here: _____ Minutes
(You are limited to 7 minutes)

PERSONAL EXPERIENCE AND
CHARACTERISTICS INVENTORY
PART D

This section takes 90 minutes to complete and has 236 questions. The Postal Service evaluates your personal experience, characteristics and tendencies. You will be asked your likes and dislikes, whether you have experience in certain areas. You really can't prepare for this section; it's your personal profile. if you answer the questions honestly the Postal Service will be able to identify the job that is best suited to your characteristics.

The answers are multiple choice. The question *"Do you like to work in groups?"* would have the answers (A) Strongly Agree, (B) Agree, (C), Disagree, (D) Strongly Disagree. A question similar to *"Are you willing to work rotating shifts?"* would have the answers (A) Very Often, (B) Often, (C) Sometimes, (D) Rarely.

Content and Structure

Part D is divided into two groups. The first group of questions includes multiple choice questions or statements with the following possible answers:

A. Strongly Agree	OR	A. Very Often
B. Agree		B. Often
C. Disagree		C. Sometimes
D. Strongly Disagree		D. Rarely

The second group of questions can have as few as four to as many as nine answer choices. You choose the answer that best describes your personal feelings and concerns.

Several typical question/statements are listed below so that you will know what to expect:

S1.   You like to work independently without interruptions.

A. Strongly Agree
B. Agree
C. Disagree
D. Strongly Disagree

S2.   You like to carefully prepare for events or activities in advance.

A. Very Often
B. Often
C. Sometimes
D. Rarely

S3.   What type of activities do you like the most?

    A. activities that require planning and attention
    B. activities that require little planning
    C. activities that are physical and challenging
    D. activities that are done while sitting
    E. activities that don't require much thought
    F. outdoor activities
    G. not sure

Answer the questions honestly and pick the answer that represents your thoughts. If several answers seem to fit pick the one and **ONLY ONE** reply that best represents how you feel about the question or statement. There are no right or wrong answers on this part of the exam. You can select only one answer for each question. Use your entire background, including work experience, volunteer work, school work, military service, anything from your background that will help you relate to the question.

If you complete this section early you can turn
in your booklet and leave the exam room.

You need to be careful with this section. The design of the questions can reveal whether you are trying to manipulate the exam. Questions are reworded or come from a different perspective, and it is impossible to remember all your answers and then evaluate what each question may mean to the examiners. The questions were designed by professionals, and the Postal Service has not released any information on how this section is evaluated and scored. These types of tests are typically used to evaluate work ethics, attitudes, teamwork, customer service, skills, performance, and productivity.

SAMPLE ANSWER SHEETS

The next four pages have two complete sets of answer sheets that you can use for the practice exams. You can also make up additional practice exam questions and make copies of the answer sheets for additional practice. If you don't have a copy machine handy you can remove the next two pages and use the answer sheet for the practice exams. You will still have another set of answer sheets on pages 151 and 152.

The answer sheet layout is not identical to what you will find in the exam. Both sides of the actual exam answer sheet are used. Your personal information will be placed at the top of the front and answer sheet and Part A and B answers are placed at the bottom. The back of the actual sheet is used to mark your answers for Part C and D. Our layout is different to accommodate the practice tests.

SAMPLE ANSWER SHEET (1)

Part A- Address Checking

1 Ⓐ Ⓑ Ⓒ Ⓓ	16 Ⓐ Ⓑ Ⓒ Ⓓ	31 Ⓐ Ⓑ Ⓒ Ⓓ	46 Ⓐ Ⓑ Ⓒ Ⓓ
2 Ⓐ Ⓑ Ⓒ Ⓓ	17 Ⓐ Ⓑ Ⓒ Ⓓ	32 Ⓐ Ⓑ Ⓒ Ⓓ	47 Ⓐ Ⓑ Ⓒ Ⓓ
3 Ⓐ Ⓑ Ⓒ Ⓓ	18 Ⓐ Ⓑ Ⓒ Ⓓ	33 Ⓐ Ⓑ Ⓒ Ⓓ	48 Ⓐ Ⓑ Ⓒ Ⓓ
4 Ⓐ Ⓑ Ⓒ Ⓓ	19 Ⓐ Ⓑ Ⓒ Ⓓ	34 Ⓐ Ⓑ Ⓒ Ⓓ	49 Ⓐ Ⓑ Ⓒ Ⓓ
5 Ⓐ Ⓑ Ⓒ Ⓓ	20 Ⓐ Ⓑ Ⓒ Ⓓ	35 Ⓐ Ⓑ Ⓒ Ⓓ	50 Ⓐ Ⓑ Ⓒ Ⓓ
6 Ⓐ Ⓑ Ⓒ Ⓓ	21 Ⓐ Ⓑ Ⓒ Ⓓ	36 Ⓐ Ⓑ Ⓒ Ⓓ	51 Ⓐ Ⓑ Ⓒ Ⓓ
7 Ⓐ Ⓑ Ⓒ Ⓓ	22 Ⓐ Ⓑ Ⓒ Ⓓ	37 Ⓐ Ⓑ Ⓒ Ⓓ	52 Ⓐ Ⓑ Ⓒ Ⓓ
8 Ⓐ Ⓑ Ⓒ Ⓓ	23 Ⓐ Ⓑ Ⓒ Ⓓ	38 Ⓐ Ⓑ Ⓒ Ⓓ	53 Ⓐ Ⓑ Ⓒ Ⓓ
9 Ⓐ Ⓑ Ⓒ Ⓓ	24 Ⓐ Ⓑ Ⓒ Ⓓ	39 Ⓐ Ⓑ Ⓒ Ⓓ	54 Ⓐ Ⓑ Ⓒ Ⓓ
10 Ⓐ Ⓑ Ⓒ Ⓓ	25 Ⓐ Ⓑ Ⓒ Ⓓ	40 Ⓐ Ⓑ Ⓒ Ⓓ	55 Ⓐ Ⓑ Ⓒ Ⓓ
11 Ⓐ Ⓑ Ⓒ Ⓓ	26 Ⓐ Ⓑ Ⓒ Ⓓ	41 Ⓐ Ⓑ Ⓒ Ⓓ	56 Ⓐ Ⓑ Ⓒ Ⓓ
12 Ⓐ Ⓑ Ⓒ Ⓓ	27 Ⓐ Ⓑ Ⓒ Ⓓ	42 Ⓐ Ⓑ Ⓒ Ⓓ	57 Ⓐ Ⓑ Ⓒ Ⓓ
13 Ⓐ Ⓑ Ⓒ Ⓓ	28 Ⓐ Ⓑ Ⓒ Ⓓ	43 Ⓐ Ⓑ Ⓒ Ⓓ	58 Ⓐ Ⓑ Ⓒ Ⓓ
14 Ⓐ Ⓑ Ⓒ Ⓓ	29 Ⓐ Ⓑ Ⓒ Ⓓ	44 Ⓐ Ⓑ Ⓒ Ⓓ	59 Ⓐ Ⓑ Ⓒ Ⓓ
15 Ⓐ Ⓑ Ⓒ Ⓓ	30 Ⓐ Ⓑ Ⓒ Ⓓ	45 Ⓐ Ⓑ Ⓒ Ⓓ	60 Ⓐ Ⓑ Ⓒ Ⓓ

Part B – Forms Completion

1 Ⓐ Ⓑ Ⓒ Ⓓ	16 Ⓐ Ⓑ Ⓒ Ⓓ
2 Ⓐ Ⓑ Ⓒ Ⓓ	17 Ⓐ Ⓑ Ⓒ Ⓓ
3 Ⓐ Ⓑ Ⓒ Ⓓ	18 Ⓐ Ⓑ Ⓒ Ⓓ
4 Ⓐ Ⓑ Ⓒ Ⓓ	19 Ⓐ Ⓑ Ⓒ Ⓓ
5 Ⓐ Ⓑ Ⓒ Ⓓ	20 Ⓐ Ⓑ Ⓒ Ⓓ
6 Ⓐ Ⓑ Ⓒ Ⓓ	21 Ⓐ Ⓑ Ⓒ Ⓓ
7 Ⓐ Ⓑ Ⓒ Ⓓ	22 Ⓐ Ⓑ Ⓒ Ⓓ
8 Ⓐ Ⓑ Ⓒ Ⓓ	23 Ⓐ Ⓑ Ⓒ Ⓓ
9 Ⓐ Ⓑ Ⓒ Ⓓ	24 Ⓐ Ⓑ Ⓒ Ⓓ
10 Ⓐ Ⓑ Ⓒ Ⓓ	25 Ⓐ Ⓑ Ⓒ Ⓓ
11 Ⓐ Ⓑ Ⓒ Ⓓ	26 Ⓐ Ⓑ Ⓒ Ⓓ
12 Ⓐ Ⓑ Ⓒ Ⓓ	27 Ⓐ Ⓑ Ⓒ Ⓓ
13 Ⓐ Ⓑ Ⓒ Ⓓ	28 Ⓐ Ⓑ Ⓒ Ⓓ
14 Ⓐ Ⓑ Ⓒ Ⓓ	29 Ⓐ Ⓑ Ⓒ Ⓓ
15 Ⓐ Ⓑ Ⓒ Ⓓ	30 Ⓐ Ⓑ Ⓒ Ⓓ

Part C - Coding

1	Ⓐ Ⓑ Ⓒ Ⓓ	13	Ⓐ Ⓑ Ⓒ Ⓓ	25	Ⓐ Ⓑ Ⓒ Ⓓ
2	Ⓐ Ⓑ Ⓒ Ⓓ	14	Ⓐ Ⓑ Ⓒ Ⓓ	26	Ⓐ Ⓑ Ⓒ Ⓓ
3	Ⓐ Ⓑ Ⓒ Ⓓ	15	Ⓐ Ⓑ Ⓒ Ⓓ	27	Ⓐ Ⓑ Ⓒ Ⓓ
4	Ⓐ Ⓑ Ⓒ Ⓓ	16	Ⓐ Ⓑ Ⓒ Ⓓ	28	Ⓐ Ⓑ Ⓒ Ⓓ
5	Ⓐ Ⓑ Ⓒ Ⓓ	17	Ⓐ Ⓑ Ⓒ Ⓓ	29	Ⓐ Ⓑ Ⓒ Ⓓ
6	Ⓐ Ⓑ Ⓒ Ⓓ	18	Ⓐ Ⓑ Ⓒ Ⓓ	30	Ⓐ Ⓑ Ⓒ Ⓓ
7	Ⓐ Ⓑ Ⓒ Ⓓ	19	Ⓐ Ⓑ Ⓒ Ⓓ	31	Ⓐ Ⓑ Ⓒ Ⓓ
8	Ⓐ Ⓑ Ⓒ Ⓓ	20	Ⓐ Ⓑ Ⓒ Ⓓ	32	Ⓐ Ⓑ Ⓒ Ⓓ
9	Ⓐ Ⓑ Ⓒ Ⓓ	21	Ⓐ Ⓑ Ⓒ Ⓓ	33	Ⓐ Ⓑ Ⓒ Ⓓ
10	Ⓐ Ⓑ Ⓒ Ⓓ	22	Ⓐ Ⓑ Ⓒ Ⓓ	34	Ⓐ Ⓑ Ⓒ Ⓓ
11	Ⓐ Ⓑ Ⓒ Ⓓ	23	Ⓐ Ⓑ Ⓒ Ⓓ	35	Ⓐ Ⓑ Ⓒ Ⓓ
12	Ⓐ Ⓑ Ⓒ Ⓓ	24	Ⓐ Ⓑ Ⓒ Ⓓ	36	Ⓐ Ⓑ Ⓒ Ⓓ

Part C - Memory

37	Ⓐ Ⓑ Ⓒ Ⓓ	49	Ⓐ Ⓑ Ⓒ Ⓓ	61	Ⓐ Ⓑ Ⓒ Ⓓ
38	Ⓐ Ⓑ Ⓒ Ⓓ	50	Ⓐ Ⓑ Ⓒ Ⓓ	62	Ⓐ Ⓑ Ⓒ Ⓓ
39	Ⓐ Ⓑ Ⓒ Ⓓ	51	Ⓐ Ⓑ Ⓒ Ⓓ	63	Ⓐ Ⓑ Ⓒ Ⓓ
40	Ⓐ Ⓑ Ⓒ Ⓓ	52	Ⓐ Ⓑ Ⓒ Ⓓ	64	Ⓐ Ⓑ Ⓒ Ⓓ
41	Ⓐ Ⓑ Ⓒ Ⓓ	53	Ⓐ Ⓑ Ⓒ Ⓓ	65	Ⓐ Ⓑ Ⓒ Ⓓ
42	Ⓐ Ⓑ Ⓒ Ⓓ	54	Ⓐ Ⓑ Ⓒ Ⓓ	66	Ⓐ Ⓑ Ⓒ Ⓓ
43	Ⓐ Ⓑ Ⓒ Ⓓ	55	Ⓐ Ⓑ Ⓒ Ⓓ	67	Ⓐ Ⓑ Ⓒ Ⓓ
44	Ⓐ Ⓑ Ⓒ Ⓓ	56	Ⓐ Ⓑ Ⓒ Ⓓ	68	Ⓐ Ⓑ Ⓒ Ⓓ
45	Ⓐ Ⓑ Ⓒ Ⓓ	57	Ⓐ Ⓑ Ⓒ Ⓓ	69	Ⓐ Ⓑ Ⓒ Ⓓ
46	Ⓐ Ⓑ Ⓒ Ⓓ	58	Ⓐ Ⓑ Ⓒ Ⓓ	70	Ⓐ Ⓑ Ⓒ Ⓓ
47	Ⓐ Ⓑ Ⓒ Ⓓ	59	Ⓐ Ⓑ Ⓒ Ⓓ	71	Ⓐ Ⓑ Ⓒ Ⓓ
48	Ⓐ Ⓑ Ⓒ Ⓓ	60	Ⓐ Ⓑ Ⓒ Ⓓ	72	Ⓐ Ⓑ Ⓒ Ⓓ

SAMPLE ANSWER SHEET (2)

Part A- Address Checking

1 Ⓐ Ⓑ Ⓒ Ⓓ	16 Ⓐ Ⓑ Ⓒ Ⓓ	31 Ⓐ Ⓑ Ⓒ Ⓓ	46 Ⓐ Ⓑ Ⓒ Ⓓ
2 Ⓐ Ⓑ Ⓒ Ⓓ	17 Ⓐ Ⓑ Ⓒ Ⓓ	32 Ⓐ Ⓑ Ⓒ Ⓓ	47 Ⓐ Ⓑ Ⓒ Ⓓ
3 Ⓐ Ⓑ Ⓒ Ⓓ	18 Ⓐ Ⓑ Ⓒ Ⓓ	33 Ⓐ Ⓑ Ⓒ Ⓓ	48 Ⓐ Ⓑ Ⓒ Ⓓ
4 Ⓐ Ⓑ Ⓒ Ⓓ	19 Ⓐ Ⓑ Ⓒ Ⓓ	34 Ⓐ Ⓑ Ⓒ Ⓓ	49 Ⓐ Ⓑ Ⓒ Ⓓ
5 Ⓐ Ⓑ Ⓒ Ⓓ	20 Ⓐ Ⓑ Ⓒ Ⓓ	35 Ⓐ Ⓑ Ⓒ Ⓓ	50 Ⓐ Ⓑ Ⓒ Ⓓ
6 Ⓐ Ⓑ Ⓒ Ⓓ	21 Ⓐ Ⓑ Ⓒ Ⓓ	36 Ⓐ Ⓑ Ⓒ Ⓓ	51 Ⓐ Ⓑ Ⓒ Ⓓ
7 Ⓐ Ⓑ Ⓒ Ⓓ	22 Ⓐ Ⓑ Ⓒ Ⓓ	37 Ⓐ Ⓑ Ⓒ Ⓓ	52 Ⓐ Ⓑ Ⓒ Ⓓ
8 Ⓐ Ⓑ Ⓒ Ⓓ	23 Ⓐ Ⓑ Ⓒ Ⓓ	38 Ⓐ Ⓑ Ⓒ Ⓓ	53 Ⓐ Ⓑ Ⓒ Ⓓ
9 Ⓐ Ⓑ Ⓒ Ⓓ	24 Ⓐ Ⓑ Ⓒ Ⓓ	39 Ⓐ Ⓑ Ⓒ Ⓓ	54 Ⓐ Ⓑ Ⓒ Ⓓ
10 Ⓐ Ⓑ Ⓒ Ⓓ	25 Ⓐ Ⓑ Ⓒ Ⓓ	40 Ⓐ Ⓑ Ⓒ Ⓓ	55 Ⓐ Ⓑ Ⓒ Ⓓ
11 Ⓐ Ⓑ Ⓒ Ⓓ	26 Ⓐ Ⓑ Ⓒ Ⓓ	41 Ⓐ Ⓑ Ⓒ Ⓓ	56 Ⓐ Ⓑ Ⓒ Ⓓ
12 Ⓐ Ⓑ Ⓒ Ⓓ	27 Ⓐ Ⓑ Ⓒ Ⓓ	42 Ⓐ Ⓑ Ⓒ Ⓓ	57 Ⓐ Ⓑ Ⓒ Ⓓ
13 Ⓐ Ⓑ Ⓒ Ⓓ	28 Ⓐ Ⓑ Ⓒ Ⓓ	43 Ⓐ Ⓑ Ⓒ Ⓓ	58 Ⓐ Ⓑ Ⓒ Ⓓ
14 Ⓐ Ⓑ Ⓒ Ⓓ	29 Ⓐ Ⓑ Ⓒ Ⓓ	44 Ⓐ Ⓑ Ⓒ Ⓓ	59 Ⓐ Ⓑ Ⓒ Ⓓ
15 Ⓐ Ⓑ Ⓒ Ⓓ	30 Ⓐ Ⓑ Ⓒ Ⓓ	45 Ⓐ Ⓑ Ⓒ Ⓓ	60 Ⓐ Ⓑ Ⓒ Ⓓ

Part B – Forms Completion

1 Ⓐ Ⓑ Ⓒ Ⓓ	16 Ⓐ Ⓑ Ⓒ Ⓓ
2 Ⓐ Ⓑ Ⓒ Ⓓ	17 Ⓐ Ⓑ Ⓒ Ⓓ
3 Ⓐ Ⓑ Ⓒ Ⓓ	18 Ⓐ Ⓑ Ⓒ Ⓓ
4 Ⓐ Ⓑ Ⓒ Ⓓ	19 Ⓐ Ⓑ Ⓒ Ⓓ
5 Ⓐ Ⓑ Ⓒ Ⓓ	20 Ⓐ Ⓑ Ⓒ Ⓓ
6 Ⓐ Ⓑ Ⓒ Ⓓ	21 Ⓐ Ⓑ Ⓒ Ⓓ
7 Ⓐ Ⓑ Ⓒ Ⓓ	22 Ⓐ Ⓑ Ⓒ Ⓓ
8 Ⓐ Ⓑ Ⓒ Ⓓ	23 Ⓐ Ⓑ Ⓒ Ⓓ
9 Ⓐ Ⓑ Ⓒ Ⓓ	24 Ⓐ Ⓑ Ⓒ Ⓓ
10 Ⓐ Ⓑ Ⓒ Ⓓ	25 Ⓐ Ⓑ Ⓒ Ⓓ
11 Ⓐ Ⓑ Ⓒ Ⓓ	26 Ⓐ Ⓑ Ⓒ Ⓓ
12 Ⓐ Ⓑ Ⓒ Ⓓ	27 Ⓐ Ⓑ Ⓒ Ⓓ
13 Ⓐ Ⓑ Ⓒ Ⓓ	28 Ⓐ Ⓑ Ⓒ Ⓓ
14 Ⓐ Ⓑ Ⓒ Ⓓ	29 Ⓐ Ⓑ Ⓒ Ⓓ
15 Ⓐ Ⓑ Ⓒ Ⓓ	30 Ⓐ Ⓑ Ⓒ Ⓓ

Part C - Coding

1	Ⓐ Ⓑ Ⓒ Ⓓ	13	Ⓐ Ⓑ Ⓒ Ⓓ	25	Ⓐ Ⓑ Ⓒ Ⓓ
2	Ⓐ Ⓑ Ⓒ Ⓓ	14	Ⓐ Ⓑ Ⓒ Ⓓ	26	Ⓐ Ⓑ Ⓒ Ⓓ
3	Ⓐ Ⓑ Ⓒ Ⓓ	15	Ⓐ Ⓑ Ⓒ Ⓓ	27	Ⓐ Ⓑ Ⓒ Ⓓ
4	Ⓐ Ⓑ Ⓒ Ⓓ	16	Ⓐ Ⓑ Ⓒ Ⓓ	28	Ⓐ Ⓑ Ⓒ Ⓓ
5	Ⓐ Ⓑ Ⓒ Ⓓ	17	Ⓐ Ⓑ Ⓒ Ⓓ	29	Ⓐ Ⓑ Ⓒ Ⓓ
6	Ⓐ Ⓑ Ⓒ Ⓓ	18	Ⓐ Ⓑ Ⓒ Ⓓ	30	Ⓐ Ⓑ Ⓒ Ⓓ
7	Ⓐ Ⓑ Ⓒ Ⓓ	19	Ⓐ Ⓑ Ⓒ Ⓓ	31	Ⓐ Ⓑ Ⓒ Ⓓ
8	Ⓐ Ⓑ Ⓒ Ⓓ	20	Ⓐ Ⓑ Ⓒ Ⓓ	32	Ⓐ Ⓑ Ⓒ Ⓓ
9	Ⓐ Ⓑ Ⓒ Ⓓ	21	Ⓐ Ⓑ Ⓒ Ⓓ	33	Ⓐ Ⓑ Ⓒ Ⓓ
10	Ⓐ Ⓑ Ⓒ Ⓓ	22	Ⓐ Ⓑ Ⓒ Ⓓ	34	Ⓐ Ⓑ Ⓒ Ⓓ
11	Ⓐ Ⓑ Ⓒ Ⓓ	23	Ⓐ Ⓑ Ⓒ Ⓓ	35	Ⓐ Ⓑ Ⓒ Ⓓ
12	Ⓐ Ⓑ Ⓒ Ⓓ	24	Ⓐ Ⓑ Ⓒ Ⓓ	36	Ⓐ Ⓑ Ⓒ Ⓓ

Part C - Memory

37	Ⓐ Ⓑ Ⓒ Ⓓ	49	Ⓐ Ⓑ Ⓒ Ⓓ	61	Ⓐ Ⓑ Ⓒ Ⓓ
38	Ⓐ Ⓑ Ⓒ Ⓓ	50	Ⓐ Ⓑ Ⓒ Ⓓ	62	Ⓐ Ⓑ Ⓒ Ⓓ
39	Ⓐ Ⓑ Ⓒ Ⓓ	51	Ⓐ Ⓑ Ⓒ Ⓓ	63	Ⓐ Ⓑ Ⓒ Ⓓ
40	Ⓐ Ⓑ Ⓒ Ⓓ	52	Ⓐ Ⓑ Ⓒ Ⓓ	64	Ⓐ Ⓑ Ⓒ Ⓓ
41	Ⓐ Ⓑ Ⓒ Ⓓ	53	Ⓐ Ⓑ Ⓒ Ⓓ	65	Ⓐ Ⓑ Ⓒ Ⓓ
42	Ⓐ Ⓑ Ⓒ Ⓓ	54	Ⓐ Ⓑ Ⓒ Ⓓ	66	Ⓐ Ⓑ Ⓒ Ⓓ
43	Ⓐ Ⓑ Ⓒ Ⓓ	55	Ⓐ Ⓑ Ⓒ Ⓓ	67	Ⓐ Ⓑ Ⓒ Ⓓ
44	Ⓐ Ⓑ Ⓒ Ⓓ	56	Ⓐ Ⓑ Ⓒ Ⓓ	68	Ⓐ Ⓑ Ⓒ Ⓓ
45	Ⓐ Ⓑ Ⓒ Ⓓ	57	Ⓐ Ⓑ Ⓒ Ⓓ	69	Ⓐ Ⓑ Ⓒ Ⓓ
46	Ⓐ Ⓑ Ⓒ Ⓓ	58	Ⓐ Ⓑ Ⓒ Ⓓ	70	Ⓐ Ⓑ Ⓒ Ⓓ
47	Ⓐ Ⓑ Ⓒ Ⓓ	59	Ⓐ Ⓑ Ⓒ Ⓓ	71	Ⓐ Ⓑ Ⓒ Ⓓ
48	Ⓐ Ⓑ Ⓒ Ⓓ	60	Ⓐ Ⓑ Ⓒ Ⓓ	72	Ⓐ Ⓑ Ⓒ Ⓓ

Answer Key
Practice Exams

Address Checking Page 118 - 120		**Forms Completion** Pages 122 - 131
1. C	31. A	1. B
2. A	32. B	2. C
3. D	33. C	3. B
4. A	34. C	4. D
5. D	35. D	5. C
6. B	36. B	6. C
7. A	37. B	7. C
8. B	38. C	8. C
9. D	39. A	9. B
10. A	40. D	10. C
11. D	41. C	11. C
12. D	42. B	12. D
13. C	43. D	13. B
14. D	44. A	14. C
15. A	45. C	15. A
16. B	46. B	16. A
17. B	47. D	17. C
18. C	48. A	18. C
19. C	49. C	19. C
20. B	50. B	20. B
21. A	51. A	21. B
22. B	52. D	22. B
23. C	53. C	23. B
24. D	54. B	24. C
25. A	55. D	25. C
26. C	56. A	26. B
27. B	57. C	27. C
28. D	58. B	28. C
29. B	59. B	29. B
30. A	60. A	30. D

Answer Key
Practice Exams
Coding & Memory Pages 135 - 146

Coding	Memory (1)	Memory (2)
1. C	37. A	37. C
2. B	38. D	38. B
3. D	39. B	39. D
4. D	40. C	40. C
5. B	41. A	41. C
6. A	42. B	42. A
7. D	43. D	43. C
8. C	44. D	44. B
9. B	45. D	45. D
10. A	46. A	46. B
11. A	47. B	47. A
12. C	48. B	48. D
13. B	49. D	49. A
14. D	50. C	50. C
15. B	51. C	51. D
16. A	52. A	52. C
17. D	53. B	53. B
18. C	54. D	54. A
19. A	55. A	55. C
20. B	56. B	56. B
21. D	57. C	57. C
22. C	58. C	58. A
23. A	59. A	59. C
24. D	60. D	60. C
25. B	61. A	61. A
26. C	62. D	62. A
27. C	63. C	63. B
28. A	64. B	64. D
29. A	65. B	65. C
30. D	66. A	66. A
31. B	67. D	67. B
32. C	68. D	68. A
33. B	69. B	69. C
34. A	70. D	70. C
35. D	71. B	71. D
36. C	72. A	72. D

Chapter Six
The Interview Process

There are several types of interviews you may encounter. The most common interview is called a *Structured Interview*. Most traditional interviews are based on this format. Below are some descriptions of the different types of interviews and what you can expect in each of them.[1]

TYPES OF INTERVIEWS

- *Screening Interview*. A preliminary interview either in person or by phone, in which an agency or company representative determines whether you have the basic qualifications to warrant a subsequent interview.

- *Structured Interview*. In a structured interview, the interviewer explores certain predetermined areas using questions which have been written in advance. The interviewer has a written description of the experience, skills and personality traits of an "ideal" candidate. Your experience and skills are compared to specific job tasks. This type of interview is very common, and most traditional interviews are based on this format.

- *Unstructured Interview*. Although the interviewer is given a written description of the "ideal" candidate, in the unstructured interview the interviewer is not given instructions on what specific areas to cover.

- *Multiple Interviews*. Multiple interviews are commonly used with professional jobs. This approach involves a series of interviews in which you meet individually with various representatives of the organization.

---

[1] The Job Search Guide, U.S. Department of Labor.

- *Stress Interview.* The interviewer intentionally attempts to upset you to see how you react under pressure. You may be asked questions that make you uncomfortable or you may be interrupted when you are speaking. Although it is uncommon for an entire interview to be conducted under stress conditions, it is common for the interviewer to incorporate stress questions as a part of a traditional interview. Examples of common stress questions are given later in this chapter.

- *Targeted Interview.* Although similar to the structured interview, the areas covered are much more limited. Key qualifications for success on the job are identified and relevant questions are prepared in advance.

- *Situational Interview.* Situations are set up which simulate common problems you may encounter on the job. Your responses to these situations are measured against pre-determined standards. This approach is often used as one part of a traditional interview rather than as an entire interview format.

- *Group Interview.* You may be interviewed by two or more agency or company representatives simultaneously. Sometimes, one of the interviewers is designated to ask "stress" questions to see how you respond under pressure.

  NOTE: Many government agencies including the Postal Service have initiated quality of worklife and employee involvement groups to build viable labor/management teams and partnerships. In this environment agencies may require applicants to be interviewed by several groups that often include peers and subordinates.

The interview strategies discussed below can be used effectively in any type of interview you may encounter.

BEFORE THE INTERVIEW

Prepare in advance. The better prepared you are, the less anxious you will be and the greater your chances for success.

- *Role Play.* Find someone to role play the interview with you. This person should be someone with whom you feel comfortable and with whom you can discuss your weaknesses freely. The person should be objective and knowledgeable, perhaps a business associate.

- Use a mirror or video camera when you role play to see what kind of image you project.

Assess your interviewing skills.

■   What are your strengths and weaknesses? Work on correcting your weaknesses, such as speaking rapidly, talking too loudly or softly, and nervous habits such as shaking hands or inappropriate facial expressions.

■   Learn the questions that are commonly asked and prepare answers to them. Examples of commonly asked interview questions are provided later in this chapter. Career centers and libraries often have books which include interview questions. Practice giving answers which are brief but thorough.

■   Decide what questions you would like to ask and practice politely interjecting them at different points in the interview.

Evaluate your strengths

■   Evaluate your skills, abilities and education as they relate to the type of job you are seeking.

■   Practice tailoring your answers to show how you meet the Postal Service's needs, if you have details about the specific job before the interview.

Assess your overall appearance.

■   Find out what clothing is appropriate for your job occupation. Acceptable attire for most professional positions is conservative.

■   Have several sets of appropriate clothing available, since you may have several interviews over a few days.

■   Your clothes should be clean and pressed and your shoes polished.

■   Make sure your hair is neat, your nails clean, and you are generally well groomed.

Research the Postal Service. The more you know about the Postal Service and the job you are applying for, the better you will do on the interview. Get as much information as you can before the interview.

Professional applicants and applicants for positions that do not require entrance exams should have extra copies of their résumé or application available to take on the interview. The interviewer may ask you for extra copies. Make sure you bring along the same version of your résumé or application that you originally provided. You can also refer to your résumé to complete applications that ask for job history information (i.e., dates of employment, names of former employers and their telephone numbers, job responsibilities and accomplishments.) A blank application form is provided in Appendix B for your use.

Arrive early at the interview. Plan to arrive 10 to 15 minutes early. Give yourself time to find a restroom so you can check your appearance.

It's important to make a good impression from the moment you enter the reception area. Greet the receptionist cordially and try to appear confident. You never know what influence the receptionist has with your interviewer. With a little small talk, you may get some helpful information about the interviewer and the job opening. If you are asked to fill out an application while you're waiting, be sure to fill it out completely and print the information neatly. Prepare the sample application in Appendix C.

Don't make negative comments about anyone or anything, including former employers.

DURING THE INTERVIEW

The job interview is usually a two-way discussion between you and a prospective employer. The interviewer is attempting to determine whether you have what the Postal Service needs, and you are attempting to determine whether you would accept the job if offered. Both of you will be trying to get as much information as possible in order to make those decisions.[2]

The interview that you are most likely to face is a structured interview with a traditional format. It usually consists of three phases. The introductory phase covers the greeting, small talk and an overview of which areas will be discussed during the interview. The middle phase is a question-and-answer period. The interviewer asks most of the questions, but you are given an opportunity to ask questions as well. The closing phase gives you an opportunity to ask any final questions you might have, cover any important points that haven't been discussed and get information about the next step in the process.

Introductory Phase. This phase is very important. You want to make a good first impression and, if possible, get additional information you need about the job and the company.

- Make a good impression. You have only a few seconds to create a positive first impression which can influence the rest of the interview and even determine whether you get the job.

The interviewer's first impression of you is based mainly on non-verbal clues. The interviewer is assessing your overall appearance and demeanor. When greeting the interviewer, be certain your handshake is firm and that you make eye contact. Wait for the interviewer to signal you before you sit down.

Once seated, your body language is very important in conveying a positive impression. Find a comfortable position so that you don't appear tense. Lean

---

[2] Postal Service Handbook EL-312

forward slightly and maintain eye contact with the interviewer. This posture shows that you are interested in what is being said. Smile naturally at appropriate times. Show that you are open and receptive by keeping your arms and legs uncrossed. Avoid keeping your briefcase or your handbag on your lap. Pace your movements so that they are not too fast or too slow. Try to appear relaxed and confident.

- Get the information you need. If you weren't able to get complete information about the job in advance, you should try to get it as early as possible in the interview. Be sure to prepare your questions in advance. Knowing the following things will allow you to present those strengths and abilities that the employer wants.

  - Why does the Postal Service need someone in this position?

  - Exactly what would they expect of you?

  - Are they looking for traditional or innovative solutions to problems?

- When should you ask questions? The problem with a traditional interview structure is that your chance to ask questions occurs late in the interview. How can you get the information you need early in the process without making the interviewer feel that you are taking control?

Deciding exactly when to ask your questions is the tricky part. Timing is everything. You may have to make a decision based on intuition and your first impressions of the interviewer. Does the interviewer seem comfortable or nervous, soft-spoken or forceful, formal or casual? These signals will help you to judge the best time to ask your questions.

The sooner you ask the questions, the less likely you are to disrupt the interviewer's agenda. However, if you ask questions too early, the interviewer may feel you are trying to control the interview.

Try asking questions right after the greeting and small talk. Since most interviewers like to set the tone of the interview and maintain initial control, always phrase your questions in a way that leaves control with the interviewer. Perhaps you can say, "Would you mind telling me a little more about the job so that I can focus on the information that would be most important to the Postal Service?" If there is no job opening but you are trying to develop one, or you need more information, try saying, "Could you tell me a little more about where the Postal Service is going so I can focus in those areas of my background that are most relevant?"

You may want to wait until the interviewer has given an overview of what will be discussed. This overview may answer some of your questions or may provide some details that you can use to ask additional questions. Once the middle phase of the interview has begun, you may find it more difficult to ask questions.

Middle Phase. During this phase of the interview, you will be asked many questions about your work experience, skills, education, activities and interests, You are being assessed on how you will perform the job in relation to the agency's objectives.

All your responses should be concise. Use specific examples to illustrate your point whenever possible. Although your responses should be prepared in advance so that they are well phrased and effective, be sure they do not sound rehearsed. Remember that your responses must always be adapted to the present interview. Incorporate any information you obtained earlier in the interview with the responses you had prepared in advance, and then answer in a way that is appropriate to the question.

FREQUENTLY ASKED QUESTIONS

Question: "Tell me about yourself."

Reply: Briefly describe your experience and background. If you are unsure what information the interviewer is seeking, say, "Are there any areas in particular you'd like to know about?"

Question: "What is your weakest point?" (A stress question)

Reply: Mention something that is actually a strength. Some examples are:

"I'm something of a perfectionist."

"I'm a stickler for punctuality."

"I'm tenacious."

Give a specific situation from your previous job to illustrate your point.

Question: "What is your strongest point?"

Reply: "I work well under pressure." or

"I am organized and manage my time well."

If you have just graduated from college you might say,

"I am eager to learn, and I don't have to unlearn old techniques."

Give a specific example to illustrate your point.

Question: "What do you hope to be doing five years from now?"

Reply: "I hope I will still be working here and will have increased my level of responsibility based on my performance and abilities."

Question: "Why have you been out of work for so long?" (A stress question)

Reply: "I spent some time re-evaluating my past experience and the current job market to see what direction I wanted to take." or

"I had some offers, but I'm not just looking for another job; I'm looking for a career."

Question: "What do you know about the Postal Service? Why do you want to work here?"

Reply: This is where your research will come in handy.

"The Postal Service is a leader in mail/package delivery, and three of the Postal Service's six product lines would qualify as Fortune 500 companies:" (Mention one or two of the following.)

- Correspondence and transactions
- Business Advertising
- Expedited Delivery
- Publications Delivery
- Standard Package Delivery
- International Mail

"The Postal Service has a superior reputation, with operating revenue exceeding $65 billion a year."[3]

You might try to get the interviewer to give you additional information about the Postal Service by saying that you are very interested in learning more about the agency's objectives. This will help you to focus your response on relevant areas.

---

[3] USPS Financial Highlights, Annual Performance Plan 2003.

Question: "What is your greatest accomplishment?"

Reply: Give a specific illustration from your previous or current job where you saved the company money or helped increase its profits. If you have just graduated from college, try to find some accomplishment from your school work, part-time jobs or extra-curricular activities.

Question: "Why should we hire you?" (A stress question)

Reply: Highlight your background based on the Postal Service's current needs. Recap your qualifications, keeping the interviewer's job description in mind. If you don't have much experience, talk about how your education and training prepared you for this job.

Question: "Why do you want to make a change now?"

Reply: "I want to develop my potential." or

"The opportunities in my present company are limited."

Question: "Tell me about a problem you had in your last job and how you resolved it."

Reply: The employer wants to assess your analytical skills and see if you are a team player. Select a problem from your last job and explain how you solved it.

Some Questions You Should Ask.

✎ "What are the Postal Service's current challenges?"

✎ "Could you give me a more detailed job description?"

✎ "Why is this position open?"

✎ "Are there opportunities for advancement?"

✎ "To whom would I report?"

Closing Phase. During the closing phase of an interview, you will be asked whether you have any other questions. Ask any relevant question that has not yet been answered. Highlight any of your strengths that have not been discussed. If another interview is to be scheduled, get the necessary information. If this is the final interview, find out when the decision is to be made and when you can call. Thank the interviewer by name and say goodbye.

ILLEGAL QUESTIONS

During an interview, you may be asked some questions that are considered illegal. It is illegal for an interviewer to ask you questions related to sex, age, race, religion, national origin or marital status, or to delve into your personal life for information that is not job-related. What can you do if you are asked an illegal question? Take a moment to evaluate the situation. Ask yourself questions like:

✎ How uncomfortable has this question made you feel?

✎ Does the interviewer seem unaware that the question is illegal?

✎ Is this interviewer going to be your boss?

Then respond in a way that is comfortable for you.

If you decide to answer the question, be succinct and try to move the conversation back to an examination of your skills and abilities as quickly as possible. For example, if asked about your age, you might reply, "I'm in my forties, and I have a wealth of experience that would be an asset to your agency." If you are not sure whether you want to answer the question, first ask for a clarification of how this question relates to your qualifications for the job. You may decide to answer if there is a reasonable explanation. If you feel there is no justification for the question, you might say that you do not see the relationship between the question and your qualifications for the job and you prefer not to answer it.

AFTER THE INTERVIEW

You are not finished yet. It is important to assess the interview shortly after it is concluded. Following your interview you should:

■ Write down the name, phone number, e-mail address, and title (be sure the spelling is correct) of the interviewer.

■ Review what the job entails and record what the next step will be.

■ Note your reactions to the interview; include what went well and what went poorly.

■ Assess what you learned from the experience and how you can improve your performance in future interviews.

PHONE FOLLOW-UP

If you were not told during the interview when a hiring decision will be made, call after one week.

At that time, if you learn that the decision has not been made, find out whether you are still under consideration for the job. Ask if there are any other questions the interviewer might have about your qualifications and offer to come in for another interview if necessary. Reiterate that you are very interested in the job.

- If you learn that you did not get the job, try to find out why. You might also inquire whether the interviewer can think of anyone else who might be able to use someone with your abilities, either in another department or at another agency.

- If you are offered the job, you have to decide whether you want it. If you are not sure, thank the employer and ask for several days to think about it. Ask any other questions you might need answered to help you with the decision.

- If you know you want the job and have all the information you need, accept the job with thanks and get the details on when you start. Ask whether the Postal Service will be sending a letter of confirmation, as it is best to have the offer in writing.

Who Gets Hired?

In the final analysis, the Postal Service will hire someone who has the abilities and talents which fulfill its needs. It is up to you to demonstrate at the interview that you are the person the agency wants.

Chapter Seven
Veterans Preference

Veterans can take advantage of special-emphasis Civil Service hiring programs including the *Veterans Preference*[1] and the *Veterans Recruitment Act (VRA)*. Unknown to many, military dependents and spouses of active duty personnel receive hiring preference for government jobs under the *Military Spouse Preference Program* and the *Family Member Preference Program*.

In 1973 I took advantage of a special-emphasis hiring program and was discharged nine months early from the U.S. Air Force under the **Palace Chase** program. I was hired full time as an avionics technician for the Air National Guard. The Palace Chase program helped reduce the size of the military as the Vietnam war was ending.

The federal government, including the Postal Service, has a long and outstanding record of employing veterans. Veterans hold a far higher percentage of jobs in the government than they do in private industry. In large part, this is due to laws providing veterans' preference and special appointing authorities for veterans, as well as the fact that agencies recognize that hiring veterans is just good business.

Over 24% of all federal employees are veterans.

When filling a competitive service job from *outside* the Civil Service, agencies may:

- Appoint a well-qualified candidate from a competitive list of eligibles developed by OPM or by an agency with delegated examining authority; or

- Appoint someone who is eligible under one of a number of special appointing authorities (e.g., the VRA or Schedule B authorities, and others authorized by either law or executive order).

---

[1] Authorized by law, Title 5 USC, Section 2108 and Section 3501.

Alternatively, filling jobs from among "status" candidates, agencies may:

- Appoint someone from an agency-developed merit promotion list (when these jobs are open to candidates outside the agency, the agency must allow eligibles under the Veterans Employment Opportunities Act of 1998, as amended to apply); or

- Reassign a current agency employee, transfer an employee from another agency, or reinstate a former federal employee.

VETERANS PREFERENCE

Beginning with the Civil War, veterans of the armed forces have been given some degree of preference in appointments for federal jobs. Veterans preference is a way to help make up for the economic loss suffered by those who answered the nation's call to arms. When an agency advertises job vacancies through the Office of Personnel Management or locally through direct hire authority, the agency must select from the top-rated eligible applicants. The official may not pass over a veterans preference eligible, however, and appoint a non-preference eligible lower on the list unless the reasons for passing over the veteran are sufficient.

Veterans preference gives special consideration to eligible veterans looking for federal employment.[2] Veterans who are disabled or who served on active duty in the United States armed forces during certain specified time periods or in military campaigns are entitled to preference over nonveterans both in hiring into the federal Civil Service and in retention during *reductions in force*. There are two classes of preference for honorably discharged veterans:

Five-Point Preference

Five-point preference is given to those honorably separated veterans (this means an honorable or general discharge) who served on active duty (not active duty for training) in the armed forces:

- During any war (this means a war declared by Congress, the last of which was World War II); **or**

- For more than 180 consecutive days, other than for training, any part of which occurred after January 31, 1955 and before October 15, 1976; **or**

- During the period April 28, 1952, through July 1, 1955; **or**

- During the Gulf War from August 2, 1990, through January 2, 1992; **or**

---

[2] Reference OPM's "Vet Info Guide" available online at http://www.opm.gov/veterans/html/vetsinfo.htm.

- For more than 180 consecutive days, any part of which occurred during the period beginning September 11, 2001, and ending on the date prescribed by presidential proclamation or by law as the last day of Operation Iraqi Freedom; **or**

- In a campaign or expedition for which a campaign medal has been authorized, such as El Salvador, Lebanon, Grenada, Panama, Southwest Asia, Somalia, and Haiti.

A campaign medal holder or Gulf War veteran who originally enlisted after September 7, 1980, or entered on active duty on or after October 14, 1982, without having previously completed 24 months of continuous active duty must have served continuously for 24 months or the full period called or ordered to active duty.

Effective October 1, 1980, military retirees at or above the rank of major or equivalent are not entitled to preference unless they qualify as disabled veterans.

Ten-Point Preference

Ten-point preference is given to:

- Those honorably separated veterans who 1) qualify as disabled veterans because they have served on active duty in the armed forces at any time and have a present service-connected disability or are receiving compensation, disability retirement benefits, or pension from the military or the Department of Veterans Affairs; or 2) are Purple Heart recipients;

- The spouse of a veteran unable to work because of a service-connected disability;

- The unmarried widow of certain deceased veterans;

- The mother of a veteran who died in service or who is permanently and totally disabled.

When applying for federal jobs, eligible veterans should claim preference on their application or résumé. Applicants claiming 10-point preference must complete **form SF-15**, Application for 10-Point Veteran Preference. Veterans who are still in the service may be granted five points tentative preference on the basis of information contained in their applications, but they must produce a DD Form 214 prior to appointment to document entitlement to preference.

Note: Reservists who are retired from the reserves but don't receive retired pay are not considered "retired military" for purposes of veterans preference.

The Veterans Preference Advisor system allows veterans to examine the preferences for which they might be entitled with regard to federal jobs. This system was developed by the Veterans Employment and Training Service.

To explore the Veterans Preference program, visit OPM's Web site at http://www.opm.gov/veterans and download the Veterans Preference Guide.

> ## PURPLE HEART RECIPIENTS ARE CONSIDERED TO HAVE A SERVICE-CONNECTED DISABILITY

How Preference Applies in Competitive Examination

Veterans who are eligible for preference and who meet the minimum qualification requirements of the position have five or 10 points added to their passing score on a civil service examination. For scientific and professional positions at the GS-9 grade or higher, names of all eligibles are listed in order of ratings, augmented by veterans preference points, if any. For all other positions, the names of 10-point preference eligibles who have a service-connected disability of 10 percent or more are placed ahead of the names of all other eligibles. Other eligibles are then listed in order of their earned ratings, augmented by veterans preference points. A preference eligible is listed ahead of a nonpreference eligible with the same score.

What Does This Mean?

If you apply for a federal job, your knowledge, skills and abilities will be rated on a point system. You will receive points for related education, experience, special skills, awards, and written test if required. To qualify for a position you must have a score of 70 to 100 points. If an eligible five-point preference candidate accumulates 90 points, five additional points are awarded on preference for a total score of 95. Therefore, the preference veteran, in most cases, must be hired before an agency can hire anyone with 95 points or less in this example. If that same veteran accumulated 100 points, his final score — with preference — would be 105 points. A 10-point preference veteran would have a total score of 110. Vets who ace the exam will go to the top of the list, since only veterans preference veterans can exceed 100 points on the exams.

The agency must select from the top three candidates (known as the rule of three) and may not pass over a preference eligible in favor of a lower-ranking non-preference eligible without sound reasons that relate directly to the veteran's fitness for employment. The agency may, however, select a lower-ranking preference eligible over a compensably disabled veteran within the rule of three.

A preference eligible who is passed over on a list of eligibles is entitled, upon request, to a copy of the agency's reasons for the pass-over and the examining office's response.

If the preference eligible is a 30 percent or more disabled veteran, the agency must notify the veteran and OPM of the proposed pass-over. The veteran has 15 days from the date of notification to respond to OPM. OPM then decides whether to approve the pass-over based on all the facts available and notifies the agency and the veteran.

Filing Applications After Examinations Close

A 10-point preference eligible may file an application at any time for any position for which a nontemporary appointment has been made in the preceding three years; for which a list of eligibles currently exists that is closed to new applications; or for which a list is about to be established. Veterans wishing to file after the closing date should contact the agency that announced the position for further information.

SPECIAL APPOINTING AUTHORITIES

The following special authorities permit the noncompetitive appointment of eligible veterans in the federal Civil Service. Use of these special authorities is entirely discretionary with the agency; no one is **entitled** to one of these special appointments:

VETERANS' RECRUITMENT APPOINTMENT (VRA)

The VRA is a special authority that agencies can use to appoint an eligible veteran without competition at any grade level through General Schedule (GS) 11 or equivalent. The VRA is an excepted appointment to a position that is otherwise in the competitive service. After two years of satisfactory service, the veteran is converted to a career-conditional appointment in the competitive service.

When two or more VRA applicants are preference eligibles, the agency must apply veterans preference as required by law. (While all VRA eligibles have served in the armed forces, they do not necessarily meet the eligibility requirements for veterans preference under section 2108 of title 5, United States Code.)

Eligibility Requirements

Eligibility requirements changed considerably under the Jobs for Veterans Act, Public Law 107-288, which amended title 38 U.S.C. 4214. The new eligibility requirements limited access to this program to veterans who served during a war, or in a campaign and to recently separated veterans as noted below:

- Disabled veterans; **or**

- Veterans who served on active duty in the armed forces during a war, or in a campaign or expedition for which a campaign badge has been authorized; **or**

- Veterans who, while serving on active duty in the armed forces, participated in a United States military operation for which an Armed Forces Service Medal was awarded; **or**

- Recently separated veterans.

There has been some confusion as to what is considered to be *"recently separated."* Agencies are limiting VRA to those within three years of discharge in some cases. Veterans claiming eligibility on the basis of service in a campaign or expedition for which a medal was awarded must be in receipt of the campaign badge or medal.

In addition to meeting the criteria above, eligible veterans must have been separated under honorable conditions (i.e., the individual must have received either an honorable or general discharge).

Clarifications

Under the eligibility criteria, not all five-point preference eligible veterans may be eligible for a VRA appointment. For example, a veteran who served during the Vietnam era (i.e., for more than 180 consecutive days, after January 31, 1955, and before October 15, 1976) but did not receive a service-connected disability or an Armed Forces Service Medal or campaign or expeditionary medal would be entitled to five-point veterans preference. This veteran, however, would not be eligible for a VRA appointment under the above criteria.

As another example, a veteran who served during the Gulf War from August 2, 1990, through January 2, 1992, would be eligible for veterans preference solely on the basis of that service. However, service during that time period, in and of itself, does not confer VRA eligibility on the veteran unless one of the above VRA eligibility criteria is met.

Lastly, if an agency has two or more VRA candidates and one or more is a preference eligible, the agency must apply veterans preference. For example, one applicant is VRA eligible on the basis of receiving an Armed Forces Service Medal (this medal does not confer veterans preference eligibility). The second applicant is VRA eligible on the basis of being a disabled veteran (which does confer veterans preference eligibility). In this example, both individuals are VRA eligible but only one of them is eligible for veterans preference. As a result, agencies must apply the procedures of 5 CFR 302 when considering VRA appointments.

How to Apply

Veterans should contact directly the federal agency personnel office where they are interested in working to find out about VRA opportunities. Complete a résumé or an Optional Application for Federal Employment OF-612 and forward it with a cover letter to selected agencies. Refer to the resources listed in Chapter Three and the Appendices for specific agency addresses and telephone numbers. Also, visit http://federaljobs.net for direct links to more than 140 federal agency recruiting sites. Chapter Six will help you draft your federal style résumé.

Send a cover letter with your application explaining that you are a VRA candidate and would like to be considered for an appointment with that agency. Send a copy of your DD-214 form with your cover letter and application.

Follow up each submission with a phone call. It helps to call an agency first and obtain a name and address to which you can send an application. Send applications to every office and department that interests you.

Agencies **do not have to hire through the VRA program**. Only if your education and work experience meets their requirements, they have openings, and like what they see will they make you an offer. Be tactful and don't be demanding.

30% OR MORE DISABLED VETERANS

These veterans may be given a temporary or term appointment (not limited to 60 days or less) to any position for which qualified (there is no grade limitation). After demonstrating satisfactory performance, the veteran may be converted at any time to a career-conditional appointment.

Terms and Conditions of Employment

Disabled veterans are given a temporary appointment with an expiration date in excess of 60 days. This appointment may be converted at any time to a career conditional appointment. Unlike the VRA, there is no grade limitation.

How to Apply

Veterans should contact the federal agency personnel office where they are interested in working to find out about opportunities. Veterans must submit a copy of a letter dated within the last 12 months from the Department of Veterans Affairs or the Department of Defense certifying receipt of compensation for a service-connected disability of 30 percent or more.

Disabled Veterans Enrolled in VA Training Programs

Disabled veterans eligible for training under the Department of Veterans Affairs' (VA) vocational rehabilitation program may enroll for training or work experience at an agency under the terms of an agreement between the agency and VA. The veteran is not a federal employee for most purposes while enrolled in the program, but is a beneficiary of the VA.

The training is tailored to individual needs and goals, so there is no set length. If the training is intended to prepare the individual for eventual appointment in the agency (rather than just work experience), OPM must approve the training plan. Upon successful completion, the veteran will be given a Certificate of Training showing the occupational series and grade level of the position for which trained. This allows any agency to appoint the veteran noncompetitively for a period of one year. Upon appointment, the veteran is given a Special Tenure Appointment which is then converted to career-conditional with OPM approval.

VETERANS EMPLOYMENT OPPORTUNITIES ACT

The Veterans Employment Opportunities Act (VEOA) was passed in 1998 and it gives veterans access to federal job opportunities that might otherwise be closed to them. The law requires that:

- Agencies allow eligible veterans to compete for vacancies advertised under the agency's merit promotion procedures when the agency is seeking applications from individuals outside its own workforce.

- All merit promotion announcements open to applicants outside an agency's workforce include a statement that these eligible veterans may apply.

The law also establishes a new redress system for preference eligibles and makes it a prohibited personnel practice for an agency to knowingly take or fail to take a personnel action if that action or failure to act would violate a statutory or regulatory veterans preference requirement.

This authority permits an agency to appoint an eligible veteran who has applied under an agency merit promotion announcement that is open to candidates outside the agency.

To be eligible a candidate must be a preference eligible or a veteran separated after three years or more of continuous active service performed under honorable conditions.

Terms and Conditions of Employment

Veterans given a VEOA appointment will be given a career or career conditional appointment in the competitive service. Veterans interested in applying under this authority should seek out agency merit promotion announcements open to candidates outside the agency. **Applications should be submitted directly to the agency.** Veterans who have career status or are reinstatement eligible are not eligible for VEOA appointments.

Positions Restricted to Preference Eligibles

Examinations for custodian, guard, elevator operator and messenger are open only to preference eligibles as long as such applicants are available.

Chapter Eight
Job Descriptions

There are over 2,000 occupational codes identified in the Postal Service's Position Directory,[1] many of which are listed in Chapter Nine. This chapter features 26 job descriptions—a cross-section of Postal Service occupations, from accountants and engineers to welders and custodians.

Mail carrier and clerk occupations are presented in Chapter Three. These job descriptions represent a cross-section of available Postal Service jobs. Many of these jobs are first offered to qualified postal employees. If they can't fill these positions in-house, they advertise jobs to the general public.

POSITION DESCRIPTIONS

Accounting Technician
Architect/engineer
Area Maintenance Technician
Automotive Mechanic
Budget and Financial Analyst
Building Equipment Mechanic
Carrier (City)
Casual
Clerk Stenographer
Computer Systems Analyst
Custodian
Data Collection Technician
Distribution Clerk
Electronics Technician

Financial Services Coordinator
Flat Sorting Machine Operator
Human Resource Specialist
Maintenance Mechanic
Mechanical Engineer
Nurse, Occupational Health
Personnel Clerk
Police Officer, Postal
Postal Inspector
Rural Carrier
Secretary
Telecommunications Specialist
Welder
Window Clerk

---

[1] Employee Master File /RDL/OCCLIST

ACCOUNTING TECHNICIAN, PS-06 Occupation Code: 0525-31XX

Ensures the proper completion of a designated major segment of accounting work in a district office; or serves as assistant to the postmaster in performing accounting and clerical duties involved in the preparation, maintenance, and consolidation of accounts and related reports in a post office.

DUTIES AND RESPONSIBILITIES

1. Performs, with assistance of accounting clerks if needed, either duty 2 or 3, in combination with duty 3. In a smaller post office having characteristics like those in the basic function, and subject to the provisions of Postal Service directives concerning internal control and separation of duties, performs any combination of duties 5 through 8.

2. In the accounting area, receives daily cash reports from all reporting units of the post office, verifies and balances reports with supporting documents, consolidates the data in one cash report, and posts the daily financial report. Items which are questionable are taken up with the reporting unit or individual in order to determine the correct entries. Reporting units are debited or credited as necessary.

3. In the budget and cost control area, receives reports and data relating to mail volume, workload, and cost ascertainment from the various reporting units, examines reports for completeness and tabulates and posts data in accordance with daily and periodic reporting requirements. Discusses with supervisor data submitted by their units in order that further necessary information and explanation may be obtained. Documents explanatory information for subsequent analysis and inclusion in management reports.

4. In addition, works closely with the supervisor in preparing weekly, biweekly, accounting period, or other periodic reports. Gives guidance and instruction to and acts as group leader for any assigned clerical assistance. May maintain accounts, reflecting trust funds, suspense items and inventories of accountable paper, stamp stock, and fixed credits. Participates with the supervisor interpreting instructions and regulations in implementing procedures pertaining to accounting. May be required to research, compile and record data for special studies and reports on various phases of postal activities as desired by the postmaster or higher authority.

5. Receives daily cash reports from all reporting units of the post office, verifies and balances reports with supporting documents, consolidates into one cash report, and posts the cashbook. Items which are questionable are taken up with the reporting unit or individual to determine the correct entries.

6. Receives reports and data relating to mail volume, workload, and cost ascertainment from the various reporting units, examines reports for completeness and accuracy, makes the necessary computations, consolidates the information in accordance with daily and periodic reporting requirements. Discusses with supervisors figures submitted by them to obtain further information and explanation as required. Prepares explanatory comments for inclusion in the reports.

7. Works closely with the postmaster in preparing required accounting period reports including operating report, financial statement, workload and mail volume reports.

8. May maintain stamp stock and fill requisitions for window clerks, stations and branches.

ARCHITECT/ENGINEER, EAS-20 Occupation Code: 0808-3020

Performs design work and assists in administering design and construction contracts within a district office.

DUTIES AND RESPONSIBILITIES

1. Provides architect/engineering consulting services, evaluates technical problems, and surveys technical alternatives for construction projects within a district office.

2. Participates in the analysis, evaluation, and determination of feasibility, costs, and technical problems related to the planning, design, installation, testings, and operation of advanced engineered systems and equipment in support of construction projects.

3. Oversees construction term contracts to ensure compliance with contract requirements and adherence to established policies and procedures.

4. Participates in the activities related to the design, construction, testing, start-up, and operation of facilities, systems, and/or equipment.

5. Participates in the preparation of requests for proposal, including specifications and drawings; participates in the evaluation of contractor bids.

6. Reviews contractor specifications and drawings for technical accuracy and compliance with contract requirements.

7. Attends preconstruction and final acceptance meetings for progress review; makes on-site inspections during installation and test, and reports discrepancies in contract work.

8. Works with architects, engineers, contractors, construction representatives, and others involved in the design and construction of postal facilities.

9. Provides technical assistance to employees and others in the development of facility projects.

AREA MAINTENANCE TECHNICIAN, PS-08 Occupation Code: 4801-20XX

Installs, maintains, repairs, removes, and disposes of postal equipment as appropriate at post offices (offices not having maintenance capability) within the geographic area served by the area maintenance office to which assigned. Installs, moves, or repairs post office screen-line equipment, lock boxes, furniture, and mechanical equipment, supervising such additional help as projects may require.

DUTIES AND RESPONSIBILITIES

1. At regional direction, moves and sets up offices in new or remodeled postal quarters; assembles, installs screen-lines, workroom, lobby, and operating equipment. Supervises carpenters and/or helpers as projects may require. Classifies or assists postmasters in classification of postal equipment for disposal or refurbishing. Under postmaster's authority, purchases materials and employs helpers as warranted.

2. Makes major and minor repairs to postal operating equipment in offices without maintenance capabilities; conducts maintenance inspections and provides operating, minor repair, and maintenance instruction to postal employees in the offices served. Whenever possible, conducts maintenance inspection and the instruction of postal employees in conjunction with emergency service trips to installations.

3. Troubleshoots, repairs, overhauls, and installs postal operating equipment such as, but not limited to, stamp vending machines, canceling machines, scales, print punch money order machines, tying machines, conveyors, safe and vault locks and other components, protective systems and devices, time clocks, and money changers. Keeps abreast of current maintenance criteria and effects service accordingly.

4. Maintains inventory of all postal operating equipment in the offices served by the area maintenance office. Makes recommendations to supervisors and/or obtains stock of operating equipment repair parts, maintaining inventories at levels prescribed by the region or the department. Maintains record of parts in stock; ships parts to territory offices as required to meet respective office needs. Keeps records of parts used, frequency of replacements, and submits reports to the regional office at prescribed intervals.

5. Installs and maintains protective systems and devices on safes and vaults in post offices. Opens safes and vaults, changes and repairs combinations, and disarms systems and devices.

6. Provides emergency service and makes minor repairs to air conditioning systems at government owned buildings not under service contracts. Prepares report of needs for the postmaster if the lessor has maintenance responsibility or the manufacturer if the system is under warranty.

7. Initiates reports to the regional office on major work assignments, shortages of equipment, and completed screen line installations. Makes reports of unsatisfactory conditions relating to equipment damage, classification, and deficiencies. Makes written recommendations for equipment improvements, operations, and fabrication changes.

8. Drives motor vehicle to respective offices to effect on-the-scene repairs and screen-line installation or modifications. Communicates with postmasters by phone, correspondence, and

personal visits to investigate reports of malfunctions, disorders, or other needs within the area maintenance office territory.

9. Performs other maintenance duties as instructed by the postmaster at the area maintenance office when not engaged in area maintenance duties.

10. Uses various hand and power tools and testing devices incident to the mechanical, electrical and electronic, and carpentry trades.

11. Observes established safety practices and procedures and instructs helpers accordingly.

AUTOMOTIVE MECHANIC, PS-06 Occupation Code: 5823-03XX

Repairs vehicles, including the removal and installation of complete motors, clutches, transmissions, and other major component parts.

DUTIES AND RESPONSIBILITIES

1. Diagnoses mechanical and operating difficulties of vehicles, repairing defects, replacing worn or broken parts.

2. Adjusts and tunes up engines, cleaning fuel pumps, carburetors, and radiators; regulates timing, and makes other necessary adjustments to maintain in proper operating condition trucks that are in service.

3. Repairs or replaces automotive electrical equipment such as generators, starters, ignition systems, distributors, and wiring; installs and sets new spark plugs.

4. Conducts road tests of vehicles after repairs, noting performance of engine, clutch, transmission, brakes, and other parts.

5. Operates standard types of garage testing equipment.

6. Performs other duties as assigned, such as removing, disassembling, reassembling, and installing entire engines; overhauling transmission, rear end assemblies, and braking systems; straightening frames and axles, welding broken parts where required; making road calls to make emergency repairs; and making required truck inspections.

BUDGET AND FINANCIAL ANALYST (DISTRICT), EAS-19 Occupation Code: 0504-5022

Performs all activities for the development and control of district operating and capital budgets; performs research and analysis of district financial operations.

DUTIES AND RESPONSIBILITIES

1. Develops, prepares, allocates, implements, monitors, and controls the district operating and capital budgets; includes current estimates of future financial performance; and integrates planning assumptions into operating budget plans.

2. Integrates all district functions into the planning process and validates budget and financial forecasts developed by managers.

3. Provides ongoing analyses to support operations management and improve overall financial and work hour performance, including the analysis and validation of major capital, facility, and program expenditures and packages.

4. Develops and implements business planning and forecasting techniques and monitors effectiveness; analyzes operating results to identify improvement opportunities and evaluate the effectiveness of cost reduction program implementation.

5. Develops and presents training for operating managers to increase their understanding of the budget process and the financial analysis techniques used for performance measurement.

6. Provides technical guidance to financial and operating employees in the development of capital investment strategies and operating expense budgets; maintains an effective financial planning and forecasting process for all district organizations.

BUILDING EQUIPMENT MECHANIC, PS-07 Occupation Code: 5306-07XX

Performs involved trouble shooting and complex maintenance work on building and building equipment systems, and preventative maintenance and preventative maintenance inspections of building, building equipment and building systems, and maintains and operates a large automated air conditioning system and a large heating system.

DUTIES AND RESPONSIBILITIES

1. Performs, on building and building equipment, the more difficult testing, diagnosis, maintenance, adjustment and revision work, requiring a thorough knowledge of the mechanical, electrical, and electronic, pneumatic, or hydraulic control and operating mechanisms of the equipment. Performs trouble shooting and repair of complex supervisory group control panels, readout and feedback circuits and associated mechanical and electrical components throughout the installation; locates and corrects malfunctions in triggering and other electro mechanical and electronic circuits.

2. Observes the various components of the building systems in operation and applies appropriate testing methods and procedures to insure continued proper operation.

3. Locates the source of, and rectifies trouble in, involved or questionable cases, or in emergency situations where expert attention is required to locate and correct the defect quickly to avoid or minimize interruptions.

4. Installs or alters building equipment and circuits as directed.

5. Reports the circumstances surrounding equipment and failures, and recommends measures for their correction.

6. Performs preventive maintenance inspections of building equipment to locate incipient mechanical malfunctions and the standard of maintenance. Initiates work orders requesting corrective actions for conditions below standard; assists in the estimating of time and materials required. Recommends changes in preventative maintenance procedures and practices to provide the proper level of maintenance; assists in the revision of preventive maintenance checklists and the frequency of performing preventive maintenance routes. In instances of serious equipment failures, conducts investigation to determine the cause of the breakdown and to recommend remedial action to prevent recurrence.

7. Uses necessary hand and power tools, specialized equipment, gauging devices, and both electrical and electronic test equipment.

8. Reads and interprets schematics, blue prints, wiring diagrams and specifications in locating and correcting potential or existing malfunctions and failures.

9. Repairs electromechanically operated equipment related to the building or building systems. Repairs, installs, modifies, and maintains building safety systems, support systems and equipment.

10. Works off ladders, scaffolds, and rigging within heights common to the facility. Works under various weather conditions outdoors.

11. Completes duties and tasks related to building equipment maintenance as required.

12. Observes established safety practices and requirements pertaining to the type of work involved; recommends additional safety measures as required.

13. In addition, may oversee the work of lower-level maintenance employees, advising and instructing them in proper and safe work methods and checking for adherence to instructions; make in-process and final operational checks and tests of work completed by lower level maintenance employees.

14. Performs other job-related tasks in support of primary duties.

CARRIER (CITY), PS-05 Occupation Code: 2310-01XX

Delivers and collects mail on foot or by vehicle under varying conditions in a prescribed area within a city. Maintains pleasant and effective public relations with route customers and others, requiring a general familiarity with postal laws, regulations, and procedures commonly used, and with the geography of the city. (Refer to Chapter Three for a complete description of Clerk and Mail Carrier occupations.)

CASUAL, EAS-07 Occupation Code: 5201-1001

Performs mail handling, mail processing, mail delivery, mail collection, mail transportation, and custodial functions, or a combination of such duties on a supplemental basis. (Refer to Chapter Three for a complete description of Clerk and Mail Carrier occupations.)

CLERK STENOGRAPHER, PS-05 Occupation Code: 0312-01XX

Performs miscellaneous office clerical, stenographic, and typing work.

DUTIES AND RESPONSIBILITIES

1. Takes dictation, in shorthand or on a shorthand writing machine, of letters, memorandums, reports, and other materials and transcribes it on the typewriter or word processor; sets up the material transcribed in accordance with prescribed format and assembles it for required initialing, signing, routing, and dispatch.

2. Types similar materials from handwritten and other drafts, and from dictating machine records.

3. Makes up file folders, keeps them in prescribed order, and places in and withdraws from them papers relating to the business of the office.

4. Makes and keeps routine records of the office.

5. Composes routine memorandums and letters relating to the business of the office, such as acknowledgments and transmittals.

6. Examines the incoming and outgoing mail of the office, routes it to the appropriate persons, and controls the time allowed for preparation of replies to incoming correspondence.

7. Receipts for and delivers salary checks and fills out various personnel forms.

8. Acts as receptionist and answers telephone calls, taking and relaying messages and furnishing routine information requested.

9. Relieves office clerks, typists, clerk typists or other clerk-stenographers during periods of their absence.

10. Operates copy machine and calculators.

COMPUTER SYSTEMS ANALYST/PROGRAMMER (PDC), DCS-20 Occupation Code: 0334-3056

Analyzes and evaluates existing and proposed systems and develops computer programs, systems, and procedures to process data.

DUTIES AND RESPONSIBILITIES

1. Translates user requirements to automate problem analysis and record keeping activities into detailed program flowcharts.

2. Prepares programming specifications and diagrams and develops coding logic flowcharts.

3. Codes, tests, debugs, and installs computer programs and procedures.

4. Reviews and updates computer programs and provides the necessary documentation for the computer operations function.

5. Prepares charts and diagrams to assist in problem analysis.

6. Prepares detailed program specifications and flowcharts and coordinates the system's installation with the user.

7. Provides technical advice and guidance to programmers assigned on a project basis; provides advice and assistance to managers involved in installing an automated system.

8. Has regular contact with contract employees and computer equipment vendors

CUSTODIAN, PS-02 Occupation Code: 3566-04XX

Performs manual laboring duties in connection with custody of an office or building.

DUTIES AND RESPONSIBILITIES

1. Performs any one or a combination of the duties listed below.

2. Moves furniture and equipment.

3. Uncrates and assembles furniture and fixtures, using bolts and screws for assembly.

4. Loads and unloads supplies and equipment.

5. Removes trash from work areas, lobbies, and washrooms.

6. Tends to lawns, shrubbery, and premises of the post office and cleans ice and snow from the sidewalks and driveways.

7. Stacks supplies in storage rooms and on shelves, and completes forms or records as required.

8. May perform cleaning duties as assigned.

DATA COLLECTION TECHNICIAN, PS-06 Occupation Code: 0301-69XX

Collects, records, and analyzes a variety of statistical data on selected operating and financial activities. Performs relief assignments for PSDS Technicians.

DUTIES AND RESPONSIBILITIES

1. Collects, records, and analyzes statistical data under any number of national data collection systems.

2. Operates computer equipment to enter data; recognizes diagnostic messages and takes appropriate actions; and performs data transfer functions through telecommunications systems.

3. Reviews input and output data to determine accuracy and compliance with national programs. Analyzes and edits data to detect and correct errors.

4. Updates national databases; maintains and updates records and files.

5. Participates in data collection activities in support of special studies or national programs.

6. Reads and interprets reference manuals and other written materials.

7. May drive a vehicle to other facilities when work assignments require.

8. Performs other job-related tasks in support of primary duties.

DISTRIBUTION CLERK, PS-05 Occupation Code: 2315-04XX

Separates mail in a post office, terminal, airport mail facility or other postal facility in accordance with established schemes, including incoming or outgoing mail or both. (Refer to Chapter Three for a complete description of Clerk and Mail Carrier occupations.)

ELECTRONICS TECHNICIAN, PS-10 Occupation Code: 0856-01XX

Carries out all phases of maintenance, troubleshooting, and testing of electronic circuitry used in equipment and systems requiring a knowledge of solid state electronics. Instructs and provides technical support on complex systems and on combinational (hardware/software) or intermittent problems.

DUTIES AND RESPONSIBILITIES

1. Performs the testing, diagnosis, maintenance, and revision work requiring a knowledge of solid state electronics.

2. Observes the various equipment and systems in operation and applies appropriate testing and diagnostic methods and procedures to ensure proper operation.

3. Locates source of equipment and system failures, rectifies trouble in involved cases, or provides instructions to be used by maintenance employees performing repair work.

4. Makes or participates with contractor representative or electronic technician in installing or altering equipment and systems as required.

5. Makes reports of equipment and system failures which require corrective action by contractor and follows up to see that appropriate action is taken.

6. Makes preventive maintenance inspections to discover incipient malfunctions and to review the standards of maintenance. Recommends changes in preventive maintenance procedures and practices as found to be necessary.

7. Programs scheme and/or scheme changes into memory units as requested by management.

8. Furnishes pertinent data to superiors and contract employees on operation and testing problems.

9. Participates in training programs: classroom, on-the-job, and correspondence, at postal facilities, trade schools, and manufacturer's plants as required. May assist in developing and implementing training programs. Instructs equal or lower level employees as required.

10. Observes established safety regulations pertaining to the type of work involved.

11. May drive vehicle or utilize other available mode of transportation to work site when necessary.

12. Provides technical support to other electronic technicians to resolve complex, combinational (hardware/software), and/or intermittent failures.

13. Performs such other duties as may be assigned.

FINANCIAL SERVICES COORDINATOR, EAS-18 Occupation Code: 0510-5050

Coordinates, analyzes, and monitors district-wide financial accounting programs and processes; coordinates the implementation of new accounting and timekeeping policies and procedures; provides technical guidance to post offices and field units in the resolution of daily accounting problems.

DUTIES AND RESPONSIBILITIES

1. Analyzes, evaluates, and determines the need for changes to district financial accounting programs and processes; identifies deficiencies and problems; and recommends and implements corrective actions to improve quality and reduce errors.

2. Provides guidance and training to post office and field unit employees concerning financial accounting procedures, including the proper recording of statements of accounts and adjustments of daily unit financial statements.

3. Resolves accounting problems, including those associated with banking, payables, and payroll adjustments.

4. Monitors revenue reporting and performs audits of financial activities to ensure financial integrity.

5. Coordinates district accounting programs and processes with the Postal Data Center and other functional areas.

6. Implements national, area, and district accounting and timekeeping policies and procedures.

7. Provides technical advice, guidance, assistance, and training to post offices and field units throughout the district area on the full range of accounting and timekeeping programs and processes.

FLAT SORTING MACHINE OPERATOR, PS-05 Occupation Code: 2315-20XX

Operates a single or multi-position, electromechanical operator-paced flat sorting machine in the distribution of flats requiring knowledge and application of approved machine distribution of directs, alphabetical or geographic groupings, by reading the ZIP code on each flat. (Refer to Chapter Three for a complete description of Clerk and Mail Carrier occupations.)

HUMAN RESOURCES SPECIALIST, EAS-15 Occupation Code: 0201-5117

Performs technical staff work in support of the implementation and administration of one or more human resources programs.

OPERATIONAL REQUIREMENTS

In addition to the following program responsibilities, oversees and coordinates the activities of a small size group of lower level employees, including making assignments, monitoring and reviewing work, providing continuing technical guidance, approving leave, and taking disciplinary action.

DUTIES AND RESPONSIBILITIES

1. PERSONNEL SERVICES: Implements and administers employee compensation and benefits programs, including wage and salaries, pay procedures and rules, performance evaluations, merits, suggestions, incentive and superior accomplishment awards, quality step increases, retirements, and insurance.

2. Provides information to and processes requests from state unemployment compensation agencies for separated employees; testifies in unemployment compensation hearings.

3. Administers employment and selection policies, procedures, and processes for bargaining, initial level supervisor, non-bargaining, and postmaster positions.

4. Coordinates entrance and in-service examination programs; oversees all procedures and processes related to examination scheduling, conducting, processing, grading, notification, and forwarding of test data.

5. SAFETY AND HEALTH: Monitors compliance with safety and health standards and regulations; conducts periodic inspections; ensures accurate accident reporting; analyzes accident rates and trends; and provides for improvement of safety awareness and accident prevention through training and promotional activities.

6. Implements Wellness Program by coordinating programs, services, and activities that promote employee health efforts.

7. Administers procedures under which employees with substance abuse and other personal problems are referred to external providers contracted under the Employee Assistance Program.

8. INJURY COMPENSATION: Provides comprehensive case management in the review and processing of injury compensation claims, including authorization and control of continuation of pay; controversion of claims; identification of possible fraud and abuse; third party claims and recovery; assignment to limited duty; and referral to the rehabilitation program, or for second opinions or fitness for duty exams.

9. TRAINING: Plans, schedules, implements, administers, coordinates, evaluates, and performs employee training, career planning and development, diagnostic testing, and counseling services; conducts workshops, orientations, and demonstrations; coordinates managerial and supervisory training; and provides guidance to employees, job trainers, and management regarding training and instructional processes.

MAINTENANCE MECHANIC, PS-05

Independently performs semiskilled preventive, corrective and predictive maintenance tasks associated with the upkeep and operation of various types of mail processing, buildings and building equipment, customer service and delivery equipment.

DUTIES AND RESPONSIBILITIES

1. Independently performs preventive maintenance and minor repairs on plumbing, heating, refrigeration, air-conditioning, low-voltage electrical systems, and other building systems and equipment.

2. Performs preventive maintenance and routine repairs on simple control circuitry, bearings, chains, sprockets, motors, belts and belting, and other moving parts or wearing surfaces of equipment.

3. Assembles, installs, replaces, repairs, modifies and adjusts all types of small operating equipment such as letter boxes, mechanical scales, stamp vending equipment, building service equipment, manhandling equipment and related equipment.

4. Under the direction of skilled maintenance employees, or clearly written instructions from either hard copy or electronic format, performs specific tasks related to disassembling equipment, replacing parts, relocating and reassembling equipment; assists higher level workers in locating and repairing equipment malfunctions.

5. Maintains an awareness of equipment operation, especially excessive heat, vibration, and noise, reporting malfunctions, hazards or wear to supervisor.

6. Uses a variety of hand and power tools, gauging devices and test equipment required, or as directed, to perform the above tasks.

7. May drive a vehicle to transport tools, equipment, employees, materials or in the normal performance of assigned duties.

8. Completes or initiates work record sheets, as required. Takes readings from meters, gauges, counters and other monitoring and measuring devices. Maintains logs and other required records; reports on breakdowns and equipment being tested.

9. Follows established safety practices and requirements while performing all duties.

10. May serve as a working leader over a group of lower-level employees assigned to a specific task.

11. Performs other duties as assigned.

MECHANICAL ENGINEER, EAS-24 Occupation Code: 0830-4012

Plans, organizes, and executes the design, construction, installation, and implementation of new systems, equipment, or controls of major magnitude and scope, in support of the mail processing objectives of the Postal Service.

DUTIES AND RESPONSIBILITIES

1. Translates operating objectives for mail processing into functional requirements for facilities, or equipment, oversees the reporting, analysis, and evaluation of data from field operating units related to mail volume, productivity, or costs; integrates this information with technical data to determine functional specifications.

2. Oversees the preparation and justification of engineering proposals and alternatives for complex mechanized systems equipment; evaluates engineered systems and related costs to determine alternatives to support mail processing objectives; provides program cost estimates; develops and recommends plans for program implementation.

3. Oversees engineering activities related to the design, construction, installation, test, and start-up of mechanized systems and equipment; provides technical management of contracts; evaluates contractor bids; makes recommendations affecting the selection of contractors; determines criteria for performance evaluation of prototype equipment; controls program costs; certifies contractor requests for payment.

4. Coordinates planning and implementation of mechanization systems and equipment programs with headquarters and field employees.

5. Provides mechanical engineering consulting services, as required.

6. Has frequent contact with contractors, professional consultants, officials of government agencies, and equipment manufacturers.

NURSE, OCCUPATIONAL HEALTH, PNS-01 Occupation Code: 0610-4001

Provides professional nursing services to employees under the general direction of a medical officer. Implements and participates in programs to provide preventative medical care and health maintenance services in support of Postal Service safety and health goals and objectives.

DUTIES AND RESPONSIBILITIES

1. Implements, monitors, and participates in occupational health programs and services within a postal facility.

2. Provides professional nursing care to employees; administers medications at the direction of a physician; and makes arrangements for physicians' care.

3. Provides continuous health or injury care, under physicians' instructions, to employees with prolonged illnesses or injuries.

4. Assists medical officer in conducting re-employment or fitness-for-duty physical examinations; performs routine examinations for items such as vision, hearing, and blood

pressure; and makes recommendations regarding suitability for employment and/or referral for additional testing and evaluation.

5. Advises or counsels employees regarding general and/or mental health care; assists employees with doctor and/or community service referrals, when necessary.

6. Prepares, updates, and maintains confidential health records for employees using the health and medical unit; compiles and analyzes various medical data and reports; and prepares regular summary reports.

7. Requisitions appropriate quantities and types of medical supplies and maintains security of supplies and equipment.

8. Regularly checks first aid boxes to ensure an adequate supply of necessary items.

9. Maintains the health/medical unit in a sanitary and orderly condition.

10. Provides continuous medical monitoring of workers exposed to potentially harmful substances.

11. Reports on-the-job injuries and other safety and health matters to appropriate postal officials.

12. Maintains familiarity with Workers Compensation and safety and personnel practices and procedures relative to occupational health programs.

13. Serves as liaison with employees, supervisors, physicians, PAR and safety employees; refers employees for participation in the PAR and other health related programs.

14. Performs related clerical duties.

15. Makes frequent contact with private physicians and representatives of hospitals and health clinics. Has occasional contact with customers, contractors' employees, and representatives of emergency services and social agencies.

16. Provides professional advice and guidance to supervisors regarding administrative procedures; provides health care advice and counseling to employees.

17. Exercises a normal regard for the safety of self and others.

PERSONNEL CLERK, PS-05 Occupation Code: 0203-14XX

Performs specialized clerical work involved in providing the central personnel services of a postal installation.

DUTIES AND RESPONSIBILITIES

1. Performs any one or a combination of the duties listed below.

2. Examines, documents, and otherwise processes official personnel actions.

3. Inducts new employees by taking their fingerprints, providing them with, and instructing them in filling out forms, administering oaths, and performing related operations.

4. Examines applications for leave by employees when the type or durations of leave desired fall within the categories required to be acted on centrally; compares the justification with the criteria for approval, and drafts memorandums or notifications of the action to be taken on the applications.

5. Examines for completeness or composes reports of personnel injuries sustained by employees in the performance of their duties and examines for completeness claims by such employees for compensation due to time lost from work because of such injuries; makes these reports and claims ready for forwarding to the appropriate government agency and composes notification to the employees or their supervisors of additional information needed and of decisions made on claims.

6. Furnishes information to employees and applicants about personnel regulations and practices, including employment in the postal installation, by personal conversations, telephone conversations, and composition of letters and memorandums.

7. Maintains various personnel records by performing such operations as posting actions taken concerning employees, adding names to and removing them from registers and rosters, and filing official papers in personnel folders.

8. Compiles various recurring and special statistical reports on personnel subjects, such as numbers of actions of various types, numbers of employees of various titles and salaries, numbers of vacancies of various titles and organizational locations.

9. In addition, may perform any of the following duties: document and otherwise process official personnel actions originating on the basis of personnel records; record the receipt of employee suggestions and initiate action for their review by appropriate supervisors; assist employees in filling out applications for retirement and documenting these forms for submission to appropriate organizations; process bids for position openings on seniority basis; and accept employment applications, and forward them to appropriate organizations.

POLICE OFFICER, POSTAL (B), PPO-06

Performs a variety of duties pertaining to the security of postal buildings, personnel, property, mail, and mail-in-transit in support of the postal security program.

DUTIES AND RESPONSIBILITIES

1. Performs a variety of duties pertaining to the security of postal buildings, personnel, property, mail, and mail-in-transit.

2. Carries a firearm and exercises standard care required by the Postal Inspection Service on firearms and use of reasonable force. Maintains assigned firearms in good condition.

3. Maintains incidents reported and daily logs of orders and basic in formation for the security force.

4. Answers the office telephone and responds to reports and inquiries.

5. Performs patrol duty, as assigned, on foot or by motor vehicle to maintain order and safeguard the facility, property, and personnel; ensures the application of security measures in manhandling areas.

6. Maintains contact with other security force personnel; responds to emergencies and other conditions, including burglaries and hold-ups, requiring immediate attention.

7. Controls access to building at an assigned post; enforces the regulations requiring identification.

8. Makes arrests and testifies in court on law violations within assigned authority.

9. Performs other job-related tasks in support of the primary duties.

POSTAL INSPECTOR (PROJECTS COORDINATOR), EAS-24

Oversees and coordinates the most complex and sensitive criminal, civil, administrative, and audit investigations, programs, projects, and studies; oversees task forces and teams of postal inspectors in the accomplishment of investigative objectives; oversees and coordinates the planning, development, implementation, and monitoring of projects, and studies within assigned area.

OPERATIONAL REQUIREMENTS

Carries firearms when engaged in official business and for self-defense; maintains established physical requirements necessary to perform law enforcement assignments; maintains eligibility to operate a motor vehicle when engaged in official business; and maintains mental and emotional standards necessary to perform law enforcement assignments.

DUTIES AND RESPONSIBILITIES

1. Oversees and coordinates the most complex-and sensitive criminal, civil, administrative, and audit investigations, programs, projects, and studies. Investigates violations of postal laws and apprehends and arrests postal offenders.

2. Oversees and supervises the activities of task forces and teams of postal inspectors, and a small group of technical and support employees. Evaluates performance and takes the necessary action to correct deficiencies, including discipline or remedial training. Provides training for new or less experienced Postal Inspection Service employees.

3. Assists U. S. Attorneys and other criminal justice employees in preparing court cases involving postal laws. Independently prepares comprehensive case presentation letters to the U. S. Attorney. Serves as a witness in court and administrative proceedings.

4. Coordinates the development, planning, and implementation of new programs and projects to improve methods, techniques, and skills of Postal Inspection Service employees.

5. Ensures that all regularly scheduled and standard inspections are properly monitored and carried out by assigned personnel.

6. Analyzes, reviews, and initially approves investigation reports, correspondence, case history information, and other documentation prepared for management review; prepares special reports and correspondence.

7. Maintains liaison with law enforcement agencies to coordinate record exchanges, case development, suspect apprehension, jurisdiction definition, security checks, and joint training.

8. Provides technical guidance and advice to postal management. Conducts conferences with postal management on the results of major audit projects and makes recommendations for service improvements, operational economies, and other areas included in the review.

9. Recommends policies and procedures that are not covered by established Postal Inspection Service methods or guidelines.

10. Oversees and coordinates the investigation into the misconduct of postal employees and the presentation of evidence to Postal management for consideration in disciplinary cases.

11. Represents the Postal Inspection Service by providing supporting information or participating in the development, implementation, and administration of technology, automation, service, operations, and training programs.

12. Reacts in emergencies to protect mail and postal assets where use of firearms and defensive techniques may be required. May work in undesirable neighborhoods and in adverse and hazardous situations.

13. Has frequent contact with the general public, witnesses, victims, complainants, suspects and offenders, informants, postal customers and contractors, federal and private attorneys, and representatives of the business community, law enforcement agencies, government agencies, armed services, and the courts. Represents the Postal Inspection Service at law enforcement, security, and civic conferences and meetings.

14. Exercises normal protective care for the use of facilities and equipment, including vehicles, weapons, and communications and technical equipment.

15. Exercises a normal regard for the safety of self and others when investigating criminal cases and apprehending or maintaining surveillance of those suspected of violating postal

laws. Exercises the standard of care required by Postal Inspection Service policies on firearms and use of reasonable force when apprehending and restraining suspects.

RURAL CARRIER, RCS-00

Cases, delivers, and collects mail along a prescribed rural route using a vehicle; provides customers on the route with a variety of services. (Refer to Chapter Three for a complete description of clerk and mail carrier occupations.)

SECRETARY, EAS-11 Occupation Code: 0318-2041

Provides secretarial support for a manager and his/her staff. Processes information in accordance with established organizational and functional area administrative practices and procedures.

DUTIES AND RESPONSIBILITIES

1. Produces reports, letters and other documentation using word processing equipment, and monitors peripheral equipment.

2. Accesses, retrieves and/or updates files and other data maintained on computers.

3. Sends and receives electronic messages, files and other documentation via the local area network.

4. Produces charts, tables and other documentation using various graphics packages.

5. Compiles information on a variety of subjects; reviews periodicals, publications, and industry related documents, bringing those of interest to manager's attention.

6. Reviews materials prepared for accuracy and proper format; ensures compliance with established collective bargaining policies.

7. Performs routine clerical duties such as, answering telephones, operating office equipment, requisitioning supplies, and coordinating printing, maintenance, and other service requests.

8. Screens, logs, and routes office mail.

9. Performs other administrative duties, such as maintaining a variety of reports, such as: time and attendance records, correspondence control, training plans, etc., and maintains office files.

TELECOMMUNICATIONS SPECIALIST, EAS-17 Occupation Code: 0393-5001

Provides analysis, coordination, and technical support for the voice and data telecommunications activities in a district.

DUTIES AND RESPONSIBILITIES

1. Analyzes voice and data telecommunications requirements, including networks and hardware; recommends new and improved services; and coordinates acquisition and implementation.

2. Prepares recommendations for system changes to improve effectiveness and reduce telecommunications costs; coordinates with national telecommunications network program specialists, and implements approved changes.

3. Coordinates the acquisition and installation of new telecommunications hardware; performs preacceptance tests to verify proper operations; makes changes to telecommunications control systems to activate or restrict specific services to designated lines, and oversees equipment repair projects.

4. Monitors all aspects of the telecommunications system, including line traffic and overall system usage; oversees the verification and certification of monthly billings, and prepares analyses and reports for management review.

5. Prepares and implements training for telecommunications system users throughout the district.

6. Troubleshoots network and equipment problems and resolves or coordinates resolution with vendors.

7. Has regular contact with representatives of local telecommunication services vendors.

8. Provides technical guidance to employees on telecommunications system operations.

WELDER, PS-06

Fabricates or repairs metal items in forge and on anvil; performs welding and brazing operations.

DUTIES AND RESPONSIBILITIES

1. Forges and fabricates or repairs tools and metal parts for building and equipment; heats metal to proper temperature in forge, hammers and bends metal to specified size and shape; hardens and tempers metals.

2. Does acetylene and electric welding on building equipment and such items as machine parts, hand truck frames, pouch racks, and conveyor equipment; also does brazing work; sets up job to be welded or brazed; sets up and adjusts proper type of welding equipment and selects proper type of rod according to the needs of the work; performs metal cutting and burning with torch.

3. Works from drawings, sketches and general instructions.

4. Uses required hand and power tools.

5. In addition, oversees helpers as assigned and may perform work incident to other trades as required.

WINDOW CLERK, PS-05

Performs a variety of services at a public window of a post office or post office branch or station. Maintains pleasant and effective public relations with customers and others, requiring a general familiarity with postal laws, regulations, and procedures commonly used. (Refer to Chapter Three for a complete description of clerk and mail carrier occupations.)

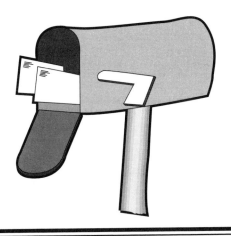

Chapter Nine
Occupation Directory

The Postal Service employs workers in over 2,000 occupational code classifications. This USPS Position Directory will assist job seekers in several ways. First, it provides a comprehensive resource for job seekers to identify potential occupations for which they may qualify. Second, it lists the average salary, total number employed for each occupation, occupational title, and the USPS Occupational Code (OCC-CODE). This is a partial directory, listing only those occupational codes that employ more than five workers in that group and a select sampling of other diverse career options.

This directory presents a pandoras box of opportunities from custodial, maintenance, and general labor trades to accountants, engineers, and computer specialists. The majority of managers' positions were excluded from this list because they are generally not entry-level positions.

After reviewing this list and identifying various occupations as potential job sources, go to the "Job Hunter's Checklist" in Appendix A. This checklist will guide you step-by-step through the USPS hiring maze.

OCCUPATION DIRECTORY[1]

OCC CODE	OCC TITLE	# EMPLOYED	AVERAGE SALARY ($)
00180016	SAFETY SPECIALIST	247	61,119
00180018	SAFETY SPECIALIST	19	66,478
00180019	SAFETY ANALYST	7	83,675
00180021	MGR SAFETY	51	75,548
00180031	SAFETY SPEC (TL)	39	67,204
00185028	SAFETY SPECIALIST	95	64,752
00720001	FORENSIC LAT PR ANL	6	63,880
00720002	FRNSC LAT PR ANLY S	5	87,039

---

[1] USPS Occupational Code Listing Report 11/14/08, Employee Master File OCCLIST

OCC CODE	OCC TITLE	# EMPLOYED	AVERAGE SALARY ($)
00800005	SECURITY CL.SPEC.	16	55,421
00800041	HL SEC COORD DIST	73	78,187
00800044	MGR NATL PREP AREA	6	89,404
01100016	PRICING ECONOMIST	11	102,219
01100017	FINANCL ECONOMIST	15	111,520
01104017	ECONOMIST	6	81,351
01605056	DIV DEV SPEC (FLD)	69	71,343
01800002	ED PSYCHOLOGIST	3	81,930
01804018	EAP COUNSELOR	4	61,719
02010053	HUMAN RESOURCES SPE	71	61,873
02010056	FMLA COORD	119	70,680
02010059	PROG MGR PAY	4	97,235
02010060	PROG MGR BENEFITS	3	104,072
02010061	PM BEN/COMP/BID SS	1	102,083
02010078	HR SPECIALIST	179	62,427
02010083	COMP SPECIALIST	5	88,285
02010085	SUPV HR SHRD SVCS	18	75,315
02010086	PER PROC SPC (HRSS)	211	58,139
02010106	PRS PR SPC TMP SS	159	41,600
02010107	HR GENERLST (PRIN)	74	79,622
02010108	HR GENERALIST	75	71,611
02010111	DIS COMPLMNT COORD	4	85,169
02010159	DIST COMP COORD	61	78,298
02010186	HR ANALYST	7	78,872
02015112	HUMAN RESOURCES ASC	144	49,433
02015116	HR ANALYST (AREA)	27	89,567
02015118	HUMAN RESOURCES SPC	7	67,652
02017094	MGR HUMAN RESOURCES	34	101,686
02017095	MGR HUMAN RESOURCES	34	96,301
02017096	MGR HUMAN RESOURCES	10	94,795
020314XX	PERSONNEL CLK	20	52,699
021205XX	ASSIGNMENT CLK	26	53,635
02230005	MGR BENEFITS PROG	11	22,400
02300002	SR DIV PROG COORD	9	85,097
02300008	WKPL ENVIRON ANLYST	64	79,506
02300019	MGR HRM (DIST)	60	75,267
02300021	HRM SPC (DIST)	48	66,433
02300025	HRM SPC (DIST)	271	60,751
02300029	MGR HRM (DIST)	9	70,283
02300030	MGR WKPL EW1IRN ANL	9	91,151
02300032	HRM ANALYST	25	77,903
02300033	MGR HRM (AO)	7	100,200
02305012	LABOR RELATIONS SPC	2	77,352
02305013	LBR REL SPEC	4	88,041
02305014	LABOR RELATIONS SPC	14	104,919
02305066	INJURY COMPNSTN SPC	2	85,307
02305074	FLD COOR QWL PROCES	1	72,085
02330004	MGR LBR RLTNS (AREA)	9	103,762
02330012	MGR COLLECTIVE BARG	11	60,750
02330017	MGR LABOR RELATIONS	68	85,329

OCC CODE	OCC TITLE	# EMPLOYED	AVERAGE SALARY ($)
02335016	LABOR RELATION SPCL	300	72,037
02335017	LABOR RELATION SPCL	50	61,817
02335018	LABOR RLTNS SPC(AO	18	77,407
02335019	LAB REL SPEC AREA	80	90,609
02335021	LABOR REL SPEC FLD	6	100,109
02350002	TRAINING SPEC	6	85,439
02350008	MGR TRAINING	74	74,587
02600001	HISPANIC PROG SPEC	16	64,046
02600016	DISPUTE RES COORD	8	83,910
02600029	EEO SVC ANALYST	21	80,914
02600030	MGR EEO DS RES (AO)	12	88,121
02600031	EEO ADR SPECIALIST	137	69,576
02600034	MGR EEO COMPLIANCE	4	98,975
02600035	EEO SYSTEMS TECH	11	44,478
03010107	OFFICE CLERK	20	52,039
03010248	PROF INTERN	11	72,982
030104XX	OFC CLK, VEHL OPRN	73	52,541
030109XX	ADMIN CLERK VMF	80	53,545
03012234	IS OPERATIONS TECH	98	48,268
030147XX	CLERK VEHICLE DISP	121	51,969
030148XX	GENERAL CLERK VMF	296	52,381
03015214	PROF/SPEC YRNEE D	69	47,760
03180004	SECRETARY	354	53,357
03180007	SECRETARY (FLD)	448	50,980
03180009	SECRETARY (AREA)	21	51,390
03182041	SECRETARY	134	48,357
03182042	SECRETARY	144	53,916
03220001	CLERK TYPIST	60	51,471
03300001	CPTR SYS SCHEDULER	14	71,189
03304013	INFO SCIENCES SPCLS	12	102,843
03320014	INFO SYSTEMS SPCLST	253	69,658
03320017	PROCESS CNTRL ASST	84	61,240
03320018	CPTR OPS SUPPT SPEC	39	53,429
03320019	CPTR OPRNS SPEC	12	67,971
03322007	TEXT&DATA SVC ASST	9	43,057
03323023	FAC COMM TECH	17	62,776
03324003	COMPUTER SYS OPRTOR	4	53,678
03340029	DISTR COMPUTING SPE	20	90,129
03340076	COMP SYS AN/PROG	14	92,903
03340081	FORENSIC COMP ANLST	12	68,730
03340102	MGR INFO SYSTMS	74	88,089
03340103	LAN ADMINISTRATOR	9	81,696
03340107	SUPV INFO SYS (BMC)	19	78,222
03340117	MAINT SOFTWARE SPEC	10	82,906
03340140	CPTR ANLST/PRG ASSC	75	62,465
03340142	COMP SYS ANALYST / PRG	116	70,683
03340146	PROG MGR INFO TECH	78	109,031
03340148	TECHNICAL SRVCS MGR	12	113,998
03343045	COMP SYS ANL PRG SR	13	87,021
03343057	CMPTR SYS AN/PR SR	161	77,340
03344019	COMP PRGMR SFTW SPC	20	86,028

OCC CODE	OCC TITLE	# EMPLOYED	AVERAGE SALARY ($)
03344020	CPTR SYSTEMS ADMIN	13	71,852
03344040	COMPTR PRGM/SFTW SP	27	88,736
03344045	INFO SYSTEMS COORDT	12	91,084
03344046	SOFTWARE SYST ADMIN	12	100,220
03344075	SYS ANLYST MIN/MIC)	21	96,622
03344082	INFORMATION SYS SPC	31	82,777
03344083	INFO SYS SPEC	24	69,897
03344090	INFORMATION SYS SPC	41	70,102
03344129	BUS SYSTEMS ANALYST	83	87,948
03344131	BUS PROJ LEADER	74	98,875
03344132	BUS SYSTEMS ENGINEER	12	99,667
03344134	DATABASE ADMIN	42	94,045
03345002	INFO SYST SEC SPEC	15	91,094
03345014	INFO SYST SEC SPEC	11	99,808
03350003	CPTR PROD SUPT TECH	29	63,104
03353008	CUST SUPPT SPEC PDC	54	55,900
03353009	CPTR SYS SPEC PDC	29	63,998
034106XX	VEH OPER MAINT ASST	138	53,643
03416031	SUPV CUST SERV SUPP	197	65,456
03430109	PM INTELLIGENT MAIL	15	101,249
03433012	MANAGEMENT ANALYST	15	72,233
03433013	MANAGEMENT ANALYST	23	62,620
03454036	PROGRAM ANALYST	11	73,226
03455098	FINANCIAL ANALYST	11	99,393
03455114	OPERATIONS SUPRT SPC	18	79,142
03455115	OPRNS SUPPRT SPCLST	35	89,783
03455118	INSP SRVC PROG SPEC	20	83,580
035992XX	OFF MACH OPER	11	52.526
0356002	SUPV REM ENCOD OPER	70	62,232
035609XX	DATA CONV OPR	4,953	30,956
035610XX	G/LDR DATA CNV OPR	147	51,436
05010030	AUDIT EVAL ANALYST	67	75,089
05010033	AUDIT EVAL SPEC	17	86,962
05045019	BUD/FIN ANLST AREA	10	78,328
05045020	SR BUD/FIN ANALYST	29	89,089
05045022	BUD/FIN ANLST DIST	148	72,824
05050092	MGR FIN CON/SUPP	77	81,332
05050093	FIN CON/SUPP ANLYS	380	71,718
05055015	FINANCIAL SYS SPCLT	10	101,912
05055019	FINANCIAL SYS ANALYS	24	87,394
05057063	MGR FIN (DIST)	31	97,868
05057065	MGR FIN (DIST)	34	103,261
05100093	SUPV ACCTG SVC CTR	37	76,683
05100021	ACCT & CON SPEC SR	38	65,832
05100022	ACCT & CON SPEC	69	60,645
05104046	SR SYS ACCT PDC	22	81,283
05104052	SYSTEMS ACCT PDC	20	69,309
05104056	ACCOUNTANT	10	101,811
05104057	ACCOUNTANT	15	84,867
05110031	AUDITOR	177	75,794
05110032	AUDITOR	9	95,633

OCC CODE	OCC TITLE	# EMPLOYED	AVERAGE SALARY ($)
05110033	AUDIT MANAGER	46	99,246
05110034	FORENSIC EXM AUDIT	8	92,009
05110037	DIR AUDITOR	17	115,648
05202020	ACCTG CLERK PDC	2	51,510
05250003	ACCT SUPP SPEC SR	13	60,220
05250004	ACCT SUPP SPEC	33	57,871
05250005	ACCT SUPP TECH	59	53,661
05250006	ACCT SPEC SR	14	65,550
05250007	ACCT SPEC	244	57,120
05300001	SUPV ACCT PAPER	79	63,526
05300005	ML ORDER ENTRY CLK	12	52,526
05300006	CUST SRVCS CLK SFS	27	53,668
053005XX	ACCT PPR SUPP CLK	148	52,595
05440007	ACCT SPEC (P)	49	57,634
05440009	ACCT TECH	114	55,498
05600006	MGR BUD/FIN ALSDIST	77	86,092
05604027	BUDGET SPECIALIST	11	100,330
05900003	MGR TACS OPRS	77	72,923
05900005	TACS T&A CLERK	413	53,661
05900009	TACS SPECIALIST	43	60,890
059001XX	TIME & ATTEND CLK	4	52,526
06020001	PHYSICIAN (CNTRCT)	15	136,111
06100001	OCCUP HEALTH NURSE	36	68,786
06104001	OCCUP HLTH NURSE	133	53,740
08010009	PROG DIR TECH ACQSN	15	104,327
08010010	PROG MGR TECH ACQSN	6	91,412
08013005	GEN ENGINEER	11	90,783
08080009	ARCHITECT/ENGINEER	23	106,719
08083017	ARCHITECT/ENGINEER	78	80,181
08083018	ARCHITECT/ENGINEER	28	89,184
081801XX	DRAFTING CLK	22	52,526
08190006	MGR ENV PRGMS (AO)	9	104,945
08190007	ENVIRON SPEC (AO)	52	86,605
08194002	ENVIRONMENTAL SPCLS	6	88,509
08304012	MECHANICAL ENGINEER	7	98,819
08304013	MECHANICAL ENGINEER	5	104,230
08550003	SR TECH SURVLNCE SP	20	77,991
08554009	ELECTRONIC ENGINEER	5	87,035
08554010	ELECTRONIC ENGINEER	3	99,229
08554011	ELECTRONIC ENGINEER	4	105,088
08554031	COMMUNICATNS ENGINR	14	91,757
08560006	ELECTRONIC TECH	7	59,410
08560020	ELECTRONIC TECH	7,668	60,479
08560021	ELECTRONIC TECH	115	62,872
08960005	OPS IND ENGR (FLD)	120	68,818
08960006	OPS IND ENGR (FLD)	66	77,726
08960007	LEAD OPS IND ENGR	8	97,078
08960008	OPS IND ENGR AREA	15	82,968
08963020	INDUSTRL ENG SR FLD	7	83,465
08964035	INDUST ENGINEER HQ	5	75,803
08964036	INDUSTRIAL ENG FLD	48	73,552

OCC CODE	OCC TITLE	# EMPLOYED	AVERAGE SALARY ($)
09050037	ATTORNEY (TEMP)	27	93,137
09050038	ATTORNEY, HONOR PRG	9	80,675
09054034	ATTORNEY	176	115,230
09056014	DEP MNG CNSL (FLD)	18	140,298
09057045	MGN CNSL (FIELD)	10	160,033
09500007	PARALEGAL SPEC (TEMP)	10	60,840
09505003	PARALEGAL SPEC	39	63,993
09860006	ADMIN ASSISTANT	16	56,132
09860007	ADMIN ASSISTANT	31	47,865
102001XX	ILLUSTRATOR	12	54,870
102005XX	SIGN PAINTER-ILLSTR	18	53,668
10350036	DISTRICT COMM COORD	12	67,785
10815055	COMMNCTN PRGMS SPCL	38	85,628
10825016	WRITER/EDITOR	6	65,606
11015042	NATIONAL ACCTS MGR	28	77,663
11015043	NATIONAL ACCTS MGR	28	86,866
11015044	NATIONAL ACCTS MGR	28	98,863
11020021	PURCH AND SUPPLY MGT	73	73,036
11020022	PURCH AND SUPLY MGT	124	86,576
11020051	CONTRT TANS SPEC	30	77,645
11020053	CONTRCT TANS SPEC	59	70,750
11020054	CONTRCT TANS SPEC	20	87,023
11020056	PURCH AND SUPPLY MGT	65	105,978
110201XX	CONTRACT TECHNICIAN	240	53,525
11025026	PURCHASING SPCLST	29	70,867
11025032	PAC CONTR SPEC	25	65,274
110250047	PURCHASING SPEC	80	65,189
110601XX	PROCUREMENT CLK	13	52,526
11065005	FACLTS CNTRCT TECHN	30	59,181
11405009	MARKETING SPECIALST	25	70,915
11405011	MARKETING SPECIALST	33	84,974
11405025	MARKETING SPECIALST	38	97,372
11700014	REAL ESTATE SPEC	20	106,792
15154024	OPRNS RESRCH ANLYST	10	100,171
15154025	OPRNS RESRCH ANLYST	7	87,349
15290002	MATH STATISTICIAN	8	111,055
15300021	MGR STAT PROGRAMS	80	74,094
15300022	SUPV STAT PROGRAMS	80	61,311
16014016	FACILITIES ENGINEER	48	72,952
16014018	MAINTENANCE MGT SPC	26	87,264
16407037	MGR MAINTENANCE	32	95,892
16407040	MGR MAINTENANCE	49	74,264
16407041	MGR MAINTENANCE	74	70,993
16704017	MAINT ENG ANALYST	28	77,080
17010002	TRAINING DEV SPEC	11	86,475
17010003	TRAINING DEV SPECTL	6	97,987
17125021	POSTL TRAINNG SPEC	4	67,517
17125022	POSTL TRAINNG SPEC	10	62,981
17125023	POSTL TRAINNG SPEC	32	77,341
18010033	INVESTIGATVE ANALYS	10	73,664
18010043	TECH OPRNS OFFICER	16	73,641

OCC CODE	OCC TITLE	# EMPLOYED	AVERAGE SALARY ($)
18020008	INVESTIGATIVE ASST	29	55,312
18110029	CRMNL INVESTIGATOR	429	75,464
18110034	SUPV CRMNL INVSTGTR	15	107,921
18110040	CRIM. INVESTIGATOR	27	96,511
18110046	CI-DAIG	12	155,514
18110047	SUPVY CRIMNL INVEST	69	95,762
19100018	QUAL ASSR/CON ANLST	10	60,181
19100019	QLTY ASR/CN ANLS SR	11	67,250
19100022	AUTOMAT OPRNS SPEC	20	74,763
200309XX	PROCR/MAT MGMT ASST	20	53,668
20035024	MATERIEL MGMT SPEC	10	71,656
20035036	MATERIAL MGMT SPCLS	71	57,824
20036025	SUPV VEH SUPPLIES C	61	64,249
20050006	SUPPLY CENTER CLERK	27	51,738
20050007	STOREKPR AUTO PARTS	99	54,504
20300002	CUSTOMER SVC CLK	20	53,728
204011XX	STOREKPR AUTO PARTS	107	53,464
215003XX	VEHICLE OPNS ASSTBM	309	54,269
21506024	MGR TRANS NETWRKS	35	88,835
21506025	MGR TRANS NETWRKS	27	77,156
21507044	MGR VHCL MAINT FCLT	40	71,883
215101XX	VEHICLE DISPATCHER	22	54,713
22100066	IT ANALYST	16	72,489
23010009	MGR PO OPERATIONS	94	91,909
23010010	POSTMASTER	3,061	61,930
23010011	POSTMASTER (1)	13	125,210
23010012	POSTMASTER (2)	22	120,573
23015102	POSTMASTER	64	24,863
23016104	POSTMASTER	594	27,615
23016106	POSTMASTER	754	30,584
23016111	POSTMASTER	4,307	44,636
23016113	POSTMASTER	5,592	50,676
23016115	POSTMASTER	2,795	56,369
23016120	POSTMASTER	2,259	75,182
23016213	POSTMASTER	214	52,177
23017004	POSTMASTER (F)	255	96,492
23017005	POSTMASTER (G)	68	106,658
23017121	POSTMASTER	1,033	79,601
23017122	POSTMASTER	752	85,263
23017137	MGR POST OFFC OPER	118	101,673
23017138	MGR POST OFFC OPER	101	88,106
23020020	MGR PROCSNG/DIST	18	95,208
23020021	MGR P/D FACILITY	38	94,062
23020022	MGR P/D FACILITY	19	81,168
23020026	SR PLANT MGR (2)	27	131,145
23020029	PLANT MGR (2)	17	130,180
23020030	PLANT MGR (3)	17	128,461
23020031	PLANT MGR (4)	8	109,034
23050040	PM RELIEF/REPLCMNT	46	21,574
23050042	PM RELIEF/REPLCMNT	434	22,214
23050068	DIST MGR (1)	27	161,188

OCC CODE	OCC TITLE	# EMPLOYED	AVERAGE SALARY ($)
23050069	DIST MGR (2)	33	152,186
23050070	DIST MGR (1)	10	142,828
23050073	PM RELIEF/REPLCMNT	602	27,927
23055023	OPERATIONS SPECLST	64	99,941
23055024	OPERATIONS SPEC	43	87,848
23055025	OPERATIONS SPEC	11	77,862
23056100	PM RELIEF/REPLCMNT	633	22,114
23056111	PM REL/REPLCMNT	4,101	24,355
23056113	PM RELIEF/REPLCMNT	5,048	24,923
23056115	PM RELIEF/REPLCMNT	1,259	27,050
23057038	MGR CUST SERVCS	90	69,163
23057039	MGR CUST SERVCS	1,200	71,905
23057064	MGR CUST SERVCS	233	70,513
23057091	MGR CUSTOMER SRVCS	546	75,527
23100002	MGR CUSTOMER SVCS	577	81,839
23100008	ASSOC SUPV - CS	752	55,284
23100010	MGR CUSTOMER SVCS	25	91,222
23100011	MGR CUST SVC OPER	8	90,419
23100012	CLRK/SPCL DLVRY MSG	466	52,528
23100015	MGR DEL/CS PROGRAMS	38	75,777
23100016	MGR DEL/CS PROGRAMS	31	83,862
23100020	OPS PROG ANLYST (A)	9	104,462
23100022	SUPV CUST SVCS	13,016	61,511
23100023	CUST SRVCS ANALYST	605	64,425
23100026	RT EXAM/ADJUST TL	18	86,078
23100027	RT EXAM/ADJUST TL	11	79,364
23100030	CC (TRANS EMPL)	6,497	41,166
23100031	CC (TRANS EMPL-MOU	6,735	41,166
23100041	CARR TECH TRNS-MOU	41	42,987
23102009	CARRIER (CITY)	182,909	51,063
23102010	CARRIER TECHNICIAN	27,217	51,529
23104013	ADDRS MGMT SYS SPEC	28	67,223
23104014	ADDRS MGMT SYS SPEC	528	57,787
23105023	OPS PROG ANLYST (A)	36	90,472
23105024	OPS PROG ANLYST (A)	10	77,733
23105026	DELIVERY/RETAIL ANL	66	66,893
23106052	MGR CUST SRVC OPER	11	84,395
23107036	MGR ADD MGMT SYST	44	74,445
23107037	MGR OPERTNS PROGS	32	95,802
23107038	MGR OPERTNS PROGS	29	102,528
23150026	ASSOC SUPV-DIST OPS	470	55,351
23150032	SACK SORT MACH OPR	23	48,997
23150036	PARCEL POST DIST-MA	186	53,061
23150051	MAIL HANDLER	245	50,306
23150052	DISTRIBUTION CLERK	82	53,599
23150063	MAIL PROC CLK	81,511	51,907
23150064	MAIL PROCESSOR	24	43,887
23150067	MGR DIST OPS	295	71,946
23150068	OPER SUPP SPEC	878	64,879
23150077	FLT SEQU PRO COOR	25	91,303

OCC CODE	OCC TITLE	# EMPLOYED	AVERAGE SALARY ($)
231501XX	MAIL HANDLER	41,940	47,330
231502XX	GRP LDR ML HANDLER	1,008	50,725
231504XX	DISTRIBUTION CLERK	28	52,137
231506XX	PARCEL POST DIST-MA	8,737	51,765
231508XX	SPEC POSTAL CLK	265	53,596
231511XX	GENERAL EXPEDITOR	4,644	53,536
231513XX	DIST CLK MACH MPLSM	28	53,889
231514XX	DIST CLK MACH SPLSM	15	53,668
231520XX	FLAT SRT MCHN OPR	2,521	52,139
23152011	MAIL FLOW CNTLR	211	55,093
231521XX	FLAT SRT MCRN OPR	437	53,230
231526XX	REVIEW CLK	621	53,655
231562XX	MAIL HANDLER TECH	977	50,476
231564XX	CONSOLE OPERATOR	8	54,870
231570XX	SACK SORT MACH OPR	13	53,668
23157128	MGR PROCSNG/DIST	47	100,587
23157131	MGR IN-PLANT SUPPT	8	123,957
23157138	SR MGR DIST OPER	43	99,919
231572XX	SACK SORT MACH OPR	670	50,162
231599XX	BULK MAIL DOCK CLK	592	53,545
23200001	SALES/SVCS ASSOC	3,905	51,808
23200003	SALES,SVC/DIST ASOC	47,088	50,269
23200004	LEAD SLS/SVCS ASSOC	3,324	53,529
23200005	BULK ML CLK	20	53,250
23200006	INFO CLK	28	53,668
232001XX	WINDOW CLK	1,249	52,512
232003XX	STAMP SUPP CLK	62	53,668
232005XX	CLERK FINANCE ST	327	53,639
232015XX	BULK ML CLK	958	53,500
232028XX	BULK ML TECH	3,017	53,521
232029XX	WINDOW SVC TECH	952	53,635
232031XX	SPEC PSTL CLK	56	53,689
232039XX	RTL SLS CK, PTL STR	8	52,900
23250003	TEMP RELIEF CARRIER	4,715	26,101
232501XX	RURAL CARRIER	68,812	52,843
232503XX	AUX RURAL CARRIER	14	50,639
232506XX	RURAL CARR RELIEF	172	44,517
232507XX	RU CAR ASC/SV RG RT	45,732	37,493
232508XX	RU CAR ASC/SV VA RT	1,173	37,473
232509XX	RU CAR ASC/SV AX RT	6,159	37,854
23300030	VEHICLE DISPATCHER	11	53,288
23300039	MGR TRANS/NETWRKS	47	70,283
23300040	SUPV TRANS OPERATNS	475	63,302
23300041	MGR TRANS/NETWORKS	51	77,225
23300043	MGR PVS OPERATIONS	23	70,546
23300044	NETWORK OPER SPEC	51	70,335
23300045	NETWORK OPER ANLYST	101	80,101
23300046	SR NTWRK OPRN ANLYS	27	92,410
23300049	NETWORKS SPECIALIST	310	60,397
23300050	AIR TRANSPTN SPEC A	21	61,518
23300051	AIR TRANS SPECF B	34	68,696

OCC CODE	OCC TITLE	# EMPLOYED	AVERAGE SALARY ($)
23300068	CORD SFC TRANS CTR	20	63,542
23300072	SUPV SUR TRNS CTR	22	61,260
233001XX	TRANSFER CLK	42	53,668
233004XX	TRANSFER CLK AMF	209	53,565
233013XX	HIGHWAY TRAN CLK	59	53,455
23302012	VEH OP & MAINT ASST	262	52,724
233022XX	SCHD EXAM VEHL RUNS	14	54,500
233042XX	RAMP CLK AMF	437	54,868
233046XX	AIR RECORDS PROC	203	53,560
23305038	TRANSPORTATION SPEC	17	87,991
23305039	TRANSPORTATION SPEC	15	102,244
23307051	MGR DIST NETWORKS	7	119,408
233077XX	EXPRS MAIL SRVC CLK	170	53,508
23350022	SUPV POSTAL POLICE	92	59,478
23350040	GENERAL ANALYST	14	63,782
23350041	GENERAL ANALYST	108	67,038
23352002	PSTL INSP (A1)	45	49,538
233524XX	PSTL POLICE OFCR(B)	581	51,114
23353002	POSTAL INSPECTOR (D)	892	78,950
23353003	PSTL INSP B	94	52,295
23353004	PSTL INSPT TEAM LDR	217	94,376
23353006	PSTL INSP C	200	59,023
23355018	POSTAL INS PROG MGR	91	93,865
23357007	INSP IN CHARGE (FLD)	19	156,275
23357032	ASST INS IN CHG FLD	39	105,093
23400023	GEN CLK	13	53,746
23400024	DIST WINDOW CLK	19	53,668
23400027	SUPV CPTR MAIL FRWD	112	62,784
23400028	MGR MAIL FORWARDING	53	68,707
23400031	OPER SUPP SPEC	45	56,772
23400033	MARKUP CLK AUTO	2,281	51,878
234001XX	GEN CLK	2,061	52,652
234002XX	DIST WINDOW CLK	16,198	52,448
234004XX	POST OFFICE CLK	69	49,208
234006XX	POSTAGE DUE CLK	246	52,522
234010XX	RCD CK-INT AIR MAIL	66	53,668
234016XX	GEN OFC CLK FRGN ML	14	53,669
234018XX	RCV CK, FRGN AIR ML	86	53,575
234024XX	POSTAGE DUE TECHN	286	53,668
234027XX	MAIL REWRAPPER	24	50,280
23403002	POSTAL OPRNS ANALYS	22	90,836
234045XX	ML PROCSG MACH OPER	1,422	50,250
234048XX	SLF SRV PST CTR TCH	291	53,626
23405043	OPER SUPP SPEC	79	77,956
23405044	OPER SUPP SPEC	263	70,453
234080XX	DSTRB WNDW&MKUP CLK	2,033	52,289
234081XX	ADMIN CLK EXP MAIL	82	52,603
234082XX	EXPRESS ML TECH	33	53,668
23450022	MAILING STAND. SPEC.	97	61,581
23450030	MAILNG REQRMNT CLK	50	52,617
23450043	SUPV BUS MAIL ENTRY	226	62,329

OCC CODE	OCC TITLE	# EMPLOYED	AVERAGE SALARY ($)
23450044	MAILPCE DSGN ANLYST	144	62,391
23450046	EXPEDITED SVC SPCLS	22	64,144
23450054	CLERK MAIL REC CTR	114	52,576
234515XX	CLMS&INQUIRY CLK	114	52,562
234523XX	CMPLNT & INQRY CLK	318	53,481
234532XX	MAILING REQRMNT CLK	393	53,677
23454016	CLASSIFICATION SPCL	14	97,071
23454017	CLASSIFICATION SPEC	14	77,983
23454019	BUSINESS ML ENTRY A	61	56,382
23455030	RETAIL SPECIALIST	169	60,680
23455035	CUST REL COORD	186	65,668
23455037	CUST REL SPECIALIST	18	71,593
234552XX	MAIL CLASS CLK MSC	11	54,870
23456052	MGR CON AFFRS & CLM	71	68,428
234570XX	STAMP DIST CLRK-SDN	23	53,668
23457051	MGR BUS MAIL ENTRY	66	74,486
235008XX	SCHEMES&SCHL CLK	48	53,493
23550008	MGR MAINTENANCE	79	67,410
23550009	MGR MAINTENANCE	36	65,487
23550010	SUPV MAINT OPRNS	1,780	66,862
23550011	MGR MAINT OPRNS	43	74,026
23550021	MGR MAINT OPS SUPP	121	73,009
23550022	SUPV MAINT OPER SUP	50	67,434
23550028	MGR MAINT OPER	176	78,607
23550029	MGR FLD MAIN OPER	122	70,477
23550030	MAINT ENG SPEC	132	73,667
23600002	FAC REQ SPEC (FSO)	36	81,570
23700024	SALES SPEC	44	72,955
23700025	SALES SPEC	73	83,001
23700092	ACCOUNT MGR	238	58,064
23700094	SR ACCOUNT MGR	54	67,230
23700199	SMALL BUSN SPEC	220	57,301
23700232	OPRNS INTEGRA SPEC	25	87,623
23700260	SALES PERFORM ANALY	25	86,908
23700270	SALES SPC	17	79,301
23700273	SALES MANAGER	17	87,300
23700274	SALES MANAGER	32	94,676
23700290	MGR BSN OPS (DIST)	60	75,878
23700291	SR BSN SPEC (AREA)	73	69,105
23700298	BSN REPRESENTATIVE	205	59,252
23700327	MGR BUSI DEVEL TM	71	70,150
23700344	SR SMALL BUSN SPEC	71	65,664
23750014	SFS CLERK	84	52,504
23800003	MGR VEHICLE MAINT	36	79,391
23800004	MGR VEHICLE MAINT	19	86,239
280503XX	MAINT ELECTRICIAN	110	54,188
341402XX	MACHINST	11	54,634
350101XX	GRP LDR CUSTODIAL	527	50,731
35021019	LABORER CUSTODIAL	12	50,292
354001XX	WINDOW CLEANER	2	51,495
356501XX	CLEANER	8	49,360

OCC CODE	OCC TITLE	# EMPLOYED	AVERAGE SALARY ($)
35660001	CUSTODIAN	14	49,617
356604XX	CUSTODIAN	546	47,262
356607XX	CUST LABORER C	61	44,932
370402XX	WELDER	62	54,008
380902XX	BODY AND FENDER REP	218	56,280
384302XX	LTR BOX MECH(MES)	153	54,272
410202XX	PAINTER	118	54,037
410404XX	SIGN PAINT/LETTERER	17	52,526
415501XX	AUTOMOTIVE PAINTER	14	54,377
420602XX	PLUMBER	31	54,147
44011013	LAB PRNTNG TEC EASC	9	50,950
450401XX	TIRE REPAIRMAN	30	51,320
460702XX	CARPENTER	74	54,462
47490001	FACILITY MAINT MECH	23	51,252
47490002	FACILITY MAINT TECH	10	55,185
47490004	MAINTENANCE MECHAN	20	51,861
474902XX	GEN MECHANIC	5	50,576
474903XX	MAINTENANCE MECH	3,575	51,659
474910XX	BLDG MNT CUSTODIAN	842	50,670
474911XX	MAINTENANCE MECHAN	96	50,821
480104XX	VENDING MACH MECH	3	53,668
480106XX	PSTL MACHS MECH	15	53,668
480120XX	AREA MAINT TECH	504	56,426
480121XX	AREA MAINT SPEC	96	54,444
52011001	CASUAL	11,368	25,160
53060002	BLDG EQUIP MECH	2,360	55,962
53060003	BLDG EQUIP MECH	10	55,957
53111002	LOCKMAKER (MES)	9	52,526
531303XX	ELEVATOR MECH	6	54,870
53500001	MAINT MECH MPE	5,655	55,485
54013001	EVELATOR/BOILER INS	35	65,387
540202XX	FIREMAN LABORER	96	51,368
541501XX	STATIONARY ENGINEER	10	54,870
543801XX	ELEVATOR OPER	64	44,866
57030002	MOTOR VEH OPER	4	50,533
57030004	TRACTOR TRAILER OP	5,530	52,599
57030005	MOTOR VEH OPERATOR	2,759	51,312
57030006	DRIVING SAFETY INST	209	53,228
570401XX	MTLS HNDL EQ OPR	69	50,639
570403XX	ML HDLR EQUIP OPER	8,991	50,560
57041003	FORKLIFT OPERATOR	11	52,526
58230001	AUTOMOTIVE TECH	2,267	51,802
58230004	LEAD AUTOMOTIVE TEC	932	55,349
58230005	LEAD AUTO TECH (AG)	270	58,516
58230006	AUTOMOTIVE MECH	171	47,454
58230007	SUPV VEH MAINT	272	63,484
582303XX	AUTOMOTIVE MECH	24	50,951
690401XX	TOOL&PARTS CLK	156	52,057
69071002	PACKER/WAREHOUSEMAN	29	50,784
695502XX	GARAGEMAN	171	50,511

Chapter Ten
Postal Inspectors

Postal Inspectors investigate criminal activities involving the security and integrity of the United States postal system. Approximately 4,000 postal inspectors, evidence technicians, support staff and uniformed postal police ensure the safety of postal employees, the postal system, and the public. The Postal Inspection Service investigates and enforces over 200 laws covering crimes that may adversely affect the mail, and provides considerable protection against identity theft and consumer fraud. The chief postal inspector and the head of the Postal Inspection Service reports directly to the postmaster general.[1]

Inspectors carry firearms, make arrests, testify in court, serve subpoenas, and write comprehensive reports. It is a demanding position, often requiring frequent and extended travel and absences from home. Postal inspectors may work under hazardous conditions, have irregular work hours, and be assigned anywhere in the country.

Beginning January 8, 2003, the Postal Inspection Service opened postal inspector recruitment for college graduates with no previous work experience. If you do not meet one of the special requirements in the *Application for U.S. Postal Inspector,* but have a conferred, four-year college degree with a minimum GPA of 3.0, or an advanced degree, you may apply to become a postal inspector. To apply, submit Form 168, *Application for U.S. Postal Inspector,* along with a copy of your college transcript.

Federal law enforcement agents in the GS-1811, Criminal Investigating Series, may apply through an expedited recruitment process by submitting a copy

---

[1]USPS O.C. List and http://postalinspectors.uspis.gov/aboutus/mission.aspx

of a current SF 50, *Notification of Personnel Action,* with their application. If the applicant has Top Secret clearance, the process may be further expedited by including a letter from their agency's security control officer certifying the clearance, the date it was originally issued and any updates, as well as copies of SF 86, *Questionnaire for National Security Positions,* for the original clearance and any updates.[2]

Overview

The United States Postal Service was founded by Benjamin Franklin, and it is one of the oldest federal law enforcement agencies. The Postal Inspection Service has a long, proud and successful history of fighting criminals who attack our nation's postal system and misuse it to defraud, endanger or otherwise threaten the American public. As the primary law enforcement arm of the Postal Service, the Postal Inspection Service is a highly specialized, professional organization performing investigative and security functions essential to a stable and sound postal system.

Congress empowered the Postal Service "to investigate postal offenses and civil matters relating to the Postal Service." Through its security and enforcement functions, the Postal Inspection Service provides assurance to American businesses for the safe exchange of funds and securities through the U.S. mail; to postal customers of the "sanctity of the seal" in transmitting correspondence and messages; and to postal employees of a safe work environment.

As fact-finding and investigative agents, postal inspectors are federal law enforcement officers who carry firearms, make arrests and serve federal search warrants and subpoenas. Inspectors work closely with U.S. Attorneys, other law enforcement agencies and local prosecutors to investigate postal cases and prepare them for court. There are approximately 1,750 postal inspectors stationed throughout the United States, covering investigations of crimes that adversely affect or fraudulently use the postal system.

To assist in carrying out its responsibilities, the Postal Inspection Service maintains a security force staffed by 830 uniformed postal police officers who are assigned to critical postal facilities throughout the country. The officers provide perimeter security, escort high-value mail shipments and perform other essential protective functions.

The Postal Inspection Service operates five forensic crime laboratories, strategically located in cities across the country. The labs are staffed with forensic scientists and technical specialists, who assist inspectors in analyzing evidentiary material needed for identifying and tracing criminal suspects and in providing expert testimony for cases brought to trial.

---

[2] Postal Inspection Web page, http://postalinspectors.uspis.gov/

The Postal Inspection Service recruits for the following positions:

- ➢ Postal inspectors
- ➢ Postal police officers
- ➢ Forensic scientists
- ➢ Information technology specialists
- ➢ Security electronic technicians
- ➢ Administrative support specialists

Requirements for U.S. Postal Inspectors[3]

U.S. postal inspectors are federal law enforcement officers. Postal inspectors have investigative jurisdiction in all criminal matters involving the integrity and security of the Postal Service.

Postal inspectors investigate criminal, civil, and administrative violations of postal laws and are responsible for protecting the revenue and assets of the Postal Service. Inspectors are required to carry firearms, make arrests, testify in court, serve subpoenas, and write comprehensive reports. They must operate motor vehicles and may undergo moderate to arduous physical exertion under unusual environmental conditions. It is essential that inspectors be in sound physical condition and be capable of performing vigorous physical activities on a sustained basis. The activities may require inspectors to perform the following: climb ladders; work long and irregular hours; occupy cramped or crowded spaces for extended periods of time; exert physical force in the arrest, search, pursuit, and restraint of another person; and protect themselves and others from imminent danger.

The duties of the position require the ability to communicate with people from all walks of life, be proficient with firearms, have skills in self-defense, and have the ability to exercise good judgment. Inspectors may be relocated according to the needs of the service.

The recruitment process is extremely thorough, and there is intense competition for relatively few positions. The recruitment and selection process must be completed prior to the applicant's 37th birthday.

This position is exempt from the Fair Labor Standards Act (FLSA) and does not qualify for overtime compensation. Postal inspector salaries are based on the Inspection Service Law Enforcement (ISLE) pay system. The ISLE pay grades and steps correspond to the General Schedule (GS) pay scale for law enforcement officers.

Candidates must:

✓ Be U.S. citizens between 21 and 36½ years of age. (Male citizens born after December 31, 1959, must have registered with the Selective Service prior to applying to become a postal inspector.

---

[3] Excerpted from http://postalinspectors.uspis.gov/employment/eligibility.aspx

- ✓ Possess a conferred four-year degree from an accredited college or university.
- ✓ Pass a comprehensive visual exam.
- ✓ Pass a hearing acuity test.
- ✓ Be in good physical condition, with weight in proportion to height, and possess emotional and mental stability. See Postal Inspector Height/Weight Chart.
- ✓ Have no felony convictions (felony charges may render candidates ineligible).
- ✓ Have no misdemeanor conviction of domestic violence (other misdemeanor charges or convictions may render candidates ineligible).
- ✓ Have a current, valid state driver's license, held for at least two years.
- ✓ Have the ability to demonstrate the following attributes, as measured by the Assessment Center evaluation:

  - ■ Write and speak English clearly.
  - ■ Schedule and complete activities in a logical, timely sequence.
  - ■ Comprehend and execute instructions written and spoken in English.
  - ■ Think clearly and comprehend verbal and nonverbal information.
  - ■ Interact with others to obtain or exchange information or services.
  - ■ Perceive or identify relevant details and associate them with other facts.

Special Knowledge

There are four special knowledge tracks that make applicants more competitive for the position of postal inspector: language skills, postal experience, specialized nonpostal skills, and academic achievement. Candidates without special knowledge will be only minimally qualified.

Language Skills

Applicants seeking to enter the recruitment process under the language skills track must have advanced competency in a foreign language deemed as needed by the Postal Inspection Service to meet its investigative mission.

Applicants must pass a formal proficiency test administered by a contractor of the Postal Inspection Service. In addition to the language requirement, applicants in this track must have one year of full-time work experience with the same company or firm within two years of the date of their application.

The current list is as follows:

Arabic	Armenian	Cambodian	Cantonese
Czech	Dutch	Egyptian	Farsi (Persian)
French	German	Greek (modern)	Haitian-Creole
Hebrew	Hindi	Hmong	Indonesian
Italian	Japanese	Korean	Lao
Mandarin	Norwegian	Polish	Portuguese
Punjabi	Russian	Serbo-Croatian	Slovak
Spanish	Swahili	Swedish	Tagalog
Thai	Turkish	Ukrainian	Urdu
Vietnamese			

Postal Experience

Candidates seeking consideration under the specialized postal experience track must within the last two years have been a U.S. Postal Service employee, contractor, or intern.

Specialized Nonpostal Experience

Applicants seeking consideration under the specialized nonpostal skill track must have experience in one of the areas of expertise designated as critical to the needs of the Postal Inspection Service. Candidates must also have one year of full-time work experience with the same company or firm within two years of the date of their application. Critical areas of expertise follow: The areas are as follows:

✓ **Military experience**. Candidates must have served at least two years in the military and received an honorable discharge. Candidates with international or bioterrorism experience preferred.

✓ **Law degree.** Candidates must have a Juris Doctor degree and one year of full-time work experience with the same company or firm within two years of the date of their application.

✓ **Certifications in auditing or investigations.** Candidates with certifications in auditing, such as Certified Public Accountant (CPA), Certified Management Accountant (CMA), Certified Internal Auditor (CIA), and Certified Information Systems Auditor (CISA), or investigative certifications in protection, security, or fraud examination, such as Certified Protection Professional (CPP) and Certified Fraud Examiner

(CFE), are eligible under this skill track. Candidates must provide proof of certification and one year of full-time work experience in this field.

✓ **Specialized Computer Education**. Candidates with a four-year degree in computer science, computer engineering, telecommunications, management information systems, electronic commerce, decision and information science, or computer information systems and one year of full-time work experience in this field are eligible under this skill track.

✓ **Specialized Computer Expertise**. Candidates who are currently employed, and have been employed for at least one year in a position specializing in computer forensics, Internet investigations, Internet security, network security, or information systems security and one year of full-time work experience in this field are eligible under this skill track.

✓ **Certifications in Computer Systems.** Candidates with a certification as a Microsoft Certified Systems Engineer (MCSE), Microsoft Certified Professional + Internet (MCP+I), Cisco Certified Network Professional (CCNP), Certified Novell Engineer (CNE), A+ Certified Computer Technician, Certified Information Systems Security Professional (CISSP), Linux certification, or Sun Systems Certified Administrator and one year of full-time work experience in this field are eligible under this skill track.

✓ **Law Enforcement.** Candidates with at least one full year of law enforcement experience as detectives, criminalists, and polygraph examiners or as patrol, probation, correction, and parole officers are eligible under this skill track, but must provide examples of the type of work conducted. (This track excludes clerical or technical support personnel.)

✓ **Bioterrorism Investigations.** Candidates with at least one full year of bioterrorism investigation experience are eligible under this skill track. Specific examples of the type of work conducted will be required.

Academic Achievement

To increase competitiveness and acquire a more diversified candidate pool, candidates may enter the recruitment process along a fourth track, academic achievement with or without work experience.

- Academic achievement with work experience. Candidates with at least one year of full-time work experience with the same company, within two years of the date of their application, are eligible under this skill track.

- Candidates with a bachelor's degree (B.A. or B.S. in any field) must have two years of full-time work experience.

- Candidates with an advanced degree (M.A., M.S., or Ph.D. in any field) must have one year of full-time work experience.

- Academic achievement without work experience. Candidates with a bachelor's degree (a B.A. or B.S. in any field) and a cumulative grade point average (GPA) of 3.0 or higher (on a 4.0 scale) or its equivalent, or an advanced degree (J.D., M.A., M.S., or Ph.D. in any field) are eligible under this skill track.

Drug Policy

The U.S. Postal Inspection Service is committed to a drug-free workplace. The unlawful use of drugs by employees is not tolerated, and those who apply for employment and illegally use or sell drugs are considered unsuitable for employment.

The Postal Inspection Service drug policy balances the need to maintain a drug-free workplace and the integrity necessary to accomplish its mission with the desirability of affording employment opportunities to the broadest segment of society, consistent with those needs. The policy is as follows:

- Candidates who have illegally used drugs while in a law enforcement or prosecutorial position, or while in a position with a high level of responsibility or public trust are considered unsuitable for employment.

- Candidates who have misrepresented their drug history in their application are considered unsuitable for employment.

- Candidates who have illegally sold a drug are considered unsuitable for employment.

- Candidates who have illegally used any drug (other than cannabis*) within the past 10 years are considered unsuitable for employment, absent compelling or mitigating circumstances.

- Candidates who have used cannabis within the past three years are considered unsuitable for employment absent compelling or mitigating circumstances.

* Cannabis may include marijuana, hashish, hash oil, and tetrahydrocannabinol (THC).

Candidates not in compliance with the Postal Inspection Service drug policy will not be considered for employment. Postal inspectors are randomly tested for illegal drug use throughout their careers.

Candidate Application Process

The applicant process for most postal inspector applicants consists of the following phases:

Phase One

- Completion of application. Applications may be completed online only during open seasons.

- Completion of a two-part on-line entrance examination. Part one of the exam is unproctored and may be completed anywhere the candidate can gain access to the Internet. (Candidates who fail part one may be eligible for one retest, provided they meet the job qualifications at the time of the retest.) A selected number candidates that are successful on part one will be invited to complete part two, as a part of an information exchange, at a designated facility.

- Participation in an information exchange. A Postal Inspection Service representative will meet with a group of invited candidates and facilitate an information exchange which includes the completion of the part two of the entrance exam, submission of paperwork to complete the comprehensive application package, a video presentation, and a question-and-answer session.

- Completion of the Comprehensive Application Packet, including forms used to initiate the National Agency Check for obtaining the Top Secret security clearance required for all postal inspectors.

- Language proficiency test, if applicable.

- Assessment center evaluation of knowledge, skills, and abilities: simulation of exercises used to assess core competencies needed by successful postal inspectors. (Candidates who fail the evaluation may be eligible for one reassessment, provided they meet the job qualifications at the time of the reassessment.)

- Polygraph examination to validate information obtained during the application process, including illegal drug use, criminal history, and integrity issues.

- Background suitability investigation.

- Management interview.

- Drug screening.

Phase Two

- Medical examination: An employment physical will be administered only to candidates who have received a contingent offer of employment. Successful completion of the employment physical is the final step in the selection process.

- Once an official appointment date has been established, the candidate begins:

- Residential Basic Inspector Training program at Potomac, Maryland. Graduation from the training program is a condition of employment.

- Six-month probation period for nonpostal candidates.

Current qualified Federal Law Enforcement Criminal Investigators (Occupational Code 1811), or equivalent, may be permitted to participate in an abbreviated applicant process, consisting of the following steps:

- Online application.

- Comprehensive application packet.

- National agency check (unless documentation is provided indicating the agent has a Top Secret security clearance.

- Polygraph interview.

- Background investigation and management interview.

- Employment physical and drug screening.

- Six-week residential Federal Investigator Orientation course. (This is an abbreviated version of the Basic Inspector Training course listed below.)

Basic Inspector Training Process

Basic Inspector Training at the Career Development Division (CDD) covers academics, firearms, physical fitness and defensive tactics, and practical exercises. Each candidate must participate fully in all program areas and achieve specific minimum academic and performance levels to graduate. Graduation from basic training is a condition of employment. Failure to meet the minimum academic and performance levels will result in the termination of the appointment.

Academics

Classroom instruction is divided into courses, or lesson blocks, which address the major areas of investigation and administration that postal inspectors are expected to perform. Three examinations will be given during training to evaluate students' understanding of the subject matter.

Firearms

Rigorous firearms training provides beginning through advanced students with the skills needed to handle firearms safely and develop shooting proficiency.

Firearms proficiency is tested twice during the program. Students must meet the standards set by the National Threat Management Committee and qualify on the Postal Inspection Service Practical Pistol Course, using the service-issued weapon. Students must also qualify on the shotgun course. The shotgun qualifications course consists of demonstrated safety, proper loading and unloading of the weapon, and firing rounds from various positions.

Physical Fitness/Defensive Tactics

All student inspectors must participate fully in both the physical fitness and defensive tactics programs.

The physical fitness program familiarizes students with various exercise options designed to improve their physical condition. Classroom time is set aside for physical fitness workouts, but students are responsible for additional workouts outside of class.

The defensive tactics program requires that students demonstrate the techniques taught and practiced through a practical exam and dynamic practical exercises. Students must develop the ability to use a level of force appropriate to the threat. After each course of instruction, students' abilities to perform assigned maneuvers are evaluated by the instructors.

Practical Exercises

Practical exercises allow students the opportunity to perform the lessons learned during classroom activities and defensive tactics in a real-life simulation.

Compensation

Postal inspectors are exempt from the Fair Labor Standards Act (FLSA) and do not qualify for overtime compensation. Salaries are based on the Inspection Service Law Enforcement (ISLE) pay scale, which corresponds to the General Schedule (GS) pay scale for law enforcement officers. Minimum-entry base pay levels range from the equivalent of a Grade 9, Step 1, to Grade 12, Step 10. The entry-level salary for transferring 1811s range from a Grade 9, Step 1, to Grade 13, Step 10. Go to www.federaljobs.net to review the federal pay scales for all major metropolitan areas.

A candidate's qualifications and current pay–excluding overtime, premiums, night differential, higher-level details, and second incomes–are considered when entry levels are established.

In addition to basic pay, postal inspectors receive locality pay and law enforcement availability pay. Inspectors in the CONUS receive locality pay (ranging from 12.64% to 30.33% in 2007) based on the cost of living in various parts of the country. Inspectors domiciled in Hawaii, Alaska, and the U.S. territories receive a territorial cost-of-living allowance (TCOLA), which is a percentage of salary that is determined and published by the Office of Personnel Management.

Candidates start earning locality pay when they begin the training academy. Overtime pay increases annual salaries by 25% and is applied upon graduation from the academy. Transferring 1811s, attending the Federal Investigator Orientation, receive overtime pay compensation while at the academy.

Relocation Expenses

Mobility is an important component of the postal inspector position. Inspectors who are required to relocate to their first duty station will receive a paid move, which includes but is not limited to the following:

- Transporting household goods

- An advance round trip to visit a new duty location to find housing

- Temporary living quarters, if necessary.

Student inspectors learn about relocation benefits while attending the training academy. Students who initiate relocation before completing training will lose relocation benefits. Postal inspectors who move later in their careers under various components of the transfer policy or as the result of a promotion are eligible to receive relocation benefits.

Additional Information

Contact one of the Postal Inspection Service division offices for additional information and to find out when jobs will be advertised in your area. A divisional office list is provided on the next page. Visit www.postalinspectors.uspis.gov frequently for updated information and new job announcements. Visit this book's companion Web site at www.postalwork.net for additional assistance and direct links to the official Postal Service sites. Explore federal law enforcement occupations, including positions with the Department of Homeland Security, at www.federaljobs.net.

U.S. Postal Inspection Service Division Offices

Miami 3400 Lakeside Dr 6th Fl Miramar FL 33027-3242 (954) 436-7200 Fax: (954) 436-7282	**New Jersey / Caribbean** PO Box 509 Newark NJ 07101-0509 (973) 693-5400 Fax: (973) 645-0600	**Denver** 1745 Stout St Ste 900 Denver CO 80202-3034 (303) 313-5320 Fax: (303) 313-5351
Houston 650 N. Sam Houston Pkwy Houston TX 77251-1276 (713) 238-4400 Fax: (713) 238-4460	**Boston** 495 Summer St Boston MA 02210-2114 (617) 556-4400 Fax: (617) 556-0400	**Atlanta** PO Box 16489 Atlanta GA 30321-0489 (404) 608-4500 Fax: (404) 608-4505
Detroit PO Box 330119 Detroit MI 48232-6119 (313) 226-8184 Fax: (313) 226-8220	**San Francisco** PO Box 882528 San Francisco CA 94188-2528 (415) 778-5800 Fax: (415) 778-5822	**Charlotte** 2901 Scott Futrell Dr. Charlotte NC 28228-3000 (704) 329-9120 Fax: (704) 357-0039
Chicago 433 W Harrison St., 6th Fl Chicago IL 60669-2201 (312) 983-7900 Fax: (312) 983-6300	**Fort Worth** 14800 Trinity Blvd. Fort Worth TX 76161 (817) 359-2700	**St. Louis** 1106 Walnut St. St. Louis MO 63199 314-539-9300
Los Angeles P.O. Box 2000 Pasadena CA 91102 626-405-1200	**Seattle** PO Box 400 Seattle WA 98111-4000 (206) 442-6300 Fax: (206) 442-6304	**Washington Metro** 10500 Little Patuxent Pkwy Columbia MD 21044 (410) 715-7700
New York Metro PO Box 555 New York NY 10116-0555 (212) 330-3844 Fax: (212) 330-2720	**Philadelphia Metro** 2970 Market St Philadelphia PA 19101 (215) 895-8450	**Pittsburgh** 1001 California Ave Rm 2101 Pittsburgh PA 15290 (412) 359-7900 Fax: (412) 359-7682

Chapter Eleven
Civil Service Job Options

The majority of jobs in the Postal Service are mail carrier and clerk positions. However, like most large corporations the Postal Service requires a broad spectrum of occupations, everything from janitors to engineers, inspectors and administrative occupations of all types. Similar or related occupations exist in the federal Civil Service. There are over 900 occupational titles in the federal sector which provide abundant employment opportunities for those willing to seek them out.

Uncle Sam employs over 2,700,000 federal civilian employees, and half are now eligible for regular or early retirement. Over a million jobs must be filled as baby boomers say so long to their federal careers. There are many reasons to consider federal employment. The average annual federal worker's compensation, pay plus benefits, is **$106,871** compared to **$53,288** for the private sector.[1] Student loan payoff, relocation, and cash incentives are now offered for hard-to-fill positions, and the benefits package is exceptional.

You need to know how to take
advantage of the federal hiring system
and recent changes to successfully land
the job you want in government.

Excellent job opportunities are available for those who know how to tap this lucrative job market. All government hiring is based on performance and qualifications regardless of your sex, race, color, creed, religion, disability, or national origin. Where else can you apply for a high-paying entry-level job that

---

[1] Bureau of Economic Analysis, National Income & Product Account Tables 6.2D and 6.5D, 2005.

offers employment at thousands of locations internationally, excellent career advancement opportunities, plus careers in hundreds of occupations?

This chapter will help you understand and explore civil service job options. Much of this chapter was excerpted from *The Book of U.S. Government Jobs*, 10th Edition, by Dennis V. Damp.

LOCATING JOB VACANCIES

Over 30,000 federal jobs are advertised on any given day. Yes, thousands of jobs are just a few key strokes away if you know where to find them. With 50 percent of the federal work force eligible for either early or regular retirement, there are abundant opportunities for all who seek them out. Jobs are available nationwide and overseas. The Office of Personnel Management (OPM) maintains the largest government online jobs database at http://www.usajobs.gov, and you can take advantage of its FREE online résumé and automated job alert services. Visit http://federaljobs.net/federal.htm to link to hundreds of agency employment Web sites to locate **ALL** available jobs. Job seekers can also call OPM's **USAJOBS** hotline for updated job information at 1-703-724-1850, TTY 978-461-8404.

The USAJOBS jobs hotline is menu driven, and you can search jobs by answering specific questions using your telephone keypad. The phone prompts help you select jobs and salary ranges of interest. If you don't have access to a computer, visit your local library to explore the easy-to-use referenced Web sites.

Not all government jobs are advertised on **USAJOBS**. Agencies with direct hire authority may advertise vacancies independently. A list of key Web sites is available in this chapter and you will find a master list of 141 agency recruitment links posted on this book's companion Web site at http://federaljobs.net.

> Individual agency personnel offices should also be contacted to obtain job announcements. Visit http://federaljobs.net for job listings and for direct links to 141 federal agency recruiting sites.

NATURE OF FEDERAL EMPLOYMENT

The federal government's essential duties include defending the United States from foreign aggression and terrorism, representing U.S. interests abroad, enforcing laws and regulations, and administering domestic programs and agencies.[5] U.S. citizens are particularly aware of the federal government when they pay their income taxes each year, but they usually do not consider the government's role when they watch a weather forecast, purchase fresh and uncontaminated groceries, travel by highway or air, or make a deposit at their bank. Workers

---

[5] The 2006-07 Career Guide to Industries, U.S. Department of Labor

employed by the federal government play a vital role in these and many other aspects of our daily lives.

This book describes federal government civilian career opportunities, including jobs with the Postal Service (an independent agency of the federal government). Armed forces career opportunities are described in the current edition of the Occupational Outlook Handbook

Over 200 years ago, the founders of the United States gathered in Philadelphia to create a Constitution for a new national government and lay the foundation for self-governance. The Constitution of the United States, ratified by the last of the 13 original states in 1791, created the three branches of the federal government and granted certain powers and responsibilities to each. The legislative, judicial, and executive branches were created with equal powers but very different responsibilities that act to keep their powers in balance.

The legislative branch is responsible for forming and amending the legal structure of the nation. Its largest component is Congress, the primary U.S. legislative body, which is made up of the Senate and the House of Representatives. This body includes senators, representatives, their staffs, and various support workers. The legislative branch employs only about 2 percent of federal workers, nearly all of whom work in the Washington, D.C., area.

The judicial branch is responsible for interpreting the laws that the legislative branch enacts. The Supreme Court, the nation's definitive judicial body, makes the highest rulings. Its decisions usually follow the appeal of a decision made by the one of the regional Courts of Appeal, which hear cases appealed from U.S. District Courts, the Court of Appeals for the Federal Circuit, or state Supreme Courts. U.S. District Courts are located in each state and are the first to hear most cases under federal jurisdiction. The judicial branch employs about the same number of people as does the legislative branch, but its offices and employees are dispersed throughout the country.

Of the three branches, the executive branch — through the power vested by the Constitution in the office of the president — has the widest range of responsibilities. Consequently, it employed 96 percent of all federal civilian employees (excluding Postal Service workers) in 2006. The executive branch is composed of the Executive Office of the President, 15 executive Cabinet departments, including the recently created Department of Homeland Security, and nearly 90 independent agencies, each of which has clearly defined duties. The Executive Office of the President is composed of several offices and councils that aid the president in policy decisions. These include the Office of Management and Budget, which oversees the administration of the federal budget; the National Security Council, which advises the president on matters of national defense; and the Council of Economic Advisers, which makes economic policy recommendations.

Each of the 15 executive Cabinet departments administers programs that oversee an aspect of life in the United States. The highest departmental official of each Cabinet department, the secretary, is a member of the president's Cabinet. The 15 departments, listed by employment size, are listed below with a brief description and total employment.

Defense: (675,744) Manages the military forces that protect our country and its interests, including the Departments of the Army, Navy, and Air Force and a number of smaller agencies. The civilian workforce employed by the Department of Defense performs various support activities, such as payroll and public relations.

Veterans Affairs: (239,299) Administers programs to aid U.S. veterans and their families, runs the veterans hospital system, and operates our national cemeteries.

Homeland Security: (154,100) Works to prevent terrorist attacks within the United States; reduce vulnerability to terrorism; and minimize the damage from potential attacks and natural disasters. Conceived after the September 11, 2001, attacks and officially established in early 2003, the DHS includes new hires, as well as workers transferring from other agencies—mostly from within the Departments of Justice, Transportation, Agriculture, and the Treasury. Agencies are housed in one of four major directorates: Border and Transportation Security, Emergency Preparedness and Response, Science and Technology, and Information Analysis and Infrastructure Protection.

Treasury: (106,925) Regulates banks and other financial institutions, administers the public debt, prints currency, and collects federal income taxes.

Justice: (106,781) Enforces federal laws, prosecutes cases in federal courts, and runs federal prisons.

Agriculture: (105,047) Promotes U.S. agriculture domestically and internationally and sets standards governing quality, quantity, and labeling of food sold in the United States.

Interior: (72,274) Manages federal lands, including the national parks and forests; runs hydroelectric power systems; and promotes conservation of natural resources.

Health and Human Services: (61,163) Sponsors medical research; approves use of new drugs and medical devices; runs the Public Health Service; and administers Medicare.

Transportation: (53,865) Sets national transportation policy; plans and funds the construction of highways and mass transit systems; and regulates railroad, aviation, and maritime operations.

Commerce: (40,079) Forecasts the weather; charts the oceans; regulates patents and trademarks; conducts the Census; compiles statistics; and promotes U.S. economic growth by encouraging international trade.

State: (34,160) Oversees the nation's embassies and consulates; issues passports; monitors U.S. interests abroad; and represents the United States before international organizations.

Labor: (16,195) Enforces laws guaranteeing fair pay, workplace safety, and equal job opportunity; administers unemployment insurance; regulates pension funds; and collects and analyzes economic data through its Bureau of Labor Statistics.

Energy: (14,795) Coordinates the national use and provision of energy; oversees the production and disposal of nuclear weapons; and plans for future energy needs.

Housing and Urban Development: (9,935) Funds public housing projects; enforces equal housing laws; and insures and finances mortgages.

Education: (4,229) Provides scholarships, student loans, and aid to schools.

WORKING CONDITIONS

Due to the broad scope of federal employment, almost every working condition found in the private sector can also be found in the federal government.[6] Most white-collar employees work in office buildings, hospitals, or laboratories, and most of the blue-collar workforce can be found in factories, warehouses, shipyards, military bases, construction sites, or national parks and forests. Work environments vary from the comfortable and relaxed to the hazardous and stressful, such as those experienced by law enforcement officers, astronauts, or air traffic controllers.

The vast majority of federal employees work full time, often on flexible "flexitime" schedules, which allow workers to tailor their own work week, within certain constraints. Some agencies also have "flexiplace" programs, which allow selected workers to perform some job duties at home or from regional centers.

The duties of some federal workers require that they spend much of their time away from the offices in which they are based. Inspectors and compliance officers, for example, often visit businesses and work sites to ensure that laws and regulations are obeyed. Few travel so far that they are unable to return home each night. Some federal workers, however, frequently travel long distances, spending days or weeks away from home. Auditors, for example, may spend weeks in distant locations.

EMPLOYMENT

The federal government, including the U.S. Postal Service, employs about 2.7 million civilian workers, or about 2 percent of the nation's workforce. The federal government is the nation's single largest employer. Because data on employment in certain agencies cannot be released to the public for national security reasons, this total does not include employment for the Central Intelligence Agency,

---

[6] Career Guide to Industries, U.S. Department of Labor, April, 2000

National Security Agency, Defense Intelligence Agency, and National Imagery and Mapping Agency.

Table 1-2
Percent distribution of employment in the federal government
and the private sector by major occupational group

Occupational Group	Federal Government	Private Sector
Total	*100*	*100*
Professional and related	32.8	19.9
Management, business, and financial	27.4	9.0
Office and administrative support	16.7	17.6
Service	10.6	19.3
Installation, maintenance, and repair	4.8	4.0
Transportation and materiel moving	3.1	7.2
Production	2.1	7.6
Construction and extraction	1.9	4.7
Sales and related	0.4	10.1
Farming, fishing and forestry	0.2	0.7

OCCUPATIONS

Although the federal government employs workers in every major occupational group, workers are not employed in the same proportions in which they are employed throughout the economy as a whole (Table 1-2). The analytical and technical nature of many government duties translates into a much higher proportion of professional, management, business, and financial occupations in the federal government, compared with most industries. Conversely, the government sells very little, so it employs relatively few sales workers.

Professional and related occupations accounted for about one-third of federal employment in 2006. The largest group of professional workers worked in life science, physical science, and social science occupations, such as biological scientists, conservation scientists and foresters, environmental scientists and geoscientists, and forest and conservation technicians. They do work such as determining the effects of drugs on living organisms, preventing fires in the national forests, and predicting earthquakes and hurricanes. The Department of Agriculture employed the vast majority of life scientists, but physical scientists were distributed throughout a variety of departments and agencies.

Many health professionals, such as licensed practical and licensed vocational nurses, registered nurses, and physicians and surgeons, were employed by the Department of Veterans Affairs (VA) in VA hospitals.

Large numbers of federal workers also held jobs as engineers, including aerospace, civil, computer hardware, electrical and electronics, industrial, mechanical, and nuclear engineers. Engineers were found in many departments of the executive branch, but they most commonly worked in the Department of Defense, the National Aeronautics and Space Administration, and the Department of Transportation. In general, they solve problems and provide advice on technical programs, such as building highway bridges or implementing agency-wide computer systems.

Computer specialists — primarily computer software engineers, network and computer systems analysts, and computer systems administrators — are employed throughout the federal government. They write computer programs, analyze problems related to data processing, and keep computer systems running smoothly. Many health professionals, such as registered nurses, physicians and surgeons, and licensed practical nurses, are employed by the Department of Veterans Affairs (VA) in one of many VA hospitals.

Management, business, and financial workers made up about 27 percent of federal employment and were primarily responsible for overseeing operations. Managerial workers include a broad range of officials who, at the highest levels, may head federal agencies or programs. Middle managers, on the other hand, usually oversee one activity or aspect of a program. One management occupation — legislators — are responsible for passing and amending laws and overseeing the executive branch of the government. Within the federal government, legislators are entirely found in Congress.

Others occupations in this category are accountants and auditors, who prepare and analyze financial reports, review and record revenues and expenditures, and investigate operations for fraud and inefficiency. Purchasing agents handle federal purchases of supplies. Management analysts study government operations and systems and suggest improvements. These employees aid management staff with administrative duties. Administrative support workers in the federal government include secretaries and general office clerks. Purchasing agents handle federal purchases of supplies, and tax examiners, collectors, and revenue agents determine and collect taxes.

Compared with the economy as a whole, workers in service occupations were relatively scarce in the federal government. About seven out of 10 federal workers in service occupations were protective service workers, such as detectives and criminal investigators, police and sheriff's patrol officers, and correctional officers and jailers. These workers protect the public from crime and oversee federal prisons.

Federally employed workers in installation, maintenance, and repair occupations include aircraft mechanics and service technicians who fix and maintain all types of aircraft. Also included are electrical and electronic equipment mechanics, installers, and repairers, who inspect, adjust, and repair electronic equipment such as industrial controls, transmitters, antennas, radar, radio, and navigation systems.

The federal government employed a relatively small number of workers in transportation, production, construction, sales and related, and farming, fishing, and forestry occupations. However, they employed almost all air traffic controllers in the country and a significant number of agricultural inspectors and bridge and lock tenders.

OUTLOOK

Employment in the federal government is projected to grow by 2.5 percent through the year 2014, while the salaried economy as a whole is expected to grow by 14 percent. Job growth generated by increased homeland security needs may be largely offset by projected slow growth or declines in other federal sectors due to governmental cost-cutting, the growing use of private contractors, and continuing devolution—the practice of turning over the development, implementation, and management of some programs of the federal government to state and local governments.

Staffing levels in government, while relatively stable in the short run, can be subject to change in the long run, due mainly to changes in public policies as legislated by Congress, which affect spending levels and hiring decisions for the various government departments and agencies. In general, over the coming decade, domestic programs are likely to see cuts in their budgets as Congress seeks to reduce the federal budget deficit, but the cuts will likely affect some agencies more than others. Any employment declines, however, generally will be carried out through attrition—simply not replacing workers who retire or leave the federal government for other reasons. Layoffs, called "reductions in force," have occurred in the past, but they are uncommon and usually affect relatively few workers. In spite of this, there still will be numerous employment opportunities in many agencies, due to the need to replace workers who leave the workforce, retire, or accept employment elsewhere.

While there will be job openings in all types of jobs over the coming decade, demand will continue to grow for specialized workers in areas related to border and transportation security, emergency preparedness, public health, and information analysis.

A study by the Partnership for Public Service, which surveyed federal department and agency hiring needs for the 2005-2006 period, found that most of the new hires in the federal government will come in five major areas. They are: security, enforcement, and compliance, which includes inspectors, investigators, police officers, airport screeners, and prison guards; medical and public health fields; engineering and the sciences, including microbiologists, botanists, physicists, chemists, and veterinarians; program management and administration; and account-ing, budget, and business, which includes revenue agents and tax examiners needed mainly by the Internal Revenue Service. The Department of Health and Human Services will need health insurance specialists and claims and customer service representatives to implement the Medicare prescription drug benefit. Patent examiners, Foreign Service officers, and lawyers also are in high demand.

Competition is expected for some federal positions, especially during times of economic uncertainty, when workers seek the stability of federal employment. In general, federal employment is considered to be relatively stable because it is not affected by cyclical fluctuations in the economy, as are employment levels in many construction, manufacturing, and other private sector industries.

GETTING STARTED

The Book of U.S. Government Jobs by Dennis V. Damp is an excellent resource that will steer you to highly informative government and private sector Internet Web sites, electronic bulletin boards, self-service job information centers, telephone job hotlines, and it explores all facets of the federal job search. This book is available at most libraries, or you can order a copy by calling 1-800-782-7424. This book will complement your federal job search.

Readers will find up-to-date information on how the federal employment system works from an insider's perspective, how to locate job announcements through various methods, and complete a thorough application package. You'll learn about special hiring programs for the physically challenged, veterans, students, and scholars, thousands of job opportunities, Civil Service exam requirements, overseas jobs, how to complete your employment application, and much more. Appendix A provides a comprehensive checklist that will take you through the entire federal employment process.

The three Appendices include an easy-to-use federal job checklist, complete lists of federal occupations, and comprehensive agency summaries and contact lists including employment office addresses and phone numbers.

This book will guide you step-by-step through the federal employment process, from filling out your first employment application to locating job announcements, networking resources and hiring agencies. Follow the guidelines set forth in this book to dramatically improve your chances of landing a federal job.

PAY AND BENEFITS

Job security, good pay, and an excellent retirement system are just a few of the top reasons most people seek federal employment. Others consider government careers because of desirable travel opportunities, training availability, diverse occupations, and the ability to locate jobs nationwide and overseas.

In December 2005, the average wage for full-time workers paid under the General Schedule was $63,812. In all pay plans, average pay was $67,186. General attorneys, who earned $105,557 on average, represented one of the higher-paid occupations, while average income for nursing assistants was only about half the average for all occupations.

The current year "Base Rate" General Schedule (GS) pay chart is posted on http://federaljobs.net — select "Pay Schedules" on the main menu. This site is the companion Web site for *The Book of U.S. Government Jobs,* and many of this book's resources and Web links are listed on this site to assist you with your job search. Updated pay tables are published on http://federaljobs.net the first week of January each year.

General Schedule (GS) pay varies from the GS-1 level at $16,630 per annum to $120,981 per annum at step 10 of the GS-15 grade, not including locality pay adjustments. The average annual salary for full-time non-postal employees increased to just over $66,000 in 2008. Starting pay depends on the level of experience, education and complexity of the position applied for.

EDUCATION REQUIREMENTS

In the federal government, 59 percent of all workers do not have a college degree. The level of required education is dependent upon the job applied for. Each job announcement lists needed skills and abilities, including education and work experience. However, the more education and work experience you have, the more competitive you will be when ranked against other applicants.

SUMMARY

It took me two years to land my first competitive federal Civil Service job. I was not aware of the employment options available at that time and I simply sent written requests for job announcements every two weeks to the local OPM office. Today there are many options available through special-emphasis hiring, case and direct hire authority, Outstanding Scholar Programs, student employment, and internships, to name a few. Also, use the many Internet sites that provide links to key job lists and informational resources such as http://federaljobs.net. Take advantage of as many of the programs and varied positions that you qualify for to expedite your career search. Don't give up or get frustrated with the paperwork that is required when applying for federal employment. Finally, I must add that it is unwise to get angry with the process; instead of getting mad, **GET INVOLVED.**

Appendix A
Job Hunter's Checklist

WHAT TO DO NOW

❑ Review Chapters One and Two to fully understand the Postal Service job market, employee benefits, salary, and how the agency hires. Also review:

  ✔ Chapter Seven for Veterans Hiring programs.

  ✔ Chapter Four for exam overviews. (all tested occupations).

  ✔ Chapter Five for the new **473 Postal Exam Study Guide**.

  ✔ Chapter Ten for postal inspector jobs.

  ✔ Chapter Eleven for related federal Civil Service occupations.

❑ Review the Postal Service occupations listed in Chapters Three, Eight and Nine. Also review Chapter Eleven for other job options. These chapters provide lists of postal jobs that you may qualify for — including job descriptions for over 40 job categories.

❑ Visit the following Web site to locate job vacancies for all occupations, including mail carrier and clerk positions in your area:

  ✔ www.usps.com/employment/ *(job vacancy lists)*
    Apply online at this site. If tests are required, you will be scheduled for exams in your area within 14 days from application date.

  NOTE: Visit this site often to locate job vacancies.

❏   See Appendix C for a national list of Customer Service District Offices that you can contact if you run into problems or need assistance.

❏   Visit www.usps.com/employment/ to locate corporate job listings that don't require entrance exams. Also, contact regional and local postal facilities including Customer Service District Sales Offices, General Mail Facilities, Sectional Center Facilities, Management Sectional Centers, or Bulk Mail Centers in your area. Don't forget to talk with your local postmaster about job opportunities in your area.

> ✔ www.usps.com/employment/ *(eCareer Center).*

> ✔ www.postalwork.net/ *(Career Center).*

> ✔ **1-478-757-3199**, TTY 1-800-800-8776 *(Postal Service Job Hot Line).* **Note:** *You must have a job announcement number to use the phone service.*

> ✔ www.postalinspectors.uspis.gov *(Postal Inspectors Web site)*

❏   Locate your school transcripts, military records, awards, and professional licenses. Collect past employment history; salary, addresses, phone numbers, dates employed, for the application. Use the PS 2591 form available online on the resource page at www.postalwork.net to review and compile the information you will need when you apply online.

APPLYING FOR A JOB

❏   When you locate a job announcement on www.usps.com/employment, apply online to complete your initial application and assessment. You can apply online for exams or by phone if you have the job announcement number. If monitored exams are required, you will be notified via e-mail and directed to select a date, location, and time where you will take the exam in your area.

❏   If no vacancies are posted, visit www.usps.com/employment frequently to check for updated postings. The Postal Service also advertises in local newspapers and at State Employment Offices. You can also call or write your local District Office's human resources department to find out when jobs will be announced for your area. Consider getting your foot in the door by taking a casual or transitional temporary position. (See page 11)

❏   Complete your online application and assessments. **ALL** requested information must be provided to rate as high as possible and be considered for a position. Collect your employment and educational history before starting your online application and draft your work descriptions offline. You can copy and paste your work descriptions into the online résumé builder when you register. They will need previous employer addresses, phone numbers, salary, dates employed, and more. Be prepared and follow all instructions.

Note: Corporate job vacancy announcements require applicants to complete write-ups for required knowledge, skills and abilities (KSAs). If you neglect to complete these statements, your application may be rejected. Review Appendix B for KSA examples. *The Book of U.S. Government Jobs*, 10th edition, by Dennis Damp, provides detailed guidance for writing federal style resumes and KSAs. This book is available at bookstores and libraries, or you can order a copy by calling 1-800-782-7424.

❑ Your application is submitted online, and you can save your profile and exam results so that you can apply for other jobs. Be sure to write down your user name and password that you establish online for future use.

❑ After applying online, you have 14 days to complete all assessments. You will be notified when and where to report for proctored exams if required. Most exams are now in two parts, an online assessment and a proctored exam at a local testing facility. **You must bring your user assessment ID and password with you to take the proctored exam**.

ADDITIONAL RESOURCES

NOTE: Internet access is required to contact the following services. Many libraries now offer online connectivity for their patrons.

❑ www.usps.com/employment **Postal Service Employment Page** – This highly informative service offers general information about the USPS and includes all recent press releases. Also visit their employment page listed above.

❑ www.secure.vitapowered.com/USPS/login.screen The U.S. Postal Service online assessment account login site. Use your login name and password that you established when you signed up for an assessment to login. If you need assistance, contact support at usps_support@panpowered.com.

❑ www.postalwork.net **Post Office Jobs & Career Center** – A popular site for exploring Postal Service careers and for direct links to key Postal Service employment information.

❑ www.federaljobs.net **Federal Civil Service Jobs and Career Center** – One of the most popular federal employment sites on the Internet today, with over 100,000 visitors each month. Visit this site to explore federal job options, including jobs with the USPS.

❑ www.usajobs.gov **Office of Personnel Management's (OPM's)** official Web site. This site posts thousands of federal government job vacancies. Visit this site to search for related Civil Service job vacancies in your area. You can also register for e-mail notification for specific job titles and occupational group vacancies.

RESULTS

❑ Your application is processed when you first register, and you have 14 days to complete all assessments. You will receive an e-mail message with instructions on how to access your test results. You can check your results as part of your candidate profile in eCareer after you complete your exam. Go to www.usps.com/employment to log into your eCareer account and review your assessment results. Selected applicants must:

   ✔ Meet basic qualifications
   ✔ Score high on the exam (if required)
   ✔ Successfully complete an interview
   ✔ Pass a drug screen

THE INTERVIEW

❑ Prepare for the interview. Review Chapter Six for guidance on how to present yourself and prepare for the interview. Most postal job books completely ignore the interview phase. If you don't impress the selecting officials, you may be passed over for the position.

CAUTION

Many postal job scams advertise toll-free job hotlines online and in newspaper classifieds. They charge fees ranging from $70 to over $200 to help you apply for jobs and include a study guide. Don't waste your money. The application process is free to all who apply, and this book provides a comprehensive 473 exam study guide in Chapter Five.

Appendix B
Corporate Positions

Corporate positions include management and supervision, administrative, professional and technical occupations. Jobs that are open to the general public are listed on the Postal Service's Web site, http://usps.com/employment/. The jobs are advertised in the following categories, with a sampling of specific occupations:

- Engineering
  - Electrical
  - Electronic
- ERM/HR
  - Educational Psychologist
  - Training
  - Human Resources
- Facilities
  - Architect Engineer
- Finance
  - Accountant
  - Economist
  - Mathematical Statistician
- Information Technology
  - Business System Analyst
  - Information System Specialist
  - Systems Analyst
- Inspection Service
  - Security Architect/Engineer
- Marketing
  - Customer Service Support Analyst
- Network Operations
  - Transportation Specialist

When you apply for a corporate position with the Postal Services, recruitment is similar to the federal Civil Service application process. The applicant is rated on his/her work experience, education, special knowledge, skills and abilities (KSAs). Job announcements are advertised on the USPS Web site, and the applicant must follow the job announcement application instructions precisely to be considered for the position. Any omissions can cause your application to be rejected. Many highly qualified applicants are excluded because of administrative errors or omissions.

This chapter guides you through the application process so that you can complete your application or Postal Service style résumé that will get the attention of the selecting official. The PS Form 2591, *"Application for Employment,"* was formerly required until the Postal Service initiated their eCareer online recruiting process recently. Applicants must prepare their résumés and applications in accordance with specific guidelines. The Postal Service has developed the following enhanced application services:

    ✎   Diverse methods to collect information from job applicants – written, telephone, and online techniques
    ✎   Applicant choices in how they submit applications
    ✎   Web site for job vacancies, www.usps.com/employment
    ✎   Customer Service District Sales Offices (see Appendix C)
    ✎   Online applications for all job vacancies through eCareer

The application information is listed on the PS 2591 form. Download this form online at www.postalwork.net/resources.htm and use it as a guide to prepare your online application. Write your work experiences on your desktop using Word, WordPerfect or any word processor, spell and grammar check the document and then copy and paste the write-ups into the online résumé builder afer you register online. Use the form to collect your employment history and education so that when you go online you will have all the information needed to complete the application.

LOCATING JOB ANNOUNCEMENTS

Corporate jobs are advertised at http://usps.com/employment. Search the listings and follow the links to the currently available job announcements. Jobs are listed in the categories noted on the previous page. The Postal Service posts announcements in federal, state, and municipal buildings open to the public; they advertise on the Internet, in local newspapers, and conducts and participates in job fairs, open houses, or other activities to reach the community.[1] I also suggest that if you visit the Web site noted above and don't find jobs in occupations you are qualified for, call the human resources department at your local customer Service District Office (see Appendix C) and ask when they anticipate hiring for your occupation.

---

[1] Handbook EL-312, September 2001, paragraph 223.12

You may also wish to consider related occupations to get your foot in the door. For example, if you are interested in an administrative position and the Postal Service is hiring carriers and clerks, apply for these entry-level positions. If you are selected for the position you will have more opportunities within the system, since most administrative jobs are first advertised to current employees. If none meet the qualification standards for the position or there are insufficient bidders, the position is then advertised to the local public. You may also find related lower-paying jobs that will get your foot in the door as well. It all depends on what you can afford to do in this case. However, before deciding, look at target occupations and salaries to determine if it will be worth your while to sacrifice initial salary for greater future salary and upward mobility potential.

APPLYING FOR JOBS

Many talented job seekers are frustrated by the paperwork and give up prematurely. If you take the time to thoroughly complete your application and seek out all available job vacancies, your chances for employment will increase substantially. All forms and KSA statements listed in the job announcement must be submitted with your package. If you need forms, most can now be downloaded off the Internet.

Don't limit your search to applying for only one job vacancy. Seek out all available job vacancies and continue to send in applications with every opportunity. The more often you apply, the greater your chances. If you are having difficulty identifying jobs that fit your training, experience, and abilities, review the qualification standards in this book and view the Occupational directory in Chapter Ten.

COMPLETING YOUR APPLICATION

Previously, most postal job announcements, in the section titled "HOW TO APPLY," stated, *"Applicants must complete and submit a résumé or Form 2591, Application for Employment, plus a separate statement of qualifications for each knowledge, skill, or ability (KSA) to the application address on or before the closing date."* Now, most require online applications. Even though you typically submit an online application, I suggest that you use the PS Form 2591. Download this form online at www.postalwork.net/resources.htm and use the form as a guide to collect required employment history and education. When you go online you will have the information needed to complete the application.

Step One

Collect key data for your application. You will need the names, addresses, and contact phone numbers for previous and present employers. Locate or start compiling work histories, salary for each position, starting and stop dates. You will also need transcripts from schools and the dates attended including major undergraduate subjects. Include special qualifications such as licenses, skills with machines, patents or inventions, publications, honors, awards and fellowships received. Use the PS 2591 as your guide. Make up a folder and compile needed data for when you sit down and start your application.

You should also include volunteer work, temporary details and other significant activities that were not work-related. For example, if you managed a Little League team you could capture management and organizational skills from that activity. Include this as a separate "Work History" entry under Section "C" on the application.

Step Two

Review the job announcement throughly before completing your online application. Highlight all keywords under the "Requirements" statements. Underline words that identify the key duties of the position. Do this with all job announcements and then incorporate relevant key words and duties in your "Work History" description of duties, responsibilities and accomplishments in your work descriptions. If you have that skill or a related skill, include it in your application. The more you focus your application to key duties and responsibilities, the higher your rating will be. This will also help you complete required KSA statements.

Step Three

Complete your online application and assessments. Your work history should go back a minimum of 10 years or to your 16th birthday, whichever is earlier. Don't limit your work history to your last four employers. Expand it to include any and all related work history, relevant volunteer and community service experience or temporary details that showcase required knowledge, skills and abilities including military experience if applicable.

When describing your experience, use bullets to capture key KSAs. You have to show what you actually accomplished to achieve the stated skill or knowledge. Many who apply for federal jobs simply restate the skill, duty or accomplishment instead of describing how they attained them. If you don't provide specific examples, you won't receive points for those items. Take your time and be thorough.

Step Four

In most cases you will be required to submit a detailed description of how you achieved each knowledge, skills and abilities statement listed on the job announcement.

Understanding and Completing KSAs

Give a description of what you did to meet this KSA. Include in each KSA any of these relevant elements:

- Education
- Training
- Experience
- Volunteer work
- Outside activities
- Awards, licenses, etc.

You must include a narrative that indicates the degree to which you possess the KSA and include as many of the bullets listed above that apply in that narrative. For each work example or accomplishment listed, describe the situation, problem, or objective of the assignment, what was done, and the results obtained. Following the narrative, the applicant must indicate the duration (date) of the activity, and the name and telephone number of a person who can verify the information provided, if available. Applicants may attach copies of any relevant documents that will help substantiate their statements, such as performance evaluations, awards, or work products. The applicant's narrative must indicate exactly how these documents relate to the KSA.

Formatting Your KSAs

You can format your KSAs in a narrative form starting with "I" or use bullets that start with a forceful verb such as "organized, directed, managed, coordinated, analyzed, or conducted" to provide action to your statements. If you don't refer directly to an experience block, be sure to summarize the experience and provide the time and place where you performed that function. If you are applying for a supervisory position, mention the number of people you supervised, their status, such as part time or full time, and pay grade if applicable.

After writing your KSAs, review them a number of times, asking yourself "What did I do," "When did I do it," "Where did I perform these functions," and don't forget the proverbial question, "How often and how much did I do it." If you didn't answer these questions, edit your work until it is included. Add examples either in the narrative or by attaching an example, which is permitted in most cases.

Another factor many applicants overlook is the depth of training completed. Include correspondence study, online courses, seminars, classes, lectures, computer-based instruction, on-the-job training, every facet of training that you received, including software programs that you taught yourself.

Include special licenses, registration exams, or certifications that you obtained in your specialty. If you are a medical assistant and passed the Registered Medical Assistant (RMA) exam, annotate that on your application and in your KSAs. If you are in the trades and have various equipment operator's licenses, list items such as "Fork Lift Operator" certification; list whatever is relevant to the job announcement.

The following KSAs are provided as examples to show formatting techniques. Sample Supplemental Qualification Statements are provided for two elements.[2] If special forms are not provided or if specific formats are not specified on the job announcement, you can follow the sample outline to submit your narratives. Notice the use of bullets and short concise statements. You want the selecting official to focus on your key qualifications and good formatting techniques. The use of bullets, bold and underlined type will focus the reader's attention to your information. If you run everything together, it is difficult for the selecting official to identify key elements that you accomplished to satisfy the rating factors. Include all required information, and be sure to add your name, job announcement number and position title at the top of each page.

Sample KSAs

The following samples were excerpted from *The Book of U.S. Government Jobs*, 10th Edition. They present a format that you can use to draft your KSAs. Note that each KSA is on a separate page and that on each page you can address related knowledge, skills and abilities from multiple employers. You can use multiple pages for each KSA if needed. It is important to note that a rating of "no demonstration" on any of the KSAs will exclude an applicant from consideration for that position.[3]

Many applicants wonder why KSAs are needed when they already addressed their work experience. KSAs are used by selecting officials to differentiate among the best qualified for the position. They present specific strengths and can point out weaknesses between candidates for the same position. It is important to take the time to draft clear and concise descriptions to improve your chances for the position. To keep the KSAs to one page, you can change the formatting and font size. However, don't use a font size of less than 10 points because it is too difficult to read. I like to use a 11 or 12 point font size when writing applications. If you have significant accomplishments to add to a description, include them even if the KSA is more than one page.

---

[2] KSA examples excerpted from *The Book of U.S. Government Jobs,* 10th Edition, with permission.

[3] Handbook EL-312, paragraph 754.41, September 2001

Job Title: Administrative Officer
Announcement Number: XX-178A
Applicant's Name: John Smith
SSN: XXX-XX-XXXX

KSA #1 *Demonstrated ability to organize and coordinate work within schedule constraints and handle emergent requirements in a timely manner.*

I performed the following duties in my current position (Block C1):

- Managed the office suspense lists for all office supervisors. Transcribed meeting minutes and compiled action item lists, annotated due dates and listed responsible parties. Sent reminders to responsible parties, kept list current and reported accomplishments to the office manager weekly.
- Planned and coordinated two annual shareholder meetings for over 700 stock owners, key management and staff. Drafted the itinerary, set up the registration booth, arranged for morning breakout sessions, planned lunch and the shareholders meeting from 1:00 to 3:00 p.m. Also staffed the shareholders information booth after the meeting.

Award: Received an award for exemplary service for planning and organizing the 2001 meeting, <u>copy attached</u>.

- Required to frequently complete short notice work assignments including reports, transcribing meeting minutes, and payroll accounting tasks. I am the chief headquarters payroll clerk and I provide backup to 12 field offices. If any of the field office clerks or supervisors are not available, I complete their payroll reports prior to the cutoff time.

- Responsible for notifying management of pending funding shortfalls and providing justification for additional fund requests. I analyzed budget reports for trends, calculated spend rates and recommended reallocation of funds to satisfy pending or potential shortages.

Training:

1. Certificate: 24-hour Meeting Preparation and Planning seminar, March 2000
2. 40-hour Time Management Course, RMC Services, April 2002

Job Title: Administrative Officer
Announcement Number: XX-178A
Applicant's Name: John Smith
SSN: XXX-XX-XXXX

KSA #2 *Demonstrated ability to monitor important and complex projects concurrently.*

Performed these duties in my present position from 1/1/99 to the present (Block C1):

- Budget analyst duties – Trend tracking, monitor and control of the Office's annual budget of $350,000. Performed budget data entry, compiled reports, tracked trends, anticipated fund shortages in various program areas and drafted requests for additional funds for management's signature. Audited program areas to ensure fund expenditures were justified and properly classified.
- Payroll chief clerk – Ensured timely submission of all payroll data before the cutoff date each pay period, entered amendments, and researched pay problems for 37 employees. I advised management of problems and notified them when to review and approve the attendance for each pay period.

Training: 80-hour accounting software class, by Peachtree, January 1999.

Performed the following duties in my previous position as Administrative Officer, GS-0341-7, with the USDA from 10/4/96 to 12/31/98 (Block C2):

- Organizational Charts & Staffing – Processed revisions to and generated complex organizational charts based on input from the management team. Reviewed proposed changes to ensure they conformed to authorized levels and that positions were properly classified. Concurrently, prepared, and tracked personnel actions for 124 employees and provided support in various program areas including payroll, benefits, staffing, and budget.
- Office of Workmen's Compensation Program (OWCP) Program – Conducted annual (OWCP) seminars for managers and supervisors. Seminars included guidance on procedures, claims processing and post-accident interventions. Provided guidance to immediate supervisors of injured employees and maintained the OSHA 200 log for all accidents.

Award: Cash award, June 1998, for managing the OWCP program, copy attached.

Training: 60-hour Position Management and Position Classification Course, 012-V-933, Graduate School, USDA, Washington D.C., June 1997.

Job Title: Administrative Officer
Announcement Number: XX-178A
Applicant's Name: John Smith
SSN: XXX-XX-XXXX

KSA #3 *Knowledge of Microsoft Word, Excel, Powerpoint, and Lotus Notes/other e-mail software.*
Performed these duties in present position from 1/1/99 to the present (Block C1):

■ Proficient in Microsoft Office, Word, Excel, Powerpoint and Lotus, and I use Lotus notes for office e-mail. Developed a 34-page Powerpoint presentation (copy attached) for our CEO to use at the 2004 annual stockholders meeting in Memphis. The presentation received rave reviews and I was asked to develop similar presentations for other meetings. Worked closely with accounting to compile the data and then integrated it into a succinct visual presentation. I use Microsoft Word for correspondence.

■ Conducted Microsoft Word and Excel mini-training sessions for those less proficient in the office. Typically sessions ran 1 to 2 hours in length. Attended various software system seminars including Microsoft Office, Peachtree Accounting, and our new Lotus Notes e-mail program.

Volunteer Work: Performed these duties while working as a volunteer for United Way over past 6 years. Approximately 12 hours a week. (Block E):

■ Developed our chapter's Web site (http://www.xxxxxxxxxx.org) using Microsoft Frontpage 98. I consider myself very proficient in Web site development, and I learned Frontpage through self study and experimentation. This Web site consists of 48 pages and two databases. We used a secure server for confidential requests. I'm the Webmaster. Contact the United Way Chairperson, Ms. Mary Jones, for verification at XXX-123-4567.

Performed the following duties in my previous position as Administrative Officer, GS-0341-7, with the USDA from 10/4/96 to 12/31/98(Block B):

■ Proficient in VISO. I used VISO to generate ORG charts while at the USDA.

■ Proficient in several payroll and T&A software systems including IPPS, the USDA's Integrated Personnel and Payroll System.

Training Certificates: 24-hour <u>VISO software course</u> and a 16-hour <u>IPPS software course,</u> both completed at our regional office, May 1998.

Job Title: Administrative Officer, GS-341-05/11
Announcement Number: XX-178A
Applicant's Name: John Smith
SSN: XXX-XX-XXXX

KSA #4 *Demonstrated ability to effectively communicate orally and in writing, to include writing and preparing memorandums, letters, and other official correspondence.*

Performed these duties in present position from 1/1/99 to the present (Block C1):

- **Written Guidance** – Developed Standard Operation Procedures (SOPs) for program areas including payroll administration, office suspense tracking, monitor and control, and general procedures. Adopted by the regional office for use throughout the organization, sample attached. I also wrote numerous internal memorandums within my program areas that provided direction for specific functions and clarified company policy issues.

  Prepare transmittal forms for project files, letters to share holders, fax cover letters, e-mail messages to team leads and customers, flip charts for meetings, Power Point presentations, proof and edit management draft correspondence, and prepare replies to organizational reports.

- **Oral Communications** – In current capacity I teach office software to small groups, brief management team of progress at meetings, give presentations at inter-office meetings and to small groups of shareholders.

Volunteer Work

- I speak at various fundraisers for our local United Way and prepare written presentations to our work group and chairperson. I organized and hosted a dozen fund raisers since 1994. Contact the United Way chairperson, Ms. Mary Jones, for verification at 890-123-4567.

Education: Completed 12 semester hours, three courses in communications, at Duquesne University in 1997; <u>Report Writing</u>, <u>Oral Communications I</u> and <u>Effective Writing Techniques</u>.

Training:

1) **Competent Toastmaster.** Joined Toastmasters International in 1995. Obtained Competent Toastmaster status in 1997. Chapter president, Dan McCormick, 321-6543-0987. Certificate attached.

2)   **Certificate;** <u>Constructive Communications with the Public</u>, USDA Course 01501, June 1996. <u>Interpersonal Communications</u>, Seminar 1996, sponsored by OPM.

KSA CHECKLIST

Use this list to ensure that you have included key information.[4] It's important to consider these areas when drafting your KSA statements. When you first start to draft your KSAs, don't worry about the specifics such as exact dates, contact information, etc. You can add that later. It is best to simply write down anything and everything, even the least significant events. After you get it all down, add specifics and put them in logical sequence. Review and rewrite your KSAs at least three times, and more if needed. Let your draft sit overnight and review it again the next day. You will be surprised at what you left out on the first draft.

❑ **Experience** – Include experience for all offices, departments or agencies that you worked for to show depth and range of experience. For example, include that you tracked inter-office correspondence at multiple locations, or that you tracked budgets for headquarters. Also show expertise in what you do well, such as having A++ certification, maintain LANS/WANS for several locations, thoroughly familiar with Peachtree accounting software, proficient at office organization, etc.

❑ **Supervision** – If you don't have a supervisory background, did you work independently with minimal supervision and make decisions for your program areas? If so, state that in your KSA. Were you assigned to be an acting supervisor on several occasions? Do you draft memorandums and letters for your supervisor's signature? Do you manage/supervise programs or projects?

❑ **ComplexityFactors** – Did you write reports or work on large projects, coordinating activities for various groups? Does your job impact the safety of others, and what standards do you follow and utilize in your present and past jobs? Do you have certifications, licenses, specific training, or accreditation that would help you land this job?

❑ **Achievements and Impact** – How did you show initiative and creativity in your office while working under adverse conditions? Were you responsible for major programs, products, or activities? If so list them. What did you do to save time, money and resources or to improve the work environment?

❑ **Awards/Recognition** – Include all awards, monetary rewards, letters of achievement, time-off awards, or write-ups in your office newsletter. Include scholastic nominations as well, and any service awards or recognition received from volunteer work.

---

[4] Excerpted from *The Book of U.S. Government Jobs*, 10th Edition

❏ **Contacts** – If you dealt with headquarters staff, the general public, EPA or OSHA inspectors, local authorities, or government officials, list them in your KSAs.

❏ **Fashionable Trends** – Mention current trends such as "Business Process Engineering (BPE), Model Work Environment (MWE) initiatives, Management by Objectives (MBO), Partnership, Quality Work Groups," etc. If you have exposure to these and other initiatives list them in your write-up.

OVERVIEW

Now that you have your application and KSAs completed, you are ready to submit your package. Follow the instructions in the job announcement. Your application must reach the listed address on or before the specified closing date. If it is received after the closing date your application will not be considered.

If selected for the position, you will have to complete other forms such as a "Pre-Employment Screening – Authorization and Release Form," PS Form 2181-A. A copy of this form is included in Appendix C for your review.

KEYS TO SUCCESS

There are three basic ingredients to successfully finding federal employment for qualified applicants:

- Invest the time and energy needed to seek out all openings.
- Correctly fill out all required application forms.
- Don't give up if you receive your first rejection.

You can learn from rejections by contacting the selecting official. Ask what training and/or experience would enhance your application package for future positions. If they specify certain training or experience, then work to achieve the desired skills.

NETWORKING

Networking is a term used to define the establishment of a group of individuals who assist one another for mutual benefit. You can establish your own network by talking to personnel specialists, contacting Customer Service District Office human resources departments, conducting informational interviews, and by bidding on all applicable job announcements. By following the guidelines outlined in the book and using your innate common sense, your chances of success are increased substantially.

Visit http://federaljobs.net to explore viable Civil Service options in the competitive sector and to use the many resources offered on this site, including direct links to hundreds of federal agency employment Web sites. You will also find updates to this book posted on http://federaljobs.net as changes occur.

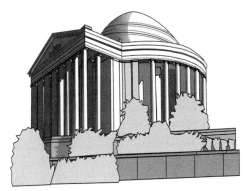

Appendix C
Customer Service and Sales District Offices

In addition to the national headquarters, there are Customer Service and Sales District (CSSD) offices supporting approximately 37,000 post offices, branches, and stations throughout the United States. The Postal Service has approximately 765,000 employees and handles over 200 billion pieces of mail annually, generating more than $75 billion in operating revenues.

> *If you need to determine when jobs will be advertised in your area or to check on test results, call your local CSSD.*

Government jobs offer abundant opportunities in all 50 states and U.S. territories. With more than 37,000 postal facilities, individuals have an excellent opportunity to apply for positions in thousands of small towns and in all major metropolitan areas.

CUSTOMER SERVICE AND SALES DISTRICTS

To determine what job vacancies are available and when exams are scheduled, visit **www.usps.com/employment** or call **1-478-757-3199**. You can also contact General Mail Facilities (GMF), Sectional Center Facilities (SCF), Management Sectional Centers (MSC), or Bulk Mail Centers in your area, or the Customer Service and Sales District (CSSD) office nearest you, to inquire when jobs will be advertised in your area. The Postal Service has established nine

Customer Service District areas: Eastern, Great Lakes, Capital Metro Operations, New York Metro, Northeast, Pacific, Southeast, Southwest, and Western. The following list, updated January 2, 2009, provides the district manager's name, address, phone and fax numbers. Call this number and have them transfer you to the Human Resources Department. Human Resources (HR) is responsible for advertising job vacancies and scheduling required proctored exams.

Disabled veterans can apply at any time regardless of whether or not vacancies exist. This list does not include testing centers. Under the new **eCareer** recruiting initiative, proctored exams are conducted by third party contractors that are certified to administer postal exams. Examinations can be scheduled at designated testing facilities nationwide.

CUSTOMER SERVICE DISTRICTS

EASTERN AREA

Karen E. Schenck
District Manager
Appalachian District
P.O. Box 59992
Charleston, WV 25350-9992
(304) 561-1200
(304) 561-1209 (FAX)

Chu Falling Star
District Manager
Cincinnati District
1591 Dalton St
Cincinnati, OH 45234-9990
(513) 684-5360
(513) 684-5197 (FAX)

Donald Marshall, III
District Manager
Northern Ohio District
2200 Orange Ave., Rm 210
Cleveland, OH 44104-9993
(216) 443-4573
(216) 443-4577 (FAX)

Joshua Colin
District Manager
Columbus District
850 Twin Rivers Drive
Columbus, OH 43216-9993
(614) 469-4300

(14) 469-7605 (FAX)

Charles P. McCreadie
District Manager
Erie District
2700 Legion Road
Erie, PA 16515-9997
(814) 836-7201
(814) 836-7215 (FAX)

Edward B. Burke
District Manager
Central Pennsylvania District
1425 Crooked Hill Road
Harrisburg, PA 17107-0001
(717) 257-2104
(717) 257-2302 (FAX)

Chris Christenbury
District Manager
Kentuckiana District
PO Box 31000
Louisville, KY 40231-1000
(502) 454-1814
(502) 454-1990 (FAX)

Elizabeth Schaefer
District Manager
Pittsburgh District
1001 California Ave.,
  Rm 2001

Pittsburgh, PA 15290-9996
(412) 359-7771
(412) 321-3373 (FAX)

Frank Neri
District Manager
Philadelphia Metro District
2970 Market St., Rm. 306A
Philadelphia, PA
  19104-9997
(215) 895-8607
(215) 895-8611 (FAX)

Joanna Korker
District Manager
South Jersey District
PO Box 9001
Bellmawr, NJ 08099-9998
(856) 933-4400
(856) 933-4440 (FAX)

GREAT LAKES AREA

Peter Allen
District Manager
Central Illinois District
6801 West 73rd St
Bedford Park, IL
  60499-9998
(708) 563-7807
(708) 563-2013 (FAX)

Gloria Tyson
District Manager
Chicago District
433 West Harrison
Chicago, IL 60607-9998
(312) 983-8030
(312) 983-8010 (FAX)

Nancy Rettinhouse
District Manager
Detroit District
1401 W. Fort St
Detroit, MI 48233-9992
(313) 226-8605
(313) 226-8005 (FAX)

Danita Aquiningoc
District Manager
Gateway District
1720 Market St., Rm 3027
St. Louis, MO 63155-9900
(314) 436-4114
(314) 436-4565 (FAX)

E. Lynn Smith
District Manager
Greater Indiana District
3939 Vincennes Road
PO Box 9850
Indianapolis, IN 46298-9850
(317) 870-8201
(317) 870-8688 (FAX)

Charles E. Howe
District Manager
Greater Michigan District
PO Box 999997
Grand Rapids, MI
49599-9997
(616) 336-5300
(616) 336-5399 (FAX)

Robert Howe
District Manager
North Illinois District
500 E. Fullerton Ave.
Carol Stream, IL 60199-9998
(630) 260-5225
(630) 260-5130 (FAX)

Kelly Sigmon
District Manager
Southern Michigan District
P.O. Box 9000
Birmingham, MI 48009-9000
(248) 546-4100
(248) 546-4102 (FAX)

David Martin
District Manager
Lakeland District
PO Box 5000
Milwaukee, WI 53201-5000
(414) 287-2238
(414) 287-2296 (FAX)

*CAPITAL METRO
OPERATIONS*

Mike Harrow
District Manager
Baltimore District
900 East Fayette St., Rm 309
Baltimore, MD 21233-9990
(410) 347-4314
(410) 347-4289 (FAX)

Henry L. Dix, Jr.
District Manager
Capital District
900 Brentwood Road, N.E.
Washington, DC 20066-9998
(202) 636-2210
(202) 636-5301 (FAX)

Nicholas Rinaldi
District Manager
Greater SC District
PO Box 929998
Columbia, SC 29292-9998
(803) 926-6469
(803) 926-6470 (FAX)

Mike Furey
District Manager
Northern Virginia District
8409 Lee Highway
Merrifield, VA 22081-9996
(703) 698-6464
(703) 698-6500 (FAX)

Russell D. Garbner, Jr.
District Manager
Greensboro District
418 Gallimore Dairy Road
P.O. Box 27499
Greensboro, NC 27498-9900
(336) 668-1201
(336) 668-1366 (FAX)

David C. Fields, Sr.
District Manager
Mid-Carolinas District
2901 Scott Futrell Drive
Charlotte, NC 28228-9980
(704) 424-4400
(704) 424-4489 (FAX)

Jacob Cheeks
District Manager
Richmond District
1801 Brook Road
Richmond, VA 23232-9990
(804) 775-6365 or 6364
(804) 775-6058 (FAX)

*NEW YORK METRO
AREA*

Jesus Galvez
District Manager
Caribbean District
585 FD Roosevelt Ave.,
   Ste 201
San Juan, PR 00936-9998
(787) 662-1800
(787) 622-1803 (FAX)

Vito J. Cetta
District Manager
Central NJ District
21 Kilmer Road
Edison, NJ 08899-9998
(732) 819-3264
(732) 819-3837 (FAX)

Ken Hale
District Manager
Long Island District
PO Box 7800
Islandia, NY 11760-9998

(631) 582-7410
(631) 582-7413 (FAX)

Robert A. Daruk
District Manager
New York District
421 8th Ave., Rm 3018
New York, NY 10199-9998
(212) 330-3600
(212) 330-3934 (FAX)

Maria Morse
District Manager
**Northern New Jersey
    District**
494 Broad Street, Rm 307
Newark, NJ 07102-9300
(973) 468-7111
(973) 468-7215 (FAX)

Lorraine G. Castellano
District Manager
Triboro District
142-02 20th Avenue
Flushing, NY 11351-9998
(718) 321-5144
(718) 321-5999 (FAX)

Joseph Lubrano
District Manager
Westchester District
PO Box 9800
White Plains, NY 10610
(914) 697-7104
(914) 697-7128 (FAX)

NORTHEAST AREA

Margaret (Peg) Weir
District Manager
Albany District
30 Old Karner Road
Albany, NY 12288-9992
(518) 452-2201
(518) 452-2309 (FAX)

Charles K. Lynch
District Manager
Boston District
25 Dorchester Ave.

Boston, MA 02205-0098
(617) 654-5107
(617) 654-5816 (FAX)

Edward F. Phelan
District Manager
Connecticut District
141 Weston St.
Hartford, CT 06101-9996
(860) 524-6137
(860) 524-6199 (FAX)

William Boughton
District Manager
Maine District
151 Forest Ave., #7000
Portland, ME 04104-7000
(207) 828-7109
(207) 828-7105 (FAX)

John W. (Mike) Powers III
District Manager
Massachusetts District
74 Main St.
North Reading, MA 01889
(978) 664-7603
(978) 664-5998 (FAX)

Deborah C. Essler
District Manager
**New Hampshire/
    Vermont District**
955 Goffs Falls Road
Manchester, NH 03103-9990
(603) 644-3800
(603) 644-3896 (FAX)

Robert M. Koestner
District Manager
**Southeast New England
District**
24 Corliss St.
Providence, RI 02904-9998
(401) 276-6950
(401) 276-6967 (FAX)

Kimberly Peters
District Manager
Western NY District
1200 William St.

Buffalo, NY 14240-9990
(716) 846-2532
(716) 846-2407 (FAX

PACIFIC AREA

Daryl Ishizaki
District Manager
Honolulu District
3600 Aolele St.
Honolulu, HI 96820-3600
(808) 423-3700
(808) 423-3708 (FAX)

Gregory Graves
District Manager
Los Angeles District
7001 South Central Ave.
Los Angeles, CA
    90052-9998
(323) 586-1200
(323) 586-1248 (FAX)

Kim Fernandez
District Manager
Bay-Valley District
1675 7th St.
Oakland, CA 94615-9987
(510) 874-8222
(510) 874-8301 (FAX)

Rosemarie Fernandez
District Manager
Sacramento District
3775 Industrial Blvd.
West Sacramento, CA
    95799-0010
(916) 373-8001
(916) 373-8704 (FAX)

Dallas W. Keck
District Manager
San Diego District
11251 Rancho Carmel Dr.
San Diego, CA 92199-9990
(858) 674-0301
(858) 674-0405 (FAX)

Winfred G. Groux
District Manager
San Francisco District
PO Box 885050
San Francisco, CA 94188
(415) 550-5591
(415) 550-5327 (FAX)

Gerald K. Ahern
District Manager
Santa Ana District
3101 W. Sunflower
Santa Ana, CA 92799-9993
(714) 662-6300
(714) 557-5837 (FAX)

Kerry Wolny
District Manager
Sierra Coastal District
28201 Franklin Parkway
Santa Clarita, CA 91383
(661) 775-6500
(661) 775-7184 (FAX)

SOUTHEAST AREA

William Mitchell
District Manager
Alabama District
351 24th St., N.
Birmingham, AL
    35203-9997
(205) 521-0201
(205) 521-0058 (FAX)

Kate Wiley
District Manager
Atlanta District
PO Box 599300
North Metro, GA
    30026-9300
(770) 717-3736
(770) 717-3735 (FAX)

Elizabeth Johnson
District Manager
Central Florida District
PO Box 999800
Mid Florida, FL 32799-9800

(407) 333-4809
(407) 333-4899 (FAX)

Gregory Gamble
District Manager
Mississippi District
PO Box 99990
Jackson, MS 39205-9990
(601) 351-7350
(601) 351-7504 (FAX)

James Nemec
District Manager
North Florida District
PO Box 40005
Jacksonville, FL 32203-0005
(904) 858-6605
(904) 858-6610 (FAX)

Tammy Autenrieth
District Manager
South Florida District
PO Box 829990
Pembroke Pines, FL 33082
(954) 436-4466
(954) 450-3015 (FAX)

Julius Locklear
District Manager
South Georgia District
451 College St.
Macon, GA 31213-9900
(478) 752-8530
(478) 752-8664 (FAX)

Timothy C. Healy
District Manager
Suncoast District
2203 N. Lois Ave., Ste. 1001
Tampa, FL 33607-7101
(813) 354-6099
(813) 877-8656 (FAX)

Carolyn Chambers
District Manager
Tennessee District
811 Royal Parkway
Nashville, TN 37229-9998
(615) 885-9252
(615) 885-9317 (FAX)

SOUTHWEST AREA

Jeffery (Jeff) Taylor
District Manager
Arkansas District
420 Natural Resources Dr.
Little Rock, AR 72205-9800
(501) 228-4100
(501) 228-4105 (FAX)

Matthew Lopez
District Manager
Albuquerque District
500 Marquette Ave., NW
    Ste. 900
Albuquerque, NM 87102
(505) 346-8501 or 3950
(505) 346-8503 (FAX)

Linda Welch
District Manager
Dallas District
951 W. Bethel Road
Coppell, TX 75099-9998
(972) 393-6787
(972) 393-6198 (FAX)

Victor H. Benavides
District Manager
Fort Worth District
4600 Mark IV Parkway
Fort Worth, TX 76161-9100
(817) 317-3301
(817) 317-3320 (FAX)

Kelvin Williams
District Manager
Houston District
PO Box 250001
Houston, TX 77202-0001
(713) 226-3717
(713) 226-3755 (FAX)

Carolyn Weisiger
District Manager
Louisiana District
701 Loyola Ave.
New Orleans, LA
    70113-9800

(504) 589-1950
(504) 589-1432 (FAX)

Julie Gosdin
District Manager
Oklahoma City District
3030 NW Expressway St.
Oklahoma City, OK 73198
(405) 553-6211
(405) 357-6663 (FAX)

Manuel "Manny" Arguello
District Manager
Rio Grande District
One Post Office Drive
San Antonio, TX 78284
(210) 368-5548
(210) 368-5511 (FAX)

WESTERN AREA

Lawrence K. James
District Manager
Arizona District
4949 E. Van Buren St.
    Rm. 211C
Phoenix, AZ 85026-9900
(602) 225-5401
(602) 225-3286 (FAX)

Dianne P. Horbochuk
District Manager
Alaska District
3720 Barrow St.
Anchorage, AK 99599-0001
(907) 261-5418
(907) 273-54866(FAX)

John J. DiPeri
District Manager
Big Sky District
841 S. 26th St.
Billings, MT 59101-8800
(406) 657-5701
(406) 657-5788 (FAX)

Michael C. Holloway
District Manager
Central Plains District
PO Box 249500
Omaha, NE 68124-9500
(402) 255-3900
(402) 255-3897 (FAX)

Selwyn D. Epperson
District Manager
Colorado/Wyoming District
7500 East 53rd Place,
Rm 1131
Denver, CO 80266-9998
(303) 853-6160
(303) 853-6099 (FAX)

Clarion (Clem) E. Felchle
District Manager
Dakotas District
PO Box 7500
Sioux Falls, SD 57117-7500
(605) 333-2601
(605) 333-2777 (FAX)

Douglas H. Morrow
District Manager
Hawkeye District
PO Box 189800
Des Moines, IA 50318-9800
(515) 251-2106
(515) 251-2050 (FAX)

Mark A. Martinez
District Manager
Mid-America District
300 W. Pershing Rd., Ste. 210
Kansas City, MO 64108-9000
(816) 374-9105
(816) 374-9153 (FAX)

Johnray Egelhoff
District Manager
Nevada-Sierra District
1001 E. Sunset Road
Las Vegas, NV 89199-1000

(702) 361-9300
(702) 361-9508 (FAX)

Anthony C. Williams
District Manager
Northland District
100 South lst St., Rm. 409
Minneapolis, MN
    55401-9990
(612) 349-3505
(612) 349-6377 (FAX)

Kim Anderson
District Manager
Portland District
P.O. Box 3609
Portland, OR 97208-3609
(503) 294-2502
(503) 276-2020 (FAX)

Kenneth S. McArthur
District Manager
Salt Lake City District
1760 W. 2100 S.
Salt Lake City, UT
    84199-8800
(801) 974-2947
(801) 974-2339 (FAX)

Katherine Nash
District Manager
Seattle District
415 First Ave. N.
Seattle, WA 98109-9997
(206) 442-6270
(206) 442-6006 (FAX)

Lloyd H. Wilkinson
District Manager
Spokane District
707 W. Maine Ave., Ste 600
Spokane, WA 99299-1000
(509) 626-6703
(509) 626-6920 (FAX)

Index

Notes